PANDITRAJ ATOMBAPU SHARMA
An Agastya in Eastern India

About the Editors

Dr. Kakchingtabam Ruhinikumar Sharma (MA, PhD) is Assistant Professor and Head, Department of History, Ideal Girls' College (Government of Manipur), Akampar, Imphal-East, Manipur. He can be contacted at <kruhinikumar@gmail.com>

Prof. Shukhdeba Sharma Hanjabam (MSW, PhD) is Professor and Head, Department of Social Work, Indira Gandhi National Tribal University, Amarkantak, Madhya Pradesh, India. He completed his PhD. from School of Social Work, Tata Institute of Social Sciences, Mumbai and post doctoral from University of Florida, Florida, USA. He can be contacted at <hanjabam@gmail.com>

PANDITRAJ ATOMBAPU SHARMA
An Agastya in Eastern India
(Panditraj Atombapu Memorial Lectures on Indic Culture and Civilisation)

Introduction by

Dr. Mohan Bhagwat

(Sarsanghachalak, Rashtriya Swayamsevak Sangh)

Edited by

Kakchingtabam Ruhinikumar Sharma

Shukhdeba Sharma Hanjabam

Published for

Intellectual Forum of North East
Manipur

Atombapu Research Centre,
Imphal, Manipur

CONCEPT PUBLISHING COMPANY PVT. LTD.
NEW DELHI-110059

ISBN: 978-93-5594-763-5

First Published 2024

Published and Printed by

Concept
Since 1974

Concept Publishing Company Pvt. Ltd.
A/15-16, Commercial Block, Mohan Garden
New Delhi-110059 (India)
T: +91-11-41101460
E: publishing@conceptpub.com, *W*: www.conceptpub.com

Cataloging in Publication--Courtesy: D.K. Agencies (P) Ltd. <docinfo@dkagencies.com>

Panditraj Atombapu Sharma : an Agastya in eastern India : Panditraj Atombapu memorial lectures on Indic culture and civilisation / edited by Kakchingtabam Ruhinikumar Sharma, Shukhdeba Sharma Hanjabam.
pages cm
"Published for Intellectual Forum of North East, Manipur, Atombapu Research Centre, Imphal, Manipur."
Includes bibliographical references and index.
ISBN 9789355947635

1. India--Civilisation. 2. Indo-Europeans. 3. Religion and culture--India. I. Sharma, Atombapu, 1989-1963, honouree. II. Sharma, Kakchingtabam Ruhinikumar, editor. III. Hanjabam, Shukhdeba Sharma, 1983- editor. IV. Intellectual Forum of North East (Manipur, India) V. Atombapu Research Centre (Imphāl, India)

LCC DS425.P36 2024 | DDC 954 23

Dedicated to

Panditraj Atombapu Sharma (1889–1963)

Introduction

"Manipur", is literally a jewel in the vast and ancient land of Bharat adorned with a beautiful and serene landscape also with equally rich hoary tradition of Human life. It has been a part and parcel of the cultural and political history of Bharat since at least fifty-five hundred years and can boast an important and significant share of contribution in arts, spirituality cultural history as well as social and political tradition of Bharat.

Unfortunately during recent century or two Bharat faced a systematic wiping out of its collective memory engineered by its British rulers. Various foreign Churches were complicit in this deep conspiracy. The diversity of language, religions, general way of living, eating, etc. and many prevalent systems of governance which actually are manifestations of the same underlying inherent unity of Bharat were used to create rifts amongst the one single people and polity of Bharat. The process still continues through the nefarious designs of powers that be in the world for which the rise of Bharat means the permanent demise of their selfish interests.

This inherent unity of Bharat was forged and kept going by the Himalayan efforts of a continuous stream of galaxy of Seers and Sages as well as scholarly and saintly personalities of Bharatiya society. Their evergreen memories continue to inspire the masses to tread the strenuous path of Dharma for glory and unity of Bharatiya society, Sanskriti and Rashtra.

Panditraj Atombapu Sharma was one such inspiration in times very near to present citizens of Bharat and particularly Manipur. He with his deep understanding of unity of Bharat and Sanskritik roots of Bharatiya society worked in Manipur and devoted his everything for the education of people in general and residents of Manipur in particular. In the post-Independence turbulent atmosphere prevailing in social life of Bharat, his life can serve as a guide light for our thoughts and actions, particularly so in Manipur. "An Agastya in Eastern India" is therefore a fitting title bestowed by late Shri Suniti Kumar Chatterji, National Professor of Humanities for his sagely life and his mission.

It is therefore a very apt and necessary happening that Shri Kakchingtabam Ruhinikumar Sharma and Shri Shukhdeba Sharma Hanjabam have collected and edited the Panditraj Atombapu memorial lectures on Indic Culture and civilization in a book form which has been published by the Concept Publishing Co. Pvt. Ltd., New Delhi for Intellectual Forum of North East, Manipur and Atombapu Research Centre, Imphal. The book will definitely inspire the people of Bharat in general and Manipur in particular and enlighten them towards the continued belonging and unity of the people of Bharat to the hoary Sanskritik tradition, Nationhood and a society that celebrates diversity.

Hearty congratulations to the authors, publishers and IFNE and ARC Imphal the forum which prompted the making of this book and best wishes for its widespread circulation.

Dr. Mohan Bhagwat
(Sarsanghachalak, Rashtriya Swayamsevak Sangh)

Preface

Though the term "culture" and "civilisation" are often used synonymously, yet it carries different connotations and have clearly defined meanings differentiating them. "Civilisation" refers to having better ways of living and sometimes making nature bend to fulfil their needs and also include among other organisation of societies into politically well-defined groups working collectively for improved conditions of life in matters of food, dress, communication, and so on. "Culture" on the other hand refers to the inner being, a refinement of heart and soul. This includes arts and sciences, music and dance and various higher pursuits of human life which are also classified as cultural activities. India as a vast country is a land of diversity in her physical and social environment and home to a sea of humanity speaking different languages, having different religions and practising different rituals. One can also see these diversities in their food habits and dress patterns along with myriad forms of dance and music. However, within all these diversities there is an underlying unity which acts as a cementing force. The intermingling of people has been steadily taking place in India over centuries. People of different racial stock, ethnic backgrounds and religious beliefs have settled down in India. Thus, the composite and dynamic character of Indian culture is a by-product of the rich contributions of all these diverse cultural groups over a long period of time. The papers contained in the present volume seek to reiterate these distinctive features of Indian culture and civilisation.

Phurailatpam Atombapu Sharma (1889–1963) more popularly known as Panditraj Atombapu Sharma was truly a product of the twentieth century Manipuri renaissance. Two broad streams of thought are discernible in the first half of the century. The first one endeavoured to discover and rediscover the past of the glory that was Manipur through the lens of folklore, myths, legends, song and poetry and the other one tried to do the same through a synthesised picture of a land, people and culture evolving out of the blending of Indic and Sinic elements. Without a doubt, it can be said that Atombapu Sharma was a multifaceted personality. Apart from being an established teacher and scholar, he also dabbled in many social and religious activities.

Though much of his works remained confined within the state of Manipur because of the geographical isolation of the state from the rest of India, many of his writings could be placed on par with those of the established works of the nineteenth and early twentieth centuries. He considered Manipur an inseparable part of the Vedic world and went so far as to putting up a strong argument on how the Vedic religion first appeared in Manipur and afterwards spread to Burma and other neighbouring countries. One may not completely concur with the assertions made by Atombapu, but for him Manipur constituted an inseparable unit of the Vedic world view—its history, culture and civilisation. To him, Manipuri culture is the syncretism of Vedic and native Meitei elements where the later belief system forms the core of the former. For these strong views, Atombapu was criticised and vilified by certain sections of the community as the movement for native revivalist movement gained momentum over the years. However, it cannot be denied that Atombapu's writings have influenced and shaped the discourse on Manipurology.

Since any academic discourse is a continuing process, the compilers of this volume are of the firm opinion that a critical engagement and re-evaluation of the works of this great scholar is the need of the hour, and therefore, this compilation has been brought out. This volume comprises of lectures delivered by eminent personalities of the country on different themes ranging from history, culture, religion, philosophy, etc.

It is worth mentioning that why the eminent persons and whose words can almost be regarded as the voice of India have readily agreed to come to such an isolated place in those days amply shows that it is not only about acknowledging the academic contribution of Panditraj Atombapu Sharma but also about honouring a great son of Manipur, who throughout his life devoted to the study of Manipur within the larger canvas of Indian culture and civilisation. We are grateful to the authorities of the Atombapu Research Centre, Imphal for reposing their faith and for entrusting us the task of compiling/editing the present volume. A compendium volume is planned in the near future for the lectures that could not be included in the present compilation.

Editors

Acknowledgements

We are grateful to the functionaries and well-wishers of Atombapu Research Centre, Imphal, Manipur for having faith in us by handing over the manuscript of the Panditraj Atombapu Memorial Lectures.

The editors feel obliged to *Param Poojaniya* Dr. Mohan Ji Bhagwat, Sarsanghachalak, Rashtriya Swayamsevak Sangh for kindly sparing his valuable time and having written a beautiful introduction to this volume.

We are indebted to Shri Pt. Phurailatpam Ibotombi Sharma, grandson of Panditraj Atombapu Sharma for helping us to locate the manuscript and to the advisors and members of IFNE for his constant support in the publication of the volume.

Editors

Panditraj Phurailatpam Atombapu Sharma

A Brief Life Sketch

Born on 31 January 1889, the Panditraj, right from an early age, showed his penchant for Sanskrit learning and at a very early age attained eminence of great scholarship in Sanskrit.

He did extensive studies of the Vedas, the *Śāstras* and the Purāṇas and desired to bring, through translations into Manipuri, the wisdom of these immortal books to the reach of the common people of Manipur. In his lifetime he translated the *Ṛgveda,* the *Śrīmad Bhāgavata* (up to 10th *skandha*) and published editions of the *Bhagavadgītā,* the *Gītā Govinda.* the *Sārasvata Vyākaraṇa* and some classic philosophical texts of the *Gauḍīya Vaiṣṇavas* with Manipuri commentaries.

His uniqueness is in his works through which he sought to establish great affinities between Manipuri pre-Hindu life and the Purāṇic and Brāhmanical life of the Hindus and thereby bringing about the great Indian Integration to Manipur.

In the words of the late Dr. Suniti Kumar Chatterji, former National Professor of India, the Panditraj

> ...was a great scholar of Sanskrit, of Brāhamanical philosophy as well as the *Brahman* way of life, and this he combined with the fullest understanding and appreciation of the Meitei background in culture and folklore and religious ideologies. He was a veritable *ṛṣi* of the present age who by the example of his life and by his preaching and his writings silently brought about a renaissance of Hindu religion and

faith among the Manipuri people, while retaining to fullest their background of Meithei culture.

Referring to these missionary works of the Panditraj, Dr. Chatterji had described him as "A Present-Day Ṛṣi: An Agastya in Eastern India".

His extensive studies of the Manipuri antiquities led him to conclude that ancient Manipur, rich in its myth and legends was comparable to the Vedic world. In the words of Dr. Chatterji,

> ... The story of the gods and heroes of Manipur as found in early Meitei literature and as expressed in the dances of Manipur, particularly the Lai-Haraoba, were equated by him with the world of the Vedas and the Purāṇas.

Through these studies, the Panditraj left invaluable works in his explanations, and interpretations of the philosophy, symbols and religious connotations of ancient Manipuri myth and folklore and as they find their expressions in the world-famous Manipuri dance was of an immense proportion.

His works include about 100 books and manuscripts in Sanskrit, Manipuri, Bengali and English. So vast was the volume of his writings that the Panditraj faced the insurmountable problem of printing and publishing them. He solved it by establishing the first ever printing press *The Churachand Printing Works*—a pioneering work of great importance in Manipur.

He was the first to publish a vernacular daily *The Dainik Manipur* (1929) and through it sought to arouse the sense of Indian nationalism in Manipur. He was also associated with the movement of the Indian National Congress in Manipur in its early stage.

The great soul passed away in 1963.

Titles and Honours Received

1. "Gaveshana Shiromani" for research work from Manipuri Sahitya Parishad.

2. "Panditraj" from Government Sanskrit Mahavidyalaya, Calcutta, 1948.
3. "Certificate of Honour" from the President of India, 1959.
4. "Presidentship" of Manipuri Sahitya Parishad for two successive years, 1960-62.
5. "Membership" of the Bharatiya Sanskrit Sangam, 1961.
6. "Sangeet Natak Akademi Award" from New Delhi, 1963 (posthumously).

Atombapu Research Centre

To carry forward the works and ideas of this great scholar, the Atombapu Research Centre was established in 1965 in memory of the Panditraj Atombapu Sharma. The objectives are:

1. To place within the easy appreach of advanced students of research a first class and up to date Oriental Library and to afford them materials for research.
2. To undertake and publish, with the cooperation of various scholars, critical edition of texts, as also original and independent works of a historical nature bearing upon Oriental Antiquities, including journals, proceedings, reports and occasional studies.
3. To arrange Panditraj Atombapu Sharma Memorial Lectures.
4. To do such other acts not inconsistent with the foregoing objects.

The Memorial Lectures

Organising the memorial lectures has been one of the important activities of the Atombapu Research Centre. First of its kind in Manipur, the first memorial lecture was delivered in 1965 by the late Dr. Suniti Kumar Chatterji, a renowned scholar and Indologist and National Professor of Humanities. A great admirer of the Panditraj, Dr. Chatterji's lectures on "Religion and Cultural Integration of India" and "Atombapu Sharma of Manipur" have been widely popular and read.

In the subsequent years, a number of scholars of eminence from all over the country have delivered the memorial lectures. Personalities who had delivered the memorial lectures with years and the topics:

1. Professor Suniti Kumar Chatterji, National Professor in Humanities, (i) *Religion & Cultural Integration of India* (1967) (ii) *Atombapu Sharma of Manipur* (1965).
2. Professor R.C. Majumdar, Eminent Historian, *Expansion of Aryan Culture in Eastern India* (1966).
3. Professor N.K. Bose, Commissioner for Scheduled Castes and Scheduled Tribes, Government of India, *Cultural History of Arts and Crafts of India* (1969).
4. Acharya Kaka Saheb Kalelkar, Padma Vibhusan & Eminent Educationist, Social Worker and Gandhian Patriarch, (i) *Mission of Bharat and its Future*, and (ii) *Gandhiji as I knew him* (1970).
5. Professor D.C. Sirkar, Eminent Historian (Carmichael Professor of Ancient Indian History and Culture), Calcutta University, *Social Life in Northern India during the Gupta and Post Gupta Period* (1973).
6. Thiru R. Nagaswami, Director of Archaeology, Government of Tamil Nadu, (i) *Social and Cultural Life of the Tamils from 6th Century to 15th Century A.D.* and (ii) *Art and Archaeology of Tamil Nadu from 6th to 15th Century A.D.* (1973).
7. Professor R.N. Dandekar, Eminent Sanskrit Scholar and Hony. Secretary, Bhandarkar Oriental Research Institute, Poona, *Vaisnavism and Saivism: A Fresh Look* (1976).
8. Dr. Svarup Damodardas, Director Bhakti Vedanta Institute (ISKCON), *Modern Science, Religion and the Fundamental Principles of Knowledge* (1977).
9. Professor Roma Choudhury, Retd. Vice-Chancellor, Ravindra Bharati University, Calcutta, Vaisnavism, *Vedanta School* (1980).

10. Dr. Subhas Chandra Malik, Centre of Advanced Studies, Simla, *Indian Civilisation: Cultural Transformation and the Individual* (1983).
11. Professor K.J. Mahale, Vice-Chancellor, Manipur University, *The Role of a University in Developing Creativity and Culture.*

Contents

Contributors' Profile

1. **Professor Suniti Kumar Chatterjee (1890–1977)** a philologist of international repute and a litterateur of a very high order, studied and researched Indo-European Linguistics, Origin and Development of Bengali Language, Slav and Austro-Asian Linguistics at London University, UK, and Sorbonne University in France. He obtained the degree of D.Litt. of the London University. He knew at least three dozens of languages, ancient and modern, Indian and foreign. Besides his eminence as a linguist, he was a specialist in Bengali literature, tribal culture of India, art and culture of Asia. A prolific writer in English, Bengali, and Hindi, some of his well-known works are *Origin and Development of Bengali Language* (in English), *Bangla Bhashatattver Bhumika* (in Bengali), *Bharat Sanskriti Kirata Janakriti* and *Aryabhasa aur Hindi* (in Hindi). He accompanied Rabindranath Tagore to the Far Eastern countries and recorded his experiences of the great cultural heritage of the area in his delightful work in Bengali *Dvipamay Bharat*. Professor Chatterjee also held many important positions. He became a National professor in 1964. He was appointed Chairman of the Sanskrit Commission, constituted by the Government of India in 1956. In that capacity, he compiled a Report which is both literature and history. He was also the President of the Bangiya

Sahitya Parishad, Calcutta in 1961 and the President of the Sahitya Akademi, 1968-72. Professor Chatterjee was a legend of his time because of his encyclopedic knowledge, photographic memory, and avid curiosity about human civilisation. (*Source*: https://ignca.gov.in/divisionss/kaldarsana/memorial-lectures/suniti-kumar-chatterjee-memorial-lecture/)

2. **Ramesh Chandra Majumdar (1888–1980) popularly known as R.C. Majumdar**, is one of the major Indian historians of the past century. In 1921 he became a professor of history and later Vice-Chancellor of the University of Dacca from 1937 to 1942. From 1950, he was the Principal of the College of Indology, Banaras Hindu University. He was elected the general president of the Indian History Congress. His work ranges from ancient Indian history (*Corporate Life in Ancient India*, 1919) to regional history (*The History of Bengal*, 1943) to Far Eastern and Southeast Asian history (*Ancient Indian Colonies in the Far East*, 1927). After extensive travels to Southeast Asia and research, he wrote detailed histories of Champa (1927), Suvarnadvipa (1938), and Kambuja Desa (1944). Initially appointed by the Government of India to helm a committee to write the history of the freedom struggle in India, he left after disagreements with the Education Ministry and published his own *The Sepoy Mutiny and the Revolt of 1857*. Later he published *History of the Freedom Movement in India* in three volumes. He also wrote *An Advanced History of India* (1960). Starting in 1951, he dedicated twenty-six long years to describing the history of the Indian people from the Vedic Period until the Independence of India in a volume series titled *The History and Culture of the Indian People* (1951-77). (*Source*: https://indianhistorycollective.com/ramesh-chandra-majumdar/)
3. **Nirmal Kumar Bose (1901–72)**, one of India's greatest sons, a humanist, a Gandhian, and a radical

anthropologist of whom social reconstruction was more important than building sociological theories—was a carry-over of the nineteenth-century Renaissance in Bengal. He was a great mind, a great visionary who was never confined to the conventional boundary of an academic discipline, be it anthropology, geography, geology, prehistory, archaeology, or even Gandhiology (if that term may be used). Professor Bose used anthropology to demonstrate India's unity in the diversity of cultures. He possessed in his heart a precious thing—the love for his countrymen—that was much greater than his passion for anthropology. Historians of world anthropology are aware of Bose's pioneer thinking and his original contribution to the concept of culture. But, regrettably and not so regrettably, Bose could not pursue it further, because in his judgement something else was more important. That was India's national Freedom Movement. He preferred to remain in the prison rather than in the luxury of intellectual pursuit. (*Source*: https://ignca.gov.in/divisionss/kalakosa/kalasamalocana/nirmal-kumar-bose-memorial-lecture/)

4. **Dattatreya Balkrishna Kalelkar (1885–1981)** popularly known as Kaka Kalelkar was a native of Kaleli village near Sawantwadi in Maharashtra which gave his surname Kalelkar. He met Mahatma Gandhi in 1915 and became a member of Sabarmati Ashram. He taught at Rashtriya Shala of Sabarmati Ashram. With Gandhi's encouragement, he played an active role in establishing Gujarat Vidyapith at Ahmedabad and became its vice-chancellor in 1928. He was imprisoned several times due to his participation in the Indian independence movement. He retired from Gujarat Vidyapith in 1939. In 1935, Kalelkar became a member of Rashtrabhasha Samiti, a committee whose objective was to popularize the Hindi-Hindustani language as the national language of India. He was active with Gandhi Smarak Nidhi

from 1948. He worked as a teacher in Shanti Niketan, as a Principal in Sabarmati Ashram, and Acharya of the National School in Baroda. He was appointed as a member of the Rajya Sabha from 1952 to 1964 and later appointed as a president of the Backward Classes Commission in 1953. He presided Gujarati Sahitya Parishad in 1959. He was bestowed with Padma Vibhushan (1964) and Sahitya Akademi Award (1965). He established Gandhi Vidyapith, Vedchhi in 1967 and served as its vice-chancellor. He died on 21 August 1981. Mahatma Gandhi called him Savai Gujarati, a quarter more than a Gujarati. (*Source*: *Kakasaheb Kalelkar Himalayan Pravas*, 1 September 2010 (First published 1 January 1924), Navajivan Publishing House).

5. **Dineschandra Sircar (1907–85) D.C. Sircar,** as he was widely known was a folklorist, numismatist, historian, and an epigraphist known particularly in India and Bangladesh for his work deciphering inscriptions. Born in a family of Ayurvedic physicians at Krishnanagar, near Faridpur, D.C. Sircar began his professional career as a Lecturer in the Department of Ancient Indian History and Culture, University of Calcutta (1937-49). Then he served the Epigraphy Branch of the Archaeological Survey of India and eventually became the Government Epigraphist. In 1962 he returned to the university as Carmichael Professor of Ancient Indian History and Culture and retired in 1972. D.C. Sircar wrote his first monograph, *The Successors of the Satavahanas in the Lower Deccan*, in 1939, and till his death in 1984, he produced no less than forty monographs, about 1,200 research articles, notes, and reviews and edited about twenty-two books. His unparalleled mastery lay in the field of deciphering and editing early Indian inscriptions, especially those in the Brāhmī script. This is best seen in about 207 articles he contributed to *Epigraphia Indica*, the specialized journal on Indian inscriptions, which he edited, as the Government Epigraphist of India.

Many academic bodies and institutions honoured D.C. Sircar for his stupendous scholarship. He was elected General President by the Indian History Congress (1980, Bombay session) and was the recipient of the Sir William Jones Memorial Plaque (Asiatic Society, Calcutta, 1972). He was a model of scholarship to be emulated by generations of future historians. (*Source*: https://en.banglapedia.org/index.php?title=Sircar%2C_Dineschandra)

6. **Ramchandra Narayan Dandekar (1909–2021) R.N. Dandekar** as widely known was born in the town of Satara in Maharashtra on 17 March 1909. Dandekar was trained in the newly-established modern Sanskrit scholarship at the Deccan College in Pune. Dandekar joined the Fergusson College in Pune in 1933 as a Professor of Sanskrit and Ancient Indian Culture. He received his doctoral degree from the Heidelberg University in 1938. In 1950, he was appointed Professor of Sanskrit and Head of the Department of Sanskrit and Prakrit Languages at the University of Poona. In 1964, he became the Director of the Centre of Advanced Study in Sanskrit and served in that capacity until his retirement in 1974. Dandekar became the Honorary Secretary of the Bhandarkar Oriental Research Institute till 1994 and from 1994 till his death, he served as the Vice-President of the Institute. He was closely associated with numerous Indian and International Organizations. However, he was closely associated with the All-India Oriental Conference, the International Congress of Orientalists, the World Sanskrit Conference, the Deccan College, and the Sanskrit Commission of the Government of India, among many others. He received numerous honors and awards, the most significant of them being the title of Padmabhusan was bestowed upon him by the President of India in 1962. Among his outstanding contributions is the monumental five-volume Vedic bibliography, a comprehensive and classified survey

of Vedic studies. As member secretary of the Sanskrit Commission appointed by the Government of India in 1956, he played a leading role in the publication of its report which even now remains a comprehensive and authoritative document providing directions for the advancement of Sanskrit studies and research in India. R.N. Dandekar represents the peak of Indian Indology in the twentieth century. (*Source*: Madhav M. Deshpande, *Professor R.N. Dandekar* (*March 17, 1909–December 11, 2001*), *Indo-Iranian Journal* 45: 109-19, 2002).

1

A Present-Day Ṛṣi: An Agastya in eastern India

Atombapu Sharma (1889-1963)

Suniti Kumar Chatterji

(a) His Career and his Activities in Various Spheres: as a Scholar, a Writer, a Teacher and as a Politician and a Journalist

In the work of Indian Integration, Pandita-raja Phurailatpam Atombapu Sarma, Vidya-ratna, Gaveshana-Siromani, was a great scholar of Sanskrit, of Brāhmanical philosophy as well as the *Brāhmaṇa* Way of Life, and this he combined with the fullest understanding and appreciation of the Meitei background in culture and folklore and religious ideologies. He was a veritable *ṛṣi* of the present age, who by the example of his life and by his preaching and his writings silently brought about a renaissance of Hindu religion and faith among the Manipuri people, while retaining to the fullest their background of Meitei culture. His work in the religio-cultural domain even in the present age would easily recall the services like those rendered, e.g. by Agastya in south India. Of course, the Pandita-raja was a man of this century, whereas Agastya belonged to fairly high antiquity, probably the middle of the first half of the first millennium before Christ, some 2,500 years from now. Agastya can be looked upon as a contemporary of Buddha, of Lao-tse and Confucius, and his importance would bring to our mind such great names as those mentioned above, besides those of Zoroaster and Socrates, and Vyāsa earlier in India (tenth century BC).

Pandit Atombapu spent his life in the small town of Imphal in Manipur, where he worked among his own people. Almost single-handed, with his erudition and his character, he brought in a new atmosphere of high culture and religious faith as well as political awakening among the Manipur people. He was not just a great Sanskrit scholar whose eminence in Sanskrit language and lore was recognised by the Government of India, far away in the distant capital city of Delhi—he was honoured by the President of India by being given the status of Sanskrit scholar of the highest rank among his compeers from mother parts of India, with a special certificate and pension. His interest in the culture of Manipur was also acknowledged by his being given an award from the official Sangit Nritya Nataka (or Music, Dance and Drama) Academy of Delhi for his knowledge of the theory and practice of Manipuri dance (1963). He manifested in his life and career that he was not only a great Sanskrit scholar in all the Brāhmanical lore in the various departments, but at the same time he kept a vital touch with the culture and traditions of the Meitei people of Manipur.

Just in the same way, Agastya in the Tamil country brought in, as can be well understood, the Brāhmanical culture of north India, and at the same time he was responsible for giving a new tone and turn to one of the basic forms of Dravidian religion which was Śaivaism; and he also helped in the development of the Tamil language and the indigenous Dravidian or Tamil approach to problems of life and literature.

We do not know much about the early life of the Pandita-raja. His life of 74 years, from 1889 to 1963, was one of manifold activity, scholarly and religious, cultural and artistic, as well as educational and political. The number of works which he wrote and which he published, works big and small, in Sanskrit, in Manipuri or Meitei, in Bengali, in English and a few in Hindi, came up to near about 100. Besides, he has left a large number of manuscripts in Manipuri, in English and in Bengali, which are awaiting identification, editing and publication. The political and cultural life of Manipur as well as the development of literature in the Manipuri language, together with a very intensive study of Hindu religion and philosophy through Manipuri, and of Manipuri antiquities and history, were all included within this great scholar's versatile genius.

A Brief Sketch of His Life is given Below

Pandita-raja Atombapu Sarma's father was Phurailatpam Nikunja Vihari Sharma, and his mother was Malati Devi. The family belongs to the Vatsya *gotra* or clan of Yajurvedic brāhmaṇas belonging to the Śukla or White Yajurvedic Kāṇva Mādhyandina Śākhā or branch. According to tradition, the family of Pandita-raja Atombapu came originally from Kanauj in northern India, just like Rādhiyā and the Vārendra brāhmaṇas in Bengal. It can very well be assumed that his ancestors sojourned in Bengal before passing into Manipur, and that could well have been in the twelfth or thirteenth century. It was in the second half of the twelfth century that some Kānyakubja brāhmaṇas, of the Rādhiyā or West Bengal group in Bengal were, specially honoured by the Bengal King Ballāla Sena by being granted special distinction for learning and devotion to religious practices, that of the *kulīna*s or persons of the highest social rank. But we cannot be sure about it all in the case of the Pandita-raja's ancestors. The thirteenth century evidently saw fresh movements of brāhmaṇas in eastern India, and it would appear that there were also repercussions of the Brāhmanical culture, about, that time in distant Manipur as well. The family tradition says that seven generations before Pandit Nikunja Vihari Sharma lived with Bhanu Nārāyaṇa, who is said to have come to Manipur at the beginning of the fifteenth century during the reign of King Kiyamba. Brāhmanical and Buddhist influences had in the meanwhile spread also to Burma. During the last decade of the fifteenth century, a Burmese king, whose name has been given as King Pong, received a symbol of Viṣṇu which fell down from the sky in the form of a *śālagrāma* or ammonite, pebble, which is commonly worshipped by the Hindus in India as symbol of Viṣṇu, and it fell like a ball of fire from the heavens. The Burmese king gave it to King Kiyamba of Manipur as a present-offering when peace was being negotiated between the two kings. King Kiyamba looked for a brāhmaṇa, who could tell him what he was to do with this symbol of Viṣṇu, and how he was to worship it. He found Bhanu Nārāyaṇa, who advised the king to carry on the worship of the sacred symbol by regular offering of milk-rice (*khīra*). From that time this *śālagrāma* stone is being regularly worshipped by the kings of Manipur. This account has been found from old records by the Pandita-raja himself. The descendants of Bhanu Nārāyaṇa who first worshipped this Viṣṇu symbol were given the title of Phuruilatpam, which means in Manipuri "Worshipper in a masonry temple (made of bricks or stones), and evidently the image of Viṣṇu was installed in a masonry temple, which must have been one of the earliest of its kind in Manipur, like the beautiful little temple of Viṣṇu (which is now almost in ruins) at the old Manipur capital of Viṣṇupur, and this temple too is ascribed to King Kiyamba (*c*.1460 AD).

The name of Atom-Bapu given to Pandita-raja was a pet name and in Manipuri it means "the youngest (Atom) brāhmaṇa Bapu)". He began his studies at home, and in due time he was invested with the sacred thread of the brāhmaṇa, and was later married. But the dates of his *upanayana* or investiture with the sacred thread and of his marriage have not been recorded. His wife was Bhagyavati Devi, who after a long and happy married life with him passed away before her husband in the year 1944. There were three sons and three daughters born to the Pandita-raja. The eldest son Dwijamani Sharma died at the age of 9, and the other sons and daughters are Deva-Kisora Sharma, Vāsudeva Sharma, Padmavati Devi, Sanatombi Devi and Dhanyavati Devi. They are all married and settled in life.

The father of the Pandita-raja, Pandit Nikuṇja Vihari Sharma, was a Sanskrit scholar and was famous specially for his knowledge of Grammar and Astrology. He studied under his father Sanskrit Grammar and Metrics as well as *kāvya*, and *alaṅkāra* (the more important compositions in literature and rhetoric), besides the *Smṛtis* or books on sacred law and *Jyotiṣa* (Astronomy and Astrology) and other branches of Sanskrit learning. Another famous Pandit of the court of the King of Manipur, Nutanesvara Sharma, who was the Raja-Vyovasthakari or Sanskrit religious scholar in charge of the Hindu religion and orthodox religious side of the administration, was another teacher of the Pandita-raja. Quite early in his youth his master conferred upon him the title of Vidyā-ratna. Later this title was confirmed by his late Highness Maharaja Sir Chuda-Chand Singh of Manipur. He was generally known in Manipur and eastern India as the Vidyā-ratna of Manipur. Later he was very much impressed by the big edition of the four Vedas published with Sanskrit commentary and Bengali translation by Pandit Durga-Das Lahiri of Bengal, and he came down to West Bengal to obtain initiation in Vedic studies from this scholar. During his early student days, Pandita-raja Atombapu Sarma followed quite a spartan discipline in his life and his ways. He would never sleep on a bedstead but just on a mat spread on the ground. He spent most of his time in his studies, and this habit continued right up to his old age, when three or four hours of sleep in 24 hours were enough for him. He was rather negligent of his health. But he had a good constitution and he passed his days without any illness, in spite of his being careless in "conserving his energies". His death was preceded by only a short illness of a couple of days. The strict regimen of the life of a brāhmaṇa of the old type was perhaps the reason for his good health and fairly long life.

He was the only son of his father. His mother had died very young, and his father was never keeping good health. Young Atombapu had to look after his father and to nurse him in illness. He regarded his father, who was also his teacher like a veritable God on earth. He was exceedingly grateful for what he had received from his father by way of education, and in spite of a busy life full of complications and difficulties he never spared himself in looking after and serving his father in many ways. Combined with his great love and respect for his father was his love of Manipur, the part of India which specially was his little motherland. He was in his talk and in his manners humility personified. He used to say:

> It is beyond my humble power to obtain even a small drop from the vast ocean of the Śāstras. I feel very humble before it all and the little that I have been able to contribute to the service of my mother Manipur is the result of my father's blessings for my sincere service to him.

In fact, he did a very great service to Manipur and its people throughout his life—his great purpose was to bring the teachings of the Sanskrit Śāstras in Manipur Hindu life and to bring about a fusion between Manipur pre-Hindu life and folklore and Brāhmanical Hinduism as in the Vedas and the Purāṇa*s*. He had no deliberate purpose for this. But it was only as a believer in the Hindu religion and its scriptures and also as a lover of the art and culture of Manipur, both of which he knew by inheritance and study, that he was able to perform this: just in the style of the old ṛṣis, who took the message of the Vedas to various parts of India and in countries outside India, and at the same time helped to conserve all that had some value in the earlier traditions and way of life in those areas. His love of Manipur and its tradition and its culture was something very remarkable, and he combined with that the great respect and affection he had for his father.

Pandita-raja started his career as a teacher quite early in his life, from the age of 15. He used to go to the residences of the disciples of the family, who were devoted to the Vaiṣṇava faith, and there he would speak in Manipuri, with his own commentaries, on the *Bhāgavata* Purāṇa dealing particularly with the life or legend of Kṛṣṇa, and on the *Bhagavadgītā*.

He was very much in demand even from his adolescence as a teacher and preacher, and every day he would go to different places, and sometimes he would have to go to ten different centres in the course of the day. At the age of 20 he became the Chief Pandit of a local Pol or Sanskrit College (Catuṣpāṭhī or Pāṭhaśālā) of the old type. At the age of 25, he was made the Teacher of Sanskrit in the English High School at Manipur, namely the Johnston High School, which was the first institution affiliated to the University of Calcutta and which taught English and modern subjects as well as Sanskrit to boys in Manipur. This School was founded as a Secondary School by Colonel (later Major General Sir) James Johnston (K.C.S.L.). British Resident, before the occupation of Manipur by the British in 1891. Sanskrit was at that time a compulsory subject in the High School, following the curriculum of the University of Calcutta; and it has been a most remarkable thing that through the instrumentality of this English School. Sanskrit was very largely promulgated among the people of Manipur—all boys who joined the school for English studies had to read Sanskrit also as their classical language; so much so that most of the senior men in the state of Manipur above 40 who were students of the Johnston High School, got both their initiation into Sanskrit and inspiration for further study from Pandita-raja Atombapu Sarma. Besides, in his own home he also used to give lessons to advanced students in Sanskrit; and this he continued right up to the last days of his life, when serious students eager to learn the Sanskrit Śāstras, including Astrology, would come to his place and sit at his feet.

Pandita-raja became interested in the Vedas, and he, started translating the Vedas with a commentary in Manipuri, the first volume only of which he could publish. As said before the work of the Bengal Pandit Durgā-Das Lahiri appears to have impressed him very much, and in April 1963 he established an Institution at Imphal called the Sanga-Veda-Asrama, with the object of teaching both the Vedas and their syncretism with the culture of Manipur. There was a number of eager and enthusiastic students who used to attend his school. But only four months after the establishment of this school, on 3 September 1968, Pandita-raja Atombapu Sarma passed away, leaving this part of his work just begun and incomplete.

Pandita-raja came to be known at the age of 30 to the then Bada-Senapati or Chief General Raja Dumbra Singh, the eldest brother of Sir Chuda-Chand Singh, the Maharaja of Manipur because of his extraordinary eminence in Sanskrit Śāstras and specially *Jyotiṣa-śāstra* (Astronomy and Astrology). The Maharaja himself became a great admirer of Pandita-raja and made him his *Rāja-Paṇḍita* or Chief Sanskrit Scholar attached to the court. In this capacity, he had the unique opportunity of visiting almost all the important holy places and towns of India. One of the first objectives of his visit was to go to Calcutta to contact Pandit Durgā-Das Lahiri for Vedic studies.

Pandita-raja Atombapu Sarma's intellectual and cultural activities were not only in study and teaching and propagation of the Sanskrit Śāstras but also in helping to develop the Manipuri language in various ways, both by translations and original works as well as by journalism, and by a general encouragement and support of Manipuri. He also took leading part in the rousing of the political consciousness of the people of Manipur, and this he achieved by journalism as well as by his speeches and active participation in political movements. He took up the early Hindu tradition of Manipur itself, and sought to give a new interpretation of early Manipuri history. This will be referred to later on.

His Highness Maharaja Sir Chuda-Chand Singh of Manipur died at Navadwip in 1941. Pandita-raja returned to Manipur and settled in his house permanently in 1942, and began to devote himself largely to translation and commentary on very great utility to popularise the advanced study of Sanskrit among the Manipuri people.

Apart from his work as a religious teacher and translator of and commentator to Sanskrit sacred texts, the Pandita-raja's achievement as a journalist was of a very high order. In

1933, the First Daily Paper in Manipuri, the *Dainik Manipur* was brought out by the Pandita-raja from his press. Then he started a monthly literary and cultural paper, the *Lalita-Manjuri Patrika*, besides a yearly almanac (mainly religious in character) in Manipuri—the *Manipur Pañcānga*, which was also started in 1933. There was no other daily paper in the Assam State of India before the *Dainik Manipur* was started. Unfortunately, this daily paper as well as the monthly journal are not published any longer. The *Dainik Manipur* helped immensely to bring about modern political consciousness to the people of Manipur, besides helping them to understand and appreciate their literature and the literature of Sanskrit. For the first time in Manipur a criticism of the British administration was started. It became a journal round which all Manipuris, not only in Manipur but also in Assam and other parts of India and in Burma, rallied. The representatives of Britain were alarmed at the activities of this daily, and it was very soon banned, and finally it ceased publication. But it is still in the consciousness of the Manipuri people, and it remains in history as having served the greatest purpose of arousing the political aspirations of the people.

The *Lalita-Manjuri Patrika* was mainly concerned with literature, and it continued to flourish longer. It may be said that this journal is the mother of modern Manipuri literature. Almost all the great Manipuri poets and prose-writers of the present age, such as Kh. Chaoba Singh Sāhitya-ratna, Hijum Aṅganghal Singh Kavi-ratna, A. Dorendrajit Singh Kavi-ratna and others were its regular contributors.

The sole responsibility for regular publication of the two papers, the daily and the monthly, was Pandita-raja's. He used to contribute by far the larger number of writings for these papers. All this time he was carrying on his teaching work at the school and also at his home—with aspirants for Sanskrit scholarship who would throng there; and there were his strenuous duties at the Mahārāja's court also, as the Court Pandit and the keeper of the religious conscience of the people, so to say.

Pandita-raja started in 1946 a new Manipuri daily known as the *Bhagyavati Patrika* in memory of his beloved wife. Two other journals, both monthlies, one called the *Bhagyavati Masika* on culture and literature, and the other the *Bhagyavati Lalita. Kidu on Music and Dance*, also followed, and this indicated the wide interests and activities of the Pandita-raja.

Meanwhile, Manipur had come more closely in touch with the rest of India, and Manipuri students began to get English education in Calcutta and Gauhati and there was now a thorough integration of Manipur with the rest of India. The Manipuri Dance became recognised and was received with acclamation as one of the most distinctive schools of Indian Dance throughout the whole of India. Initially, in this matter Rabindranath Tagore at his Santiniketan School gave the first great impetus. The *Bhagyavati Patrika* became a mouth-piece of the people of Manipur for criticising the administration both of British India and of the Manipur State. The Pandita-raja almost single handed carried on the work of these three papers, and in this way he can be described as "the Father of Manipuri Journalism", and one of the Creators of Manipur Public Life.

As early as 1946, the Pandita-raja organised an institute called the Manipuri Sangita Kala Rakshini Sabha for research in the character and history of music and dance as they prevailed in Manipur.

The Manipuri Sahitya Parishad, which was working for the development of Manipuri language and literature, out of the great regard for the researches which he was conducting, gave him the title of Gaveṣaṇa-Śiromaṇi. The Government Sanskrit Mahavidyalaya or College of Calcutta, through its Principal and its professors expressed their appreciation of Pandita-raja's work for Sanskrit, and gave him the title of Pandita-raja in 1948. In 1956, the Pandita-raja became a member of a panel of experts formed by the Government of India to select deserving candidates from young artists in Manipur for scholarships in Manipuri dancing. The Pandita-raja's work for Sanskrit was mentioned in the Government of India Sanskrit Commission's Report, and following the suggestion of the

Sanskrit Commission, when the Government of India decided upon giving Certificates of Honour with a token pension to the most distinguished Sanskrit scholars throughout the whole of India in the present day, the President of India in 1959 gave him this Certificate of Honour for Sanskrit. In 1960, the Pandita-raja accepted the Presidentship of the Manipuri Sahitya Parishad, and this office he held for two successive years. In 1961, he became a member of the Bharatiya Sanskrit Sangam. In 1963, the Sangeet Natak Akademi of India in New Delhi gave to him its award for Manipuri dance. As he passed away in September 1963, this award became a posthumous one. This was for his being a true *guru* in the art of Manipuri dancing through his profound knowledge of its whole system in both theory and practice.

In Politics also it is to be mentioned that, he became associated with the Manipur State Branch of the Indian National Congress from its very beginning. His house was used as the head office of the state Congress for a long time. The first big session of the Congress was held within the compound of the house of the Pandita-raja.

(b) Pandita-raja Atombapu's Services to Manipur and India: His Enrichment of Hinduism by Expanding Its Horizon and Its Intensity

It would be seen that the Pandita-raja's life was a very fruitful one, comprehending almost all the religious, intellectual, cultural and political activities of Manipur for nearly half a century. He was a builder of Manipur in these lines, a veritable friend, philosopher and guide of his people; and he could be thus truly described as "the father and Maker of Modern Manipur". His work of integration of Manipur history and culture with the wider world of the composite Hindu sphere of culture, was manifest in some of his research publications.

There is a theory which was propounded by the late Dr. Haran Chandra Chakladar, distinguished Anthropologist, Sanskritist and Scholar of Indology, who was lecturer in the University of Calcutta for a long number of years that there was a very early settlement of the Aryan people in eastern India—on the banks of the Brahmaputra. This view was also independently promulgated in his own way by the Pandita-raja from his own readings and interpretations of some of the Vedic texts. He described that Manipur was the scene of a very early advent of the gods—of an Aryan settlement, as we could interpret it in the modern way. In fact, according to him it was the *Pratnaukas* or the "Ancient Homeland" of the Aryan people in the area of north-eastern India. The story of the gods and heroes of Manipur as found in early Meitei literature, and as expressed in the dances of Manipur, particularly the Lai-Haraoba, were equated by him with the world of the Vedas and the Purāṇas. This was the time honoured way of integration, by finding points of agreement or contact or supplementation between the two cultures—the Aryan or Hindu and the Pre-Aryan. What he has written in these matters could veritably be described as a kind of a *Maṇipura Purāṇa*, or Purāṇic traditions with special reference to the Meitei people of Manipur. This matter has in general been discussed before. If the Pandita-raja had lived three or four or five hundred years ago, and if he had the happy idea, like many other ancient and medieval Indian saints and teachers, of rendering the whole thing in Sanskrit verse, we would have got a real *Maṇipura Purāṇa* in Sanskrit, which would take its place beside the extent Sanskrit Purāṇas or Upapurāṇas or Sthala-Purāṇas and thus be a heritage for the whole of India. But he wrote in Manipuri, and some of it was published in English and in Hindi and Bengali. But nevertheless, it remains as an imperishable testimony to his knowledge of the two cultures, and of his faith in their being in essence one single culture—a unity and not a duality. Just as in the Tamil south the *bhakti* literature of the Tamil Azhvars or Tamil Vaiṣṇava saints on the one hand and the Vedānta literature of the *Upaniṣads* and the *Gītā,* etc. On the other have been accepted by the Tamilian Vaiṣṇavas as complimentary or explanatory to each other and have been generally given the name of Ubhaya-Vedānta, or "both the Vedāntas, or the two-fold Vedānta". Similarly, the Purāṇic tales of Manipur and their points of agreement, contact and integration with the Sanskrit Purāṇa and other connected literature can be described as "Ubhaya-Purāṇa". For his having dedicated the whole life in the service of this ideal, and for his great success in this line, the late Pandita-raja Atombapu Sarma can very well be described as a Modern Ṛṣi of the Hinduism of India and, as observed before, as a veritable Agastya for eastern India.

To give a most interesting example of this kind of integration which characterised the Pandita-raja's interpretation of Hinduism and the Purāṇas. The Pandita-raja was nothing but an orthodox brāhmaṇa of the old type, with absolute faith in the truth of the Purāṇic myths and legends and semi-historical tales. Like all orthodox Sanskrit scholars, too, he would believe also in the allegorical interpretation of a great many of these myths and legends and stories, in their being repositories of deep spiritual truths and lessons. The religious philosophy of Hinduism which he believed in was that of Caitanya Vaiṣṇavism (with its affiliation to the *prasthāna-traya* or the three great masses of authority—(1) the *Śruti-prasthāna* or the Vedas including the Upaniṣads, (2) the *Smṛti-prasthāna* or the Purāṇistic texts like the *Mahābhārata* including the *Bhagavadgītā* as well as the *Rāmāyaṇa*, and all the corpus of the Purāṇas and the Dharmaśāstras, including particularly the Vaiṣṇava *Bhāgavata* Purāṇa, and (3) the *nyāya-prasthāna* or the authority of argumentative philosophy like the *Vedāntasūtras* of Bādarāyaṇa). During the sixteenth-eighteenth centuries, the story of the love of Rādhā and Kṛṣṇa came in for a full and elaborate mystic-philosophical treatment in the bands of some ten generations of Bengal Vaiṣṇava teachers at Navadvīpa and Vrindavana. This began in a way from the twelfth century, with Jayadeva's mystic-erotic poem the *Gītā-Govinda*, to which the Bengal Vaiṣṇavas gave almost the Authority of the *Bhāgavata* Purāṇa. Rūpa and Sanātana, Jīva and Raghunātha and other Goswāmīs or saint-sages of Vrindavana and Baladeva Vidyābhūṣaṇa from Orissa, who in the eighteenth century gave to Caitanya Vaiṣṇavism its philosophical affiliation to the *prasthāna-traya* by his commentaries to the *Bhagavadgītā*, the *Vedāntasūtras* and to some of the Upaniṣads, prepared a mass of literature in Sanskrit establishing the doctrines of this form of Vaiṣṇavism. One of the most noteworthy ideologies was its doctrine of Parakīyavāda, exalting the love of Rādhā as a married woman for Kṛṣṇa while her husband Abhimanyu (Ahivannu, Aihana or Ayana) was still living. The abandon of love, with its complete self-abnegation, and its recklessness of consequences, social and otherwise, for an anti-social and even immoral infatuation of a married woman for her lover, as typifying the highest form of attachment of a devotee for his God, was given a higher place in this ideology of the *parakīya* than the legitimate virtuous love of the married woman for her husband, as this latter did not entail the risks and the loss of respect and reputation and social ostracism which the other kind of love did.

Pandita-raja Atombapu Sarma was saturated with the spiritual interpretation and application of the *parakīya*; and with this he interpreted the old Manipuri story of love, and without any incongruity in the logic which he followed, he could bring in this story in perfect agreement in its spirit with the conception and justification of the *parakīya*. Already, before the times of the Pandita-raja, Manipur was associated with Śiva and Umā. They wanted to emulate Kṛṣṇa and Rādhā in performing the Rāsa dance on their own, as it has been narrated before. The great national love-romance of the Meitei people of Manipur the story of the hero Prince Khamba and the heroine Princess Thoibi, is exceedingly wide spread, and minstrels with the *pena* lute sing about it. Moving through the whole of Manipur, and the story is enacted in dances at Moirang, 27 miles to the south-west of Imphal, in the courtyard of the temple of the God Thangjing and the Goddess Lairembi. The popularity of this story has been further demonstrated by the composition of huge epic poem of some 38,000 lines by the late Hijam Aṅganghal Singh, *c.*1892–1943) and its full publication in 1964, dealing with the Khamba-Thoibi story—the Khamba Thoibi Shoreng (This has been noted before).

After many adventure and reverses in the course of their true love which never ran smooth, and after their triumph over their enemies with their machinations, the lovers finally triumphed, and were united in wedlock. But their happiness was short-lived. Khamba in his jealous love of Thoibi foolishly wanted to test her fidelity, and was inadvertently pierced by a spear by Thoibi who could not see her husband and thought he was an evil-minded molester, and when the mistake was discovered by her, she committed suicide with the same spear over the body of her dying lover-husband. They were cremated together on the same pyre. It was said that they were really gods who came down to the earth to demonstrate their great love, and they did not mean to live long on the earth and to have children like ordinary human couples. Khamba and Thoibi were looked upon as incarnations of Śiva and Umā, and their love as husband and wife was the legitimate and proper love of a married couple, as Pandita-raja explained it.

But another great Meitei love story as already there, and it was concerned with the love of a princess for a young chief, both of whom formed a deep and a compelling attachment for each other when they first met each other. The story and its *parakīya* interpretation as believed by the Pandita-raja and other Vaiṣṇavas have been given by the Pandita-raja in his brochure in English—*Manipur Sangtan Dharma* or "The Traditional Religion of Manipur", published from Imphal in 1952 (pp. 18-27). Nompok-Ningthou was a young chief in Manipur (the name meant "the Lord of the Past"—Prācīśvara in Sanskrit) loved Panthoibi the daughter of Ching-Ningthou, the Lord of the Mountains in Sanskrit Giri-rāja. While out hunting, the young chief met Panthoibi, and they immediately fell in love with each other. Panthoibi was so very much moved that she lost control over her senses—her condition was like that of Rādhā when she first saw Kṛṣṇa. Panthoibi's father was alarmed at her condition—she was so much absorbed in her love, and was listless. He and his followers had seen Nompok-Ningthou, whose strange dress (he was clad in tiger-skin, had matted hair, and snakes were on his body, and he held a trident for a spear) and strange personality alarmed them, and they thought that Panthoibi was taken ill at the sight of this apparition. But they did not understand that it was only the first dawning of an uncontrollable love (*pūrva-rāga*) in Vaiṣṇava parlance which had overpowered Panthoibi. Thinking that if she had a husband and lived with him, who would be cured of her strange malady, her father gave her to onc Khaba as his wife. But Khaba was afraid to approach her when she was brought to his home—he thought she was a Goddess, or a serpent, or a mad woman, and lived separately from her. Panthoibi and Nompok-Ningthou were seeking each other, and they finally met at Kangla, which is in the heart of the town of Imphal. This was the rendezvous which saw the union of the lovers. Khaba came to know of this, and he built a temple to Panthoibi, and he placed there her garments and hair from her head. People came to know that Nompok-Ningthou and Panthoibi were incarnations of Śiva and Pārvatī, and their purpose in enacting this love-drama was to show the importance and value of Vaiṣṇava *parakīya* love. Even now, at many places, special dances celebrating the drama of this love Śiva-Nompok-Ningthou and Umā-Panthoibi are performed by the Maidas and Maibis, the priests and priestesses of the primitive Meitei religion and by young girls and youths.

Pandita-raja Atombapu Sarma has sublimated this love story into a *līlā* or sport of Śiva and Pārvatī with its special set up in Manipur, and has linked it indissolubly with the great mystic conceptions of Śiva and Umā. Dravidian south India has similarly supplied her quota of legends enlarging the scope of the Śiva-Umā myth and symbolism, e.g. that of Mīnākṣī and of Kanya Kumari, and the stories of the *Periya-Purnāṇam* and those connected with Śiva's sons Gaṇeśa and Kārttikeya (Subramaṇya or Murugan). Pandita-raja in addition to being a devotee and a philosopher, had the soul of an artist. The Panthoibi story he found beautiful, matching the story of the great love of Rādhā and Kṛṣṇa. In his home, as in all well-to-do Manipur homes, he had his family temple, with images of

Rādhā and Kṛṣṇa and of Caitanya (Gauraṅga) and his disciple Nityānanda. There the orthodox Vaiṣṇava worship is regularly performed. But near to this family shrine of Rādhā and Kṛṣṇa, he built another little temple dedicated to Nompok-Ningthou as Śiva and Panthoibi as Umā. He had a group of two figures, made in clay, about half life-size each, beautifully modelled and resplendent with colours, depicting Nompok-Ningthou in the garb of Śiva embraced by Umā Panthoibi dressed as a Meitei Laisabi or young maiden, as a princess, with her typical skirt with red and black strines and her veil of fine muslin. In front of this beautiful group in clay sculpture, the Pandita-raja put in a large Śivaliṅga with Gaurīpaṭṭa or base, the symbol of Śiva and Umā all over India. He has arranged for regular service of worship in this temple also. Nompok-Ningthou and Panthoibi are here linked up with Śiva and Umā—they are but special incarnations or emanations of Śiva and Umā and as such they will claim the reverent homage of Hindus from all over India who believe in the Śiva-Umā conception. Here we have a beautiful and telling example of integration of a Manipuri legend with the all-comprehending images of Śiva and Umā, and by this integration the horizon of Brāhmanical Hindudom is certainly extended and enriched with a new emotional content from the world of the Meitei people: Worshippers of Śiva and Pārvatī, whether from Kashmir or Kerala, Punjab or Nepal, Bengal or Maharashtra, Karnataka or Uttar Pradesh, Bihar or Andhra or Gujarat, will easily and most naturally pay their homage make their obseisance to this concept of Śiva. Nompok-Ningthou and Umā Panthoibi at Imphal in Manipur.

The great work of the Pandita-raja is making Purāṇa-lore and Hindu philosophy easily available to the Manipuri people by bringing out the *Bhāgavata Purāṇa*, the *Bhagavadgītā*, and other works of capital importance in the Manipuri language, with the original Sanskrit text included has been worthily taken up by a batch of Manipur scholars. Already this work was started early in the eighteenth century when portions of the *Mahābhārata* and the *Rāmāyaṇa* were made accessible in Manipuri. Through the discourse of the brāhmaṇa scholars, the knowledge of the Purāṇas and the two epics was spreading in Manipur, and Pandita-raja also took his part in this work. A Manipuri version of the entire Sanskrit *Mahābhārata* has now been taken in hand, the Sanskrit text with Manipuri translation, and this is more than half achieved now (April 1964). Pandit Sri Kalachand Sastri, under the auspices of a society for the publication of the *Mahābhārata* in Manipuri, has already brought out twelve out of the proposed twenty-one volumes of this great work. When completed, this will be an achievement of which any of the major languages, not only of India but of the whole civilised world, could very well be proud. Pandit Kalachand Sastri has also published a long religious poem on the story of Kṛṣṇa—the *Vāsudeva Mahākāvya*, of some 12,000 lines (pulished 1960). All this redound to the glory and success of the spirit of integration to a pan-Indian Hindu culture, of which Pandita-raja Atombapu Sarma has been a dedicated same and seer as well as a symbol.

(c) Personal Contact with the Pandita-raja

I had the privilege of knowing this *ṛṣi* of the modern age only for a few days during my first visit to Manipur in 1948, and subsequently I had the privilege of corresponding with him and exchanging publications with him. He had a generous heart and he always remembered old friends; and for what he thought was some service rendered to him, he was infinitely grateful. From his friends and others who have known him intimately in Manipur, I can only have a confirmation of an estimate of his personality and character, namely, that he was an erudite scholar in Sanskrit, a fervent believer in Hindu philosophy, particularly in its *Vaiṣṇava* set-up, a lover of the art and culture and history and traditions of the Meitei people, a person who was for synthesis and integration, and who in his personal life was a man who never spared himself of the service of the masses; and who was moreover in private life a devoted husband and a dutiful father, and a man who bound up to him all his friend with golden chains of love and respect.

I remember the few long talks I had with him in his residence, and that I was impressed by the profundity of his religious convictions and his great simplicity and sincerity. After returning to Calcutta, I was instrumental in persuading the late Principal jātindra Bimal Chaudhuri and the scholars of the Government Sanskrit College in Calcutta to honour his scholarship and his service to Sanskrit by giving him the title of Pandita-raja, an honour he appreciated very much.

We made a reference to his erudition and his work for Sanskrit in the Report of the Government of India Sanskrit Commission (1957-58) of which I was the chairman. The Government of India through President Rajendra Prasad recognised his merit by giving him a certificate of honour, and in this way drew the attention of the rest of the Sanskrit knowing world in India to distant Manipur in the Eastern Frontier of India, which had built-up a tradition of its own in Sanskrit studies.

The father of Rabindranath Tagore, because of his scholarship and his spirit of devotion and his whole-hearted services for the revival of Upaniṣadic philosophy and the Upaniṣadic way of thought and life, was acclaimed by the people of Bengal with respect and love, and they gave him the sobriquet of *maharṣi,* a great *ṛṣi* or sage of modern times. From what the Pandita-raja did for the integration of Hinduism and the harmonisation of Manipuri life with Hindu thoughts and culture, it will be easily conceded that he too was a *ṛṣi* of the modern age. And we honour ourselves by calling him by this name.

I consider it to be a great privilege for me to come to Manipur on the occasion of the First Anniversary of his passing away—which really means for him his acquisition of immortality, and to present, along with the people of Manipur my tribute of respect to his illustrations and sacred memory.

(d) A List of His Books and Papers (in Meitei, Sanskrit, Bengali, Hindi and English)

Below is given a list of the books and booklets written, edited and published by the Pandita-raja. This had been obtained through the courtesy of his son, Sri Devakisore Sharma.

These works are either in Meitei or in Sanskrit and Meitei (with a few Bengali, English and Hindi):

1. *Srimad-Bhāgavata*-Purāṇa (*Anvaya, Anuvada* & *Vyakhya* in Manipuri)
   (i) *Skandha* I -do-
   (ii) *Skandha* II -do-
   (iii) *Skandha* III -do-
   (iv) *Skandha* IV -do-
   (v) *Skandha* V -do-
   (vi) *Skandha* VI -do-
   (vii) *Skandha* VII -do-
   (viii) *Skandha* VIII -do-
   (ix) *Skandha* IX -do-
   (x) *Skandha* I up to 78th *adhyāya* (the 1st twelve *adhyāya*s in two editions).

   The *Skandhas* I and II are in two editions.
2. *Rig-Veda Saṁhitā* (vol. I only).
3. *Kumbaba.*
4. *Gita-Govinda* of Jayadeva (in three editions *Anvaya*, *Anuvada* and *Vyakhya* in Manipuri).
5. Rāsa-*Panchadhyaya.*
6. *Gopāla-Sahasranama.*
7. *Markandeya-Chandi* (*Saptasati*).
8. *Chaitanya-Charitamrita-Sloka-Mala.*
9. *Sarasvata Vyakarana*: a magnum opus: original Sanskrit with Manipuri Commentary.
10. *Harinamamritha.*
11. *Ujjvala-Nilmani-Kirana* (based on the great work of Rūpa Gosvāmī).
12. *Hari-Bhakti*-Rāsa*mrita-Sindhu-Bindu.*
13. *Veshasrita-Vidhi.*
14. *Mala-Nirnaya.*
15. *Lakṣmī-Nārāyaṇa-Hridaya.*
16. *Gopāla-Sahasranama* (abridged edition).
17. *Sraddha-Paddhati.*

18. *Puja-Paddhati* (in two editions).
19. *Deva-Puja.*
20. *Graha-Puja.*
21. *Graha-Santi.*
22. *Sandhya-Paddhati.*
23. *Yumseng Yumang* (deals with the Smṛtiśāstra).
24. *Charchara-Panjarika.*
25. *Tarpana-Vidhi.*
26. *Hari-Bhakti Vilasa-Kana.*
27. *Gita* (abridged edition).
28. *Gita* (big edition).
29. *Gita* (medium size edition).
30. *Gita* (Manipuri only, without Sanskrit text).
31. *Maṇipura Itihasa.*
32. *Maṇipura-Puravritta.*
33. *Maṇipura-Pratibha* (in Sanskrit).
34. *Maṇipura-Pratibha* (in Manipuri).
35. *Meitei and Meitei Leipak.*
36. *Pratnaukas: The Ancient Home* of the Aryans.
37. *Manipuriya Sanātana Dharma* (in Hindi).
38. *Manipuriya Sanātana Dharma* (in English), 2 parts.
39. *Manipuriya Sanātana Dharma* (in Manipuri).
40. *A Supplement to Manipur Sanatan Dharma* (in English).
41. *Meitei Meihouron.*
42. *Harei Maye* (in English).
43. *Meitei and Meitei Leipak* (in English).
44. *Meitei Dharma Ariba.*
45. *Manipur* Rāsa, vol. I.
46. *Manipur* Rāsa, vol. II.
47. *Cheitharon Kumbaba*, I.
48. *Cheitharon Kumbaba*, II.
49. *Meitei Leima.*
50. *Meihouron Shukuk.*
51. *Pakhangba.*
52. *Meitei Kirtana.*
53. *Meitei Sidabung* (in Manipuri).
54. *Meitei Sidabung* (in English).

55. *Khagola.*
56. *Bhu-gola.*
57. *Sankirtana Maha-yajna.*
58. *Bhāgavatamrita-Kana.*
59. *Meitei* (in English).
60. *Chanakya-Slokas.*
61. *Bhava-Phala.*
62. *Paknaba Yengba* (*Totak Bichar*).
63. *Ashotottari-Phala.*
64. *Kuthi Inaba.*
65. *Dasha Yengnaba.*
66. *Jyotiṣa-Vijnana*, vol. I.
67. *Jyotiṣa-Vijnana*, vol. II.
68. *Jyotiṣa-Kamadhenu.*
69. *Masa-Phala.*
70. *Cha-Sambru.*
71. *Rasi-Phala.*
72. *Nakshatra-Phala.*
73. *Mang-Phala.*
74. *Subika Lai.*
75. *Svarodaya.*
76. *Cheithaba.*
77. *Khubakmayi Yengnaba*, vol. I.
78. *Khubakmayi Yengnaba*, vol. II.
79. *Luk Katnaba.*
80. *Nityachara.*
81. Rāsa-*Panchadyaya* (abridged edition).
82. *Bhangi Pareng Achouba.*
83. *Meitei Jagoi Chali.*
84. *Manipuriya Nartana-Thabal Chongbi.*
85. *A Brief Description of the Manipuri Dance.*
86. *A Short Introduction to the Manipuri Dance.*
87. *Siksha.*
88. *Meitei Gavam-ayana Satra.*
89. *Laipou Jagoi.*
90. *Gochura-Phala.*
91. An address to Pandit Jawaharlal Nehru.

92. Presidential Address to Manipuri Sahitya Parishad for the session 1960.
93. Presidential Address to Manipuri Sahitya Parishad for the session 1961.
94. *Meitei Sahitya.*
95. *Swami Vivekanandaji Samkshipta Parichaya* (a booklet of essays on Swami Vivekananda).

Many other smaller booklets or lectures given out from time to time in different functions are not included here.

In Manuscript

1. *Rig-Veda Saṁhitā*, vol. II.
2. *Amara-Kosha* (up to Vanaushadhi Varga).
3. *Pre-Historic Thabalchongbi* (in English).
4. *Pre-Historic Thabalchongbi* (in Bengali).
5. *Manipuri* Rāsa (in English).
6. *Manipuri* Rāsa (in Bengali).

Quite a large mass of manuscript materials in the Pandita-raja's own hand is lying unidentified.

2
India's Integration and Hindu Culture

Suniti Kumar Chatterji

General Lines of the Spread, Acceptance and Establishment of Hindu Religion and Culture

(a) *The Theory of the Expansion of a Highly Civilised Indo-European Herrenyolk: Modern European Expansion and Ancient "Aryan' Conquest—Political and Cultural*

It is now more or less accepted that Hindu culture—using "Hindu" in the widest sense, and including within this term all religious ideologies and movements which from the earliest times down to recent years originated on the soil of India—has been the most vital and enduring force to bind up the different races and peoples, pure or mixed, which are found in India into a single people—single in the sense that it possesses a specific cultural character, and feels as one people. The matter has been engaging the attention of scholars in India and abroad during the past few decades. It has now been generally established—and also accepted—that the culture of India, like all great cultures, is a great composite. A hundred years ago, people in Europe believed, and their ideas in this matter were also adopted generally by the intelligentsia (mostly people of the higher castes) in India, that the Aryans or Indo-Europeans were a remarkably gifted race, and ever since they emerged into history they formed a powerful civilising force. They originated in some unknown area in Central Asia or Southern Russia, and then they spread West and North-West, South and East; and in the various countries of Europe and Asia they became the ancestors of the great, civilised peoples of antiquity—of the Greeks and of the Italians (including the Latin), of the Iranians and the Indo-Aryans; and, besides, of the Germans or Teutons, the Celts, and the Slavs and the Balts. These last were in a comparatively backward situation in culture and organisation right down to the commencement of the first millennium AD. But they too, the Germans, the Celts, the Slavs and the Balts, because of some of their inherent qualities of mind and body as Indo-European-speaking peoples, became the inheritors of the ancient civilisation which some of their brothers and cousins developed almost to perfection in the Mediterranean area, and in distant Iran and India. The "Aryans" (or Indo-Europeans) were, to use the expression which was made widely current in Hitler's Germany, as a white race and Herrenvolk par excellence—a masterful people, who because of their basic physical, mental and moral qualities and their power of organisation, easily became conquerors and rulers over all other nations they came in contact with. In this way, the Indo-European people spread all over the world of Europe and Asia, not only in the past centuries—some three to four thousand years from now—but also during the five centuries of recent history they were able to dominate the whole of the two Americas, Africa to the South of the Sahara, and considerable parts of Asia.

(b) *The Spread and Establishment of West European Peoples as Rulers and Civilisers in the New World, Africa and Asia during the Last Five Centuries*

To obtain a share of the very profitable trade with the countries of the East and the Far East (particularly with India); Western

European nations—the Italians, the Spaniards, the Portuguese, the Dutch, the English and the French—wanted, from the early centuries of the second millennium AD, to have direct access to India by the sea, if they could find it, without it being necessary for them to traverse the overland route through Asia Minor, Mesopotamia and Iran to India, Central Asia and China. These lands were almost closed to the European peoples because of the easily understood unwillingness of the Muslim peoples of these areas—the Arabs, the Iranians and others—to permit Christian Europeans have full access to the lands of the Golden East. The story of the wealth and grandeur of the East as told by Marco Polo and other great European travellers and sojourners in the East fired the imagination of the peoples of Western Europe from the thirteenth century onwards, and urged them on to exploration and discovery. The earnest desire of the Western nations to find out a sea-route to India (when the land route, was virtually closed to them) made them direct, from the second half of the fifteenth century, their enterprise in maritime adventure. While the Portuguese under Vasco da Gama, by doubling the Cape of Good Hope (Capo da Boa Esperanza) in South Africa, managed to arrive in the year 1497, in southern India at the port of Calicut (Kozhekode) in Kerala, the Italian navigator Cristofero Colombo (Columbus) with the patronage of the King of Spain made the greatest maritime adventure of history—he sailed towards the West, and crossing the Atlantic, found himself in the West Indies, and so discovered America. Columbus was in this way instrumental in acquiring the vast lands and resources of two great continents for the benefit of Western Europe. Before Columbus there was no knowledge in Europe or Asia of the existence of the American islands and continents, except that some adventuring Scandinavians had found their way into parts of the American mainland some centuries before Columbus. The two Americas stood as a great barrier between Asia and Africa by the direct sea route, with the Pacific to their West and the Atlantic to their East.

In this way, these maritime discoveries brought in a new era of adventure and conquest, proselytisation and exploitation for the Spaniards and the Portuguese, and then for the English, the Dutch and the French, in America as well as in Africa and Asia. The Spaniards almost entirely destroyed the magnificent civilisations which the Amerindians had developed as independent systems of culture and ways of life in Mexico and Central America and in Peru, and the Red Man in America came absolutely under the control of the White Man from Western Europe. Similarly, the Black Man of Africa, i.e. of Africa to the South of the Sahara, became an easy prey to the White Man from Europe. But in Asia there were civilised nations, and in certain respects they were more civilised than the Western Europeans, 500 years ago—the Arabs, the Persians, the Indians, the Indo-Chinese, the Indonesians, the Chinese and the Japanese. But in their initiative and power of organisation, in their superiority in navigation and in the use of firearms, and in their experience of the world, and also in their unscrupulousness and fanaticism, these European adventurers could manage to get the better of the civilised peoples of Asia. Although during the first centuries of their contact with the civilised peoples of Asia, which started mainly on the platform of trade (exporting to Europe the manufactured goods of Asia and also its raw materials), there could not be any swift and spectacular conquest and destruction of the civilisations of Asia as it happened in America, nor could there be any large-scale conquests and empire-building from the very beginning. But gradually, bit by bit they created for themselves centres of influence and power in India, in Indonesia and in Indo-China, and also in the coastlands of China, and they established themselves as a force in all these countries. Owing to their loss of nerve (ultimately the result of stagnation among these old peoples of Asia, and owing also to their inner troubles, combined with their becoming more and more apprehensive of foreign ideas to the extent of excluding them from their life, it was possible, from the eighteenth century onwards, for the White Man in Asia to build-up great spheres of influence and, then empires, both colonial and imperial in their character.

This all-round success of the White Man of Europe in America, Asia and Africa gradually established the cult of the White Man's superiority in God's World, which became almost an axiom of faith with him. After the establishment of the English as the most powerful and then the paramount power in India during the first quarter of the nineteenth century, the Englishman took it for granted that as a White Man he was far superior to the Brown Man in India, in organisation and also in culture, and in mental and even in spiritual qualities. And it must be said that in certain wakes of life, particularly in the technological and organisational sides, and in their sense of the realities of geography and history, they were certainly ahead of the peoples of India and Asia. The three centuries from the end of the fifteenth century onwards witnessed a sort of establishment of a sense of European superiority, particularly amongst the Europeans themselves—although this was denied and resented and looked down upon with contempt by a good section of the Asian peoples—Muslim Arabs and Iranians, Brāhmanical Hindus, Confucian and Buddhist Chinese and others, who passionately clung to their old cultural atmosphere in their minds. But it was a case of "veni, vidi, vici" for the European Herrenvolk.

(c) *The Discovery of Sanskrit by Europe, and Its Far-reaching Consequences: A New Interpretation of History*

It was but recent history which was confined to the last few centuries. But with the discovery of Sanskrit by Europe and the gradual understanding and appreciation among the scholars of Europe of all the implications which were behind this discovery, Europe was able to broaden her ideas of history and to have for the first time some definite and clear perception of the process of world history. This, of course, was not final, but it was something new and revolutionary for the time. The study of Sanskrit gave rise in Europe to a number of new sciences, and it brought in some new ideologies which were very potent in our study of man. Thus, for instance, the establishment of the science of linguistics or comparative philology which was at first based on a comparison of Sanskrit with Avestan, Greek, Latin, Germanic, Celtic, Baltic and Slav groups of European languages, brought before us a new conception of language and culture as well as of race-movements and human history: linguistic. Palaeontology gave us some new and hitherto, unseen points of view in the study of the development of culture. The new science of comparative religion, which developed from the study of the Vedas, was equally potent in orienting in the proper direction our views about the origin and development of religion, detaching it from dogmatic Christian theology. Above all, the European peoples speaking Indo-European languages were able to build-up what at that time was the most reasonable concept of their history; and this seemed to agree so very much with the general trend of their progress throughout the entire world during the sixteenth, seventeenth, eighteenth and nineteenth centuries, that, they naturally felt that their history both ancient and recent, was only a confirmation of their faith in the divinely-appointed task of the Christian White Indo-European Herrenvolk to conquer, and rule over, and civilise and exploit all the coloured peoples of the world—Red, Yellow, Black and Brown. Just as the Spaniards, the Portuguese, the English, the Dutch and the French established themselves as ruling, proselytising and civilising. White Men among the Amerindians of America, the Negroes of Africa and the various peoples of Asia, particularly in India and Indonesia which succumbed earlier before the onslaught of the White Man, similarly in the ancient world, at least 3,000 to 4,000 years from now, the ancestors of the same Indo-European peoples of Europe; who were a white race, according to testimony they found from Greek, Sanskrit and other old literature as much as in actual present-day life, had spread themselves out from their original homeland somewhere in Central Asia or in South Russia, and as a Herrenvolk had become the dominant peoples in the whole of Europe and in considerable parts of Asia particularly in the Near-East, Iran and India. Just as the White Englishmen came and gradually established themselves in India among her brown peoples and brought to them many of the amenities of modern life and civilisation, and presented at least in the material sphere, a more advanced form of life, similarly the Aryans or Indo-Europeans (whose advent in India from some outside areas to the West of the country was becoming almost universally accepted), were the prototypes of the Englishmen as members of a white race bringing a higher civilisation for the benefit of the dark-skinned aboriginal peoples of India, the Dravidians, the Mongoloids, and the Kols or Muṇḍas (Austrics), whom the superior white men conquered and ruled over as a matter of course.

When the Aryan or Indo-European hypothesis was well-established in Europe, and popularised among the English and other peoples through the works of eminent scholars like Friedrich Max Müller and others, the intelligent and cultured European in India, who had a sense of these things; felt some sort of elation that after all his people and the very ancient and culturally advanced Aryans of India were branches of the same race, and it was the Aryans again who, like the Englishmen and other white men of a later age, were bringers of civilisation in America and Africa and in some parts of Asia; and so in India too, three to 4,000 years ago, that it was his people, the White Aryans, who were harbingers of higher life and civilisation among the dark-skinned aborigines. Some German scholars had identified themselves so very thoroughly with the Primitive Aryans (or Indo-Europeans) that they considered ancient Indo-European expansion to be just a sort, of Germanic or German Expansion (Deutsche Ausbreitung). Many Englishmen and other Europeans also thought in similar terms. The brāhmaṇas and other higher castes in India were accepted as relations in, blood and language of the peoples of Europe, and members of the dominating British ruling class in India in a sort a familiar and patronising way referred to the upper class Hindu as "our Aryan brother, the mild Hindu". The upper classes of the Hindus, in spite of a strong orthodox mentality, did not after all much dislike this attitude, as it made it quite explicit that they were within the same cultural and possibly racial orbit with the British and other European people.

From the middle of the nineteenth century, the Indian Intelligentsia belonging to the upper class as were chafing under the colonial-cum-imperial rule of England. There was a desire, which was becoming more and more articulate, to become free from the control of the British—at any rate, to acquire certain fundamental rights which they did not as yet possess, rights particularly in running the administration of the country. There were divided feelings—antagonistic towards the British rulers, and respectful towards the exponents of the great culture of Europe which intelligent Indians all admired and appreciated and were anxious to graft on their own national culture; and along with that, there was a little sense of pleasure in being considered as related to the peoples of Europe. This last sentiment they would, not in their nationalistic fervour very much like to analyse.

(d) *Origin and Establishment of "Aryanism" in India*

But there was one point to be considered. The upper classes were through the evil effects of one aspect of the caste system particularly as it became crystallised during Muslim and early British times, considering themselves, in a new racialistic way, to be superior to the peoples of the lower castes, specially the masses of the untouchables and others, although they admitted that even the lowest of the low in Hindu society had their acknowledged place or position or status within the framework of this society. But the average upper-class Hindu, educated in English, did not much dislike the idea that his ancestors brought civilisation to India and ruled over the pre-Aryan peoples, more or less in the same way that the British were doing with regard to the general mass of Indians in the nineteenth century. They therefore accepted this civilising role of Aryans, and were quite content to consider themselves as descendants of a Herrenvolk who had subjugated the earlier dark-skinned aborigines, the Dravidians, the Kola, and others, and the Yellow hill-peoples of the Himalayan slopes and of

Assam and eastern India; and they were happy with the idea that it was only the leaders of the Aryans who had organised them into the Hindu people themselves being the rulers and directors of a new society. The Aryan settlers brought to the earlier peoples of India, the non-Aryans or pre-Aryans, the light of culture and civilisation and higher thought and life. The idea was more or less tacitly accepted that whatever was great and noble and laminating and of high value for humanity—the highest philosophy of the Vedas and the Vedānta and the later religious systems as they developed in India—originated from the Aryans; and whatever was dark and base, unreasonable and ignoble, superstitious and silly was the contribution in Hinduism from the pre-Aryan peoples. This kind of reading of the history of Indian culture continued for a number of decades, and it was generally looked upon as quite a proper and correct estimate of Indian history. The orthodox brāhmaṇas, ignorant of English, however, stood aloof from this, as they did not accept the point of view of the European scholars that the Aryans came from outside with a higher civilisation. In orthodox brāhmaṇa opinion, the brāhmaṇas and the upper castes were in their origin as much the sons of India, and not outsiders, as were the pre-Aryan peoples. The lower classes, particularly to whom the stigma of this theory attached itself, were as yet uneducated and inarticulate, and they had no say in the matter; and a few people among them who were educated and came to know of this interpretation of Indian history, either kept silent because of want of positive evidence against the Aryan claims or pretentions, or they made haste to compromise with the superior Aryan people and tried to acquire, through fiction (which was piously believed in) or otherwise; the Aryan name, and attempted to exalt their castes or groups which were considered as low, as being really higher and belonging to the original Aryandom.

(e) ***The anti-Aryan Reaction among a Section of the Dravidian-Speaking Peoples***

This was so long the general consensus of opinion among both

Europeans and Indians with regard to the origin of Indian civilisation and the Indian people. But other facts began to come to light, and this made for a very large-scale revision of the above theory of history for India. It gradually came to be known that the Aryans were not the oldest and the most civilised people of the world—that when they first entered the stage of history they were in a semi-barbarous state leading a life partly nomadic and partly agricultural, and not possessing any high degree of material culture. A number of peoples who were not Indo-European or Aryan had already come to the forefront of civilisation long before the Aryans or Indo-Europeans entered the arena of history; like, for example, the Egyptians, the Sumerians and following them the Akkadians and the Assyrio-Babylonians, and various peoples of Asia Minor, and in distant India the peoples of the Mohen-jo-Daro civilisation facts relating to the origin and development of religion and culture, and to racial movements and mixtures in India gradually established the fact that the Indian or Hindu civilisation was not the gift of the Aryans alone, but it was the result of a mixture of the world of the Aryan with the various worlds of some of the most fundamental and vital the non-Aryans things in the Hindu religious concepts and practices came from the non-Aryans, to a greater extent than from the Aryans. Then, again, the discovery of the great city-civilisation of western Punjab and Sindh, which had ramifications in Gujarat and Maharashtra as well as in eastern Punjab and Uttar Pradesh and even distant Bengal, presented a highly advanced urban world which was comparable to that of the ancient Babylonians, and which certainly was something which the Aryans could not show. The semi-nomadic Aryans, like their kinsmen, the ancient Achaeans and other Hellenic Indo-European tribes of Greece, did not take to a city culture at first, and they were destroyers of cities and the great Aryan War-God and leader of the Aryan people in India. India was actually known as Purandara, which means "destroyer of cities". In the meanwhile, education was spreading, and a new orientation as to the origin of Indian culture was also in the offing. Some European as well as Indian scholars now began to accept frankly the new point of view—how Aryan and non-Aryan both combined to build-up the great culture of India; and in this culture, the non-Aryan contribution was perhaps more significant and important than the Aryan. This point of view was supported by a number of Indian scholars also, including a good proportion of those who belonged to the higher caste-groups as well; and in some cases, ample amendments were made for the establishment of what now dawned in their minds as the real truths. An historical analysis of Indian culture into its most essential components, as derived from the Aryan as well as the non-Aryan sources, has been attempted in many places. (A resume will be found in my University of Calcutta Kamala Lectures on the subject of "Indianism and the Indian Synthesis", University of Calcutta, 1963).

The non-Aryan peoples of the south, particularly those who were chafing under the predominance of the brāhmaṇas in the south Indian scene, in life and in society and in higher services and general economy, now swung the pendulum to the other side, and they began to magnify the non-Aryan elements or contributions in Indian culture, particularly Dravidian, and to minimise or discredit the contribution from the Aryan side. It was the time and opportunity for the hitherto mute non-Aryan, particularly of the less exalted classes, to hit back; and the south Indian Dravida Munnetra Kazhagam and other organisations issued this anti-brāhmaṇa, anti-Aryan and anti-north Indian challenge.

But some old-fashioned scholars—not merely learned Sanskrit *paṇḍit*s of the old school without any knowledge of or interest in the European attitude to these things are still there who nourish the feeling that it was the Aryan who gave the tone to Indian culture. In certain respects, their attitude is not to be dismissed entirely. But the non-Aryan contribution also is to be given its proper place.

(f) *The Culture of India: The Result of a Racial, Linguistic and Religio-social Fusion*

As it always happens, the actual truth is between the two extremes. This kind of via media in our appraisement of Indian culture has been admitted in the work mentioned above (*Indianism and the Indian Synthesis*). Like the warp and the woof of a piece of woven stuff, the Indian or Hindu civilisation and culture, as a finished and completed product, is the result of a profound intermingling of the Aryan and the non-Aryan, in race, in language and in the various items of material as well as mental and spiritual culture. In the evolution of this great stream of culture which appears to have commenced in north India in the Indus and Ganges Valleys, and to have taken a definite shape towards the end of the Vedic period (say, roughly 1000 BC), it was equally the work as well as the inheritance of the Dravidians and other non-Aryan peoples as that of the Aryans . The Sanskrit language, which became the great vehicle of this composite Hindu or ancient Indian Culture, is, in the first instance, an Aryan language, with its words, roots and formative and other affixes inherited from the primitive Indo-European speech. But it has been profoundly modified by the pre-Aryan speeches of India, so much so that its basic character appears to have changed in many matters. As it approximated in its spirit and expression to the non-Aryan speeches, its original purely Aryan character was largely modified, and in some instances even lost; and the highly cultured Dravidian peoples, after the spread of the composite north Indian Hindu civilisation all over India, had now no difficulty nor any animosity with regard to the acceptance by them of this Aryan speech, Sanskrit—as a language of religion and a language of culture, and to borrow words from it as and when it was necessary to do so in their own Dravidian languages.

The Aryan–non-Aryan Hindu culture of north India became a great force, and it gradually spread all over India. During the closing centuries of the first millennium BC, it was already well-established over the greater part of India, and it was spreading also in countries outside India. eastern India gradually came within the sphere of this composite Hindu culture, and by the middle of the first millennium AD it was well established as far as Bengal and Assam in the east, and had even come to Indo-China and Indonesia and found homes there. The *modus operandi* for this culture to spread among the various peoples of races and languages other than the Aryan who felt attracted by the great civilisation of the Ganges Valley, or in other words, the missionary enterprise and endeavour for this culture to spread, as doubtless there was such an endeavour, would be a subject of very great interest in our study of Indian civilisation. A great integration has taken place on the soil of India, and the beginnings of this integration are at least 3,000 years old; and in this integration, there has been the guiding hands of both the brāhmaṇa sages, scholar and priests on the one hand and the Buddhist *bhikṣus* and the Jain *yatis* on the other; and it was through Sanskrit primarily, with Pāli and some of the Prākṛts as ancillaries, that this culture could spread and be established and fortified. The Integration of India through one single culture could be described in another way as the Sanskritisation of the Indian scene.

(g) *The Role of the North Indian Brāhmaṇas in Integrating Diverse Peoples and Religions of India within One Common Pan-Indian Hindu Culture*

How did it start? We note in the first instance a great idea and a way of life among the Vedic and post-Vedic sages and seers. While they had dealings with the nobles and aristocrats of the king's courts and with the humble dwellers of cities and villages, they would themselves carry on their deepest intellectual and spiritual exercises and musings "far from the madding crowd" in their village retreats and forest hermitages. Moving away from the dwellings of men into the forest and mountain retreats—*āśramas*—was quite the rule from Vedic times. In fact, this aspect of the development of Indian culture as we see in the *Upaniṣads* and in the *Mahābhārata* was particularly stressed upon by a modern Indian poet and seer like Rabindranath Tagore. The brāhmaṇas represented in the main the Aryan strain and tradition. But one very well conceive that in many cases, Indian brāhmaṇadom reinforced by the priests and the sages of the more advanced non-Aryan peoples, since they accepted the Aryan speech and could find that the masses of non-Aryans, particularly in the vast plain lands of north India, were similarly abandoning their non-Aryan languages for the Aryan, as members of an ever-growing Aryan-speaking Hindu community.

The assimilation or acculturation or conversion of non Aryan peoples to the Brāhmanical or Hindu world has generally been on a wide tribal scale, entire groups of people slowly merging into a brāhmaṇa-organised society, and, usually they became accepted as "a tribal caste" within the Hindu community, with a high or low status according to their previous economic cultural or political level. Their priestly class, with the syncretism of the pre-Aryan world of religious mythology and philosophy were first accepted as brāhmaṇas for that particular tribal caste (as varṇa-brāhmaṇas), and their subsequent acceptance as true brāhmaṇas of Vedic or Aryan pedigree was accomplished in the ages of unrecorded history in this matter, 1,000 to 3,000 years from now.

So, it is just likely that many ideologies and practices of the sages and seers and priests of the non-Aryan worlds also joined the forces with the original Aryan bases, and what resulted was the composite Brāhmanical Hindu world. In ancient times, it would appear that there was conscious urge on the part of the thinkers of a newly-developed society—the Hindu society with its ideologies which were still fresh and fluid and were taking new shapes—to go forth and to bring their new thought, ideologies and organisations and disciplines among all and sundry. In fact, the brāhmaṇas as priests and thinkers of the growing Hindu society became the great body of unorganised missionaries, whose only urge or directive from the fount and source-head of their culture were the ideas which were promulgated through Sanskrit, and theoretically derived from the Vedas and were of divine origin or inspiration. They not only were working among their own people, but they also were spreading north and south, west and east, through the forest tracts, among the various non-Aryan speakers, and they brought to them the message of this great composite Aryan–non-Aryan culture of the north, and its tradition and its ways of thinking and ways of life.

In this way, we can say that they spread deep down into the south where there were blocs of Dravidian speakers, among whom the inroad of the Aryan language had not as yet started and where the Dravidian world was reigning in its pristine character. Similarly, among the great Tibeto-Burman blocs in the blocs in north and east Bengal, in Assam and in Nepal. We have legends of one or two great sages and saints from north India who went down to the south and worked among the Dravidian peoples, unquestionably in the centuries before Christ, this movement starting possibly during the first half of the first millennium BC.

(h) *North Indian Culture in South India*

Thus, we have the legends of Agastya, who, according to the ancient tradition accepted by the Dravidians of the south as well, was a north Indian Aryan brāhmaṇa (unless he were one of mixed origin, like Vyāsa, the reputed compiler of the Vedas, the collector of myths and legends which formed the nucleus of the Purāṇas, and the author of the *Mahābhārata* in its original form). Thus the *Ṛṣi* Agastya crossed the Vindhya Mountains from the north, and then went down to the deep south; and there he was one of the pioneers to bring north Indian Aryan Hindu thought and culture to the Dravidians of the far south. Later on, this great missionary of Brāhmanical culture and religion is said to have passed by the route of the sea to Indo-China and Indonesia—to Cambodia, Champa or Cochin, China and Java, which later, in the early centuries became a land of Hindu (Brāhmanical and Christian era, Buddhist) religion and civilisation.

Agastya's is the greatest name among these brāhmaṇa sages from north India who brought the message of this great culture to the Dravidian south. Doubtless there were many others like him, possibly a few before him, but mostly after him. In the *Rāmāyaṇa*, for example, and also in, the *Mahābhārata*, there are traditions of *Ṛṣis* from north India who were like pioneers in the domain of culture and religion and who penetrated deep down into the south and formed little settlements of their own within or on the outskirts of the virgin forests where they practised Vedic cults and the rites of the Vedic religion, and continued the tradition of Vedic and Upaniṣadic thinking. These *Ṛṣi* or brāhmaṇa settlements became the foci of Aryan culture which was generally accepted by the surrounding Dravidian and other peoples. Of course, there were some among the pre-Aryan peoples who did not understand or appreciate these newcomers from the Aryan world, and they were inimical and antagonistic, and tried to prevent them in following their Vedic religious practices. They were stigmatised as the *rākṣasa*s or *asura*s—demons who were the enemies of the Vedic and Brāhmanical gods and way of worship. It was the duty of the Aryan or Aryan-speaking princes—*kṣatriya*s and others—to take strong action (if they were in a position to do so) and to fight these "demons" and save the brāhmaṇa or *ṛṣi* settlements from molestation or destruction. These Aryan-speaking brāhmaṇas from the north, nevertheless, took with them the prestige, of this great mixed Niṣāda Dravida-Kirāta-Ārya culture which was dominating the scene in India; and through their well-regulated life of religious discipline and study they created a great impression among the Dravidian, and other peoples. They were known later on in the Tamil land as Parppar or "Sages", and ordinarily people respected them for their wisdom and personality and character. With this respect was undoubtedly mixed a great fear because people thought they had uncanny powers through their rites and sacrifices with their Vedic *mantra*s which were considered mystic and magical. Their scriptures, the Vedas came to be accepted by the Dravidians as the repository of *marai*, i.e. the supreme wisdom or knowledge of God.

These sages of Aryandom did not confine themselves to the study of their own language—the Vedic texts and Sanskrit only. But from very early times they took up the local Dravidian speech also. Thus Agastya and his disciples, according to the oldest literary tradition of Tamil, were credited with the great feat of channelling the ancient Tamil language into a stream of grammar and rhetoric. The oldest and most comprehensive grammar of Old Tamil still extant is said to have been composed by a direct pupil of Agastya, who came to be known as *Tolkappiyan* from his book the *Tolkappiyam*. In the dim and almost fabulous past, which can reasonably be brought down to the period from the beginning of the first millennium BC. Brāhmanical religion started to come down to the south. The tall, white-skinned sages from the north, clad in skin or in bark or in rough woollen or cotton cloth, did their ceremonies and worship in front of the fire; and they looked with their topknots of long hair and their long beards (in the earliest age they were golden or tawny-haired and blue-eyed) like veritable incarnations or embodiments of the fire. In their religious ideas they brought their own concepts, sometimes vague and sometimes precise, about life and Being and the Ultimate Reality. They never spared themselves in their religious penances and discipline. But they were imaginative and receptive enough, and with their intelligence and their intellectual adopting new points of view in their philosophical outlook; and pre-Aryan ways of thinking and living whenever reasonable and helpful were being taken over by them to enrich and extend their own philosophy of life. Thus, the great doctrine of rebirth and transmigration, which did not belong to the Indo-European or Aryan domain, was accepted by the sons of the Aryans in India through contact with pre-Aryan peoples. All this was responsible for bringing with them a great moral prestige, and this enabled them, after their presence in the south made the pre-Aryan peoples know them well enough, to travel deep into the heart of non-Aryandom without any fear and with the spontaneous homage of respect from all and sundry. The south Indian rulers, both Dravidian and Austric, from the very beginning revered and accepted their ministrations and gave them a most honoured place in their society, establishing them with lands in separate settlements and receiving when needed all advice and guidance from them.

In this peaceful way, the Brāhmanical culture was creating an integration with non-Aryandom. The divinities which were worshipped by the Dravidian peoples were all identified as a matter of course with the great gods of the Vedic and early Brāhmanical pantheon. The brāhmaṇas sometimes did not hesitate to take over non-Aryan words and names in connexion with their gods and rituals. Already some non-Aryan Dravidian divinities of the highest rank and Dravidian concepts were adopted into the Brāhmanical Hinduism of the north, and thus these could not be foreign or strange to the Dravidians of the south. Besides, its great value was its mobility, its progressive sprit. New ideas and ways of worship were constantly being added to it to increase its all-inclusive spirit. From the naturism of the primitive Vedic religion, we have a transformation in the *Bhāgavata* or devotional approach in the centuries during the first half of the first millennium BC. Then about that time came the Purāṇa atmosphere, with the *pūjā* ritual beside the pure Aryan *homa*, and later on the Tantra cults and the *Vāmācāra* from the first half of the first millennium AD. The Vedānta of the Upaniṣads started from after 1000 BC, and it was made to suffer a "sea-change" in the *bhakti* philosophy and cults from after 500 AD. In many cases, the old pre-Aryan religion and ritual lived on side by side with the new one brought by the brāhmaṇas. But the masses of people who began to develop sympathies for both effected a synthesis, and this we find also in the Hinduism of the Draviḍa land. The Jains and the Buddhists also took part in this. But the Brāhmanical faith and concepts possessed certain great and universal human qualities, a good deal of romance and poetry which became their greatest strength in obtaining the willing support of the people. The role of the wandering or sedentary brāhmaṇa *saṁnyasī* or householder was great in the spread of Hindu culture as an integrating force.

The brāhmaṇa was not all by himself. He was followed or accompanied by adventuring kṣatriya princes and princelings and military adventurers who came over with their families, or without their women, and they settled down in the country and easily commingling with the people by marriage became one with them. And they helped to expand and invigorate with new blood and new ideas and new ways of life the earlier pre-Aryan ruling houses.

Then there were the merchants and the artisans—men in humbler wakes of life who always from very early times were adventuring down to the south and other borders of the Aryan-speaking core in north India. We have cases of artisans of certain types migrating from the north and establishing themselves in the deep south of Dravidiandom, and the tradition continued right: down to the closing centuries of the first millennium AD and even later. We have thus the case of silk-weavers who came from the Gujarat side—the Saurashtras some of whom have still somehow kept up their north Indian Aryan language in the heart of the Tamil and Telugu country although they all speak fluently the local languages. But others very quickly forgot their language, and in a few generations became merged with the Telugu and Kannada, Tulu and Kodagu, and Tamil and Malayalam speakers. With the exception of the fact that the bulk of the people in the solid Dravidian blocs of the south still continue to speak the Dravidian languages in their general attitude to life and in their way of living and thinking and in the outward forms of life, there is a common Indianness which marks all the peoples of India; and that is based primarily on Brāhmanical Hinduism as it expressed itself in the ritual of the Vedas and of the Purāṇas and the Tantras, in the philosophy of the Upaniṣads and of the later *bhakti* schools, and, above all, in the romantic, moral and didactic and aesthetic world of the *Rāmāyaṇa* and the *Mahābhārata* and the Purāṇas.

We learn from an early history of Sindh written in the Old Sindhi language (or in the Apabhraṁśa of Sindh) and translated into Arabic before 1000 AD—a history which also includes the *Mahābhārata* story, with some variants from the Sanskrit epic—how Duryodhana from the midland of northern India, the home of the composite Brāhmanical culture, sent 2,000 brāhmaṇas to settle in Sindh, which was then beyond the pale of Aryan influence and was occupied by two tribes of unknown (possibly non-Aryan) origin—the Jatts and the Meds—to bring and establish the culture of the Brāhmanical world among the original peoples of Sindh.

(i) *Agastya and south India*

The name Agastya is exceedingly well-known in Indian myth and legend and a number of wonderful stories have become attached to his name, which are found in Purāṇa and other post-Vedic literature. It is generally presumed by these legendary stories that there was but one Agastya. But it would be more reasonable, judging from the range and variety of these stories, that there were several Agastyas, each with one exploit or story attached to him, and the sum-total of these exploits or stories were fathered upon a single mythical Agastya. In all likelihood it was a clan name—and Ṛṣi Agastya, or Agasti, to give the earlier form of it, from his name which has no satisfactory explanation in Sanskrit, may be of Dravidian or mixed Aryan-Dravidian origin (cf. T. Burrow and M.B. Emeneau, *Dravidian Etymological Dictionary*, Oxford University Press, 1961, p. 2, article "Akatti: Vedic Agasti" may be a borrowing from Dravidian in north India, and it meant the name of a flowering tree, and the name, as that for a clan absorbed in the Aryan-speaking community in Vedic times, may be totemistic in origin). The first Agastya goes back to the *Ṛgveda*, in which there are several hymns ascribed to him. There is mention of his wife Lopāmudrā, and his patronymic is given as Maitravaruṇa, the offspring of the two gods—Mitra and Varuṇa. The story of his birth from the seed of the two gods who were overcome by love at the sight of the celestial nymph Urvaśī is well-known. He is said to have spent the time of his gestation in a water-jar, from which he issued as a babe, and he is hence called *kumbhaja*, or *ghaṭa-yoni*. But a linguistic interpretation to this wild legend is possible, as has been indicated below.

The Vedic Agastya whose *floruit* was before the tenth century BC. (the estimated period for the compilation of the Vedic texts by Kṛṣṇa Dvaipāyana Vyāsa), might have been an ancestor of another Agastya, who crossed the Vindhya mountains and went down to the Tamil country, never return north India. This early pioneer who took north Indian to Brāhmanical culture to the ancestors of the Tamil and other Dravidian peoples of the deep south, peoples who were as yet untouched by the early Brāhmanical religion and culture as it was evolving in a mixed Aryan and non-Aryan atmosphere, would appear to have some dim historical background, and he might have gone to south India sometime during the middle or first half of the first millennium BC when the expansion of Brāhmanism from Āryāvarta seems to have started as a large-scale movement, and the people of north India were getting to know more closely the Dravidian and other peoples of the south. There are some stories about this Agastya which are found in south India, in early Tamil literature. Some of these stories feature in the Sanskrit Purāṇa as well, e.g. the *Skanda* Purāṇa. One is that Agastya went down along the Konkan Coast to Coorg the country of Kudaga people, near to the source of the Kāverī River, where he settled down in a hermitage. A local king, evidently Dravidian or Tamil by language and culture, named Kavera, made him his Minister, and married him to his daughter Kāverī or Kaviri. The old name of Coorg was Kutaka, then it became Kudaga, Kodaga; and it was possibly his first home in the south. From this he was known as Kutaka Muni or Kuta Muni in Sanskrit. Now, *kuta* is a common Dravidian word meaning a water-jar (modern Tamil *kudam*) of which the Sanskrit equivalent would be *kumbha* or *ghaṭa* and so Kuta Muni could be fully translated into Sanskrit as Kumbha Muni Water-jar Sage. From this, an association with the water-jar was conjectured, and the legend of his having been born out of a water-jar arose (Kumbha Muni, Kumbha-yoni, Ghaṭa-yoni, Kumbha-sambhuva, etc.); and this was linked up with the story of his having the gods Mitra and Varuṇa as his progenitors.

Agastya's marriage with Kāverī as the daughter of a local king, and also as the deity of the great River Kāverī, or Kavīrī, of the Coḷa country in the heart of the Tamil-land, is significant. It is said that the king of the Coḷa country Kandaman (about whom there are other stories, connecting him with Paraśurāma and with Agastya lived in voluntary exile in the Kutaka country, where Agastya was minister. At that time there was a river originating in the source of the present-day Kāverī in Coorg at the foot of the Sahya mountains which used to flow west and fall into the Arabian Sea. Kandaman, in whose kingdom in the Coḷa country where was no great river, and consequently the whole country was dry and was not arable, with the permission of King Kavera and help of Agastya, had the course of that river changed from the west to the east, and the river could thus be brought into the Coḷa country where it became a mighty river and flowed down to the Bay of Bengal, making the whole land fertile. The river, when it took its eastern course was named after Princes Kāverī, the wife of Agastya (this story is given in the Old Tamil Sangam Epic the *Maṇimekalai*, 1.15: I am indebted to Sri K. Sankara Sharma of the National Library, Calcutta, for this and some other items of information about Agastya from Tamil sources. See the section on the Kuveri Myth in *Religion and Society among the Coorgs of south India* by M.N. Srinivas, 2nd edn., 1965, Asia Publishing House, Bombay, pp. 243-47).

There is another south Indian legend, which makes Kāverī a beautiful maiden of a divine and mystic origin, who was loved by Agastya, but as the lover transgressed a taboo that the maiden Kāverī was not to get into the source of a particular hill-stream, she was transformed into the River Kāverī; and was lost forever to her lover Agastya, who was left forlorn (see "Tales from Indian Mythology" by A.S. Rāman, "Kutub-Popular", Bombay 1961, pp. 28-39).

There was one Agastya who went back to north India from Kutaka (Coorg), and at Naimiṣāraṇya the famous *āśrama* for *ṛṣi s* at the foot of the Himalayas, when he found some brāhmaṇas performing Vedic sacrifices by slaughtering goats (*aja* in Sanskrit), he persuaded them to use three-year old rice instead, as one of the many meanings of the word *aja* in Sanskrit was a kind of rice. We do not know how to explain this story. Is it indicative of a growing desire on the part of sore brāhmaṇas to stop animal-sacrifice oven in Vedic ritual, through the acceptance of the Jaina ideal of *ahiṁsā*? This legend as connected with one of the Agastyas must be very late.

There were legends in Indo-China and Indonesia about Agastya coming to these lands of Greater India beyond the sea—particularly in Indonesia—and there helping to establish or strengthen Brāhmanical culture. In Indonesia, Agastya is looked upon as an incarnation of Śiva as the Great Teacher—a sort of counterpart of Buddha, and as such both Śiva and Agastya were known in Indonesia as Bhaṭṭāraka Guru (Batara Guru), and in iconography Śiva-Agastya was represented as a bearded middle-aged man, like an Indian *ṛṣi*, as distinguished from the usual form of Śiva as a young Divinity (see in this connexion, O.C. Gangoly, "The Cult of Agastya and the Origin of Indian Colonial Art" in the *Quarterly Journal of the Mythic Society*, Bangalore, vol. XVII, Second Series No. 3, January 1927, pp. 169-99; and Dr. Raden Mas Poerbatjaraka's Monograph in Dutch on Agastya in the Indian Archipelago).

In south India, one Agastya has been able to establish himself in the reverence and affections of the Tamil people for the great service, he did for the language, literature and culture of the Tamils; and also, what was of more paramount and enduring value, for helping to affect the integration of the Dravidian south with the north through Brāhmanical religion and thought. This Agastya, it may be, permitted to assume, was the post-Vedic sage who left north India for good, and, as tradition has it never re-crossed the Vindhya mountains to return to north India. He may have flourished (if one is permitted to make argues in the sixth century BC during the great days of Buddha and Mahāvīra and the later *ṛṣis* of the Brāhmaṇas and the Upaniṣads and of great kings in north India like Ajātaśatru Kunika of Magadha, Udayana of Vatsa and Caṇḍa Mahāsena Pradyota of Malava. Even at the present day, the anti-Aryan ideology of the Dravida Munnetra Kazhagam in Tamil Nadu has not been able to liquidate Agastya from the heart of Tamilakam or the Tamil country.

Three things we have to remember in connection with the great integration to a common Hindudom of all the various peoples of India by the brāhmaṇa:

(1) There was, at least in the earlier stages, quite a large-scale racial fusion through intermarriage among the incoming Aryans brāhmaṇas and kṣatriyas and others—and the local pre-Aryan peoples. This was a very vital and easily a most effective way of total integration. The case of Agastya marrying Kāverī the daughter of king Kavera of Kutaka is a pointer, and it was quite typical of brāhmaṇa and pre-Aryan relations. Instances are plentiful to show how all over India such unions were common; and we have both legendary and historical (epigraphical) evidence from both within and outside India that the establishment of Hindu religion and culture by brāhmaṇas and others went hand in hand with these inter-racial unions.

(2) There was always understanding and accommodation from the side of the imaginative as well as philosophically-minded brāhmaṇa, kṣatriya and vaiśya towards the pre-Aryan cultural milieu. A great sense of the Unity of Humanity before the all-embracing Divinity or Ultimate Reality enabled them to develop this attitude most easily, and this brought in a corresponding spirit of accommodation on the other side also. Thus, Brāhmanism (or Buddhism) everywhere came to fulfil and not to destroy, and new expressions of the Indian

spirit came out on the background of the various pre-Aryan religions within India, Indo-China and Indonesia, and in Tibet, China, Vietnam, Mongolia, Korea and Japan. Chinese Buddhism did not out itself off from native Chinese religion and philosophy (both Taoism and Confucianism), and Japanese Buddhism has one of its bases in the native Japanese Shinto religion. Finally—

(3) The brāhmaṇa (and Buddhist) attitude was for conserving and developing the pre-Aryan language and literature and culture. This is how Tamil, Old Javanese, Old Khmer, Old Mon, Old Newari, Old Siamese, Old Burmese, Early Meitei or Manipuri and other languages and literatures, both within India and outside India, could have their full development with brāhmaṇa (and Buddhist) help and cooperation. Thus, all sense of Brāhmanism or Buddhism being a foreign cult or philosophy and the brāhmaṇas and *bhikṣus* or Buddhist monks an alien people was lost.

There is reference to another Agastya in a historical document, the Prah Bat Stela (Inscription in Sanskrit, from Cambodia raised by King Yaśovarman, with date corresponding to 811 AD. Here there is mention of a brāhmaṇa from Āryadeśa (India—it may be south India, but there is no certainty) named Agastya who was well-versed in the Vedas and Vedāṅgas, and he came to Cambodia and settled down there, married there and had a family, and one of his descendants was Yaśomatī, the queen of King Yaśovarman, who had two children—a son Narendra Varman and a daughter Narendra Laksmī.

Brāhmaṇa sages and scholars emulating Agastya the crosser of the Vindhyas were to be found as missionaries of culture all over India, and over the greater part of Asia also, particularly Southeast Asia and Indonesia. Agastya of the Tamil country can thus be taken as a prototype or representative of all such sages and scholars, through the centuries right down to our day.

(j) *Brāhmanical or Hindu Culture among the Kirātas People of the North and the East*

The method of the spread of Indian culture by Brāhmanical thought-leaders and spiritual adventurers, followed by members of the kṣatriya and vaiśya groups, we note also in the north and in the east, among the Kirāta, i.e. Tibeto-Burman and other Sino-Tibetan peoples, as well as among the Austro-Khmers, and the Indonesian groups, besides among the various mixed peoples of Indo-China. Even in distant Burma, traditions of brāhmaṇa and ksatriya expansion go back to the first half of the first millennium before Christ, and we have epigraphical and literary evidence of Hinduisation or integration with Indian culture in Arakan and in southern and central Burma at least as early as the fifth and sixth centuries AD. The Candra dynasty of kings of Arakan is a case in point. The quite likely that the Kulki-Chin or Meitei people of Manipur were similarly within the fold of Hindudom by 500 AD at least, although tradition would take it much earlier.

In Nepal we have an overflow of Brāhmanical culture from Uttar Pradesh and Bihar and Bengal from very early times, and though there were close connexions with Tibet and distant ones with China, and although Buddhism in its Mahayura form as backwash from Bengal and Bihar had a new lease of life in Nepal, the people there were brought within the general Indian orbit and were integrated with Hindu India, as much as any other people within the geographical limits of India. Maithili and Bengali-speaking brāhmaṇas continued the tradition, even down to the seventeenth century, of re-enforcing the Hindu culture of Nepal. Probably in the earlier centuries of the Christian era, the Tibeto-Burman-speaking Bodo tribes of the Brahmaputra Valley became completely Hinduised. The tradition of the Mahābhārata battle which goes back to the tenth century BC would seem to suggest that the spread of Brāhmanical Aryandom had come to Assam and had at last brought the ruling houses within its operation. From the *Mahābhārata* we learn that Bhagadatta was a great king of

Prāgjyotiṣa or Arsan, who was ruling over the Kirātas and the Cīnas, and he came as one of the allies of the Kauravas and fought at the Kurukṣetra battle and gave his life for Duryodhana. Brāhmaṇas from the Midland, that is to say, from Upper Gangetic India, were being settled in Bengal and eastern India, as much as there was a long stream of brāhmaṇas going down to the south during Pallava times (middle and second half of the first millennium AD).

With regard to south India, the opinion has been expressed that the fullest Hinduisation of the Tamil and other peoples of the Dravidian blocs of the south took place during the first few centuries after Christ, and this also was going on unabated during the second half of the first millennium AD when the masses in the south became most ardent followers and devotees of Viṣṇu and Śiva, with certain groups paying homage to Buddha and the Jain. The gods and goddesses of the primitive Dravidian pantheon were already being approximated to or syncretised with the Brāhmanical deities as in the Vedic pantheon, to give rise to the deities of the later Purāṇic Hindu faith. In the deep south, in Tamil-land, possibly during the second half of the first millennium AD, there was further identification and fuller integration of the world of the Tamil gods with those of brāhmaṇadom, so that Śiva and, Rudra became one, and Mal or Mayon and Viṣṇu, Korravai and Durgā, Murukan and Rāma became but the names for the same concepts of the divinities, one in Tamil and the other in Sanskrit, and a great integration thus took place. In eastern India, by 500 AD Hindu influences which were well-established as far east as East Bengal and Chittagong and Arakan, had already passed on to Burma, among the Mon or Talaing people first and then among the Mongol Tibeto-Burman peoples (like the Mranma or the Old Burmans) further to the north, and the now extinct Pyu people belonging to the same Tibeto-Burman group. The Bodos were completely Hinduised; and after the Ahoms, who were a branch of the Thai or Siamese race, conquered Assam in 1228, they also gradually fell under the Spell of Hinduism, and in five centuries their Hinduisation was a most complete, with their ruling house being declared Indravanśī kṣatriyas.

Brāhmaṇa settlers with the banner of Hindu religion and culture were also going east and south-east from India by way of the sea, and in the early centuries of the Christian era we have legends of brāhmaṇa scholars like Kauṇḍinya and Kambu going from south India to what is now Cambodia and Cochin China. Kambu went and settled in Cambodia, and his children became the Kambujas or the sons of Kambu, who gave their name to the kingdom of Cambodia. Slightly earlier, the descendants of the brāhmaṇa Kauṇḍinya had established another Hindu kingdom in Fu-nan in northern Cambodia, took wives from among the local people, and their spouses were described as *apsaras*es or nymphs and princesses of Nāga or non-Aryan ruling houses. In this way, Kambu married the apsaras Mera, and Kauṇḍinya married the Nāga princess Soma, and the offspring of these mixed marriages were the creators of the Hindu civilisation of Indo-China. Some of these brāhmaṇas are remembered by tradition even to the present day—in the marriage ceremony in Cambodia names of Kauṇḍinya and Soma are mentioned even today.

In Cambodian inscriptions in Sanskrit, from the eighth century AD onwards, long after Kauṇḍinya and Kambu, we find mention of a succession of brāhmaṇas from India going to Indo-China, settling down there as householders with wives from among the local peoples, and carrying on the Hindu traditions of spiritual and intellectual life. Thus in 715 AD, the Śaiva brāhmaṇa Sakrasvāmin, born in India, married the daughter of King Jayavarman I. Another brāhmaṇa, Divākara Bhaṭṭa, who was born near Mathura, was also married to a princess of Cambodia, the daughter of a king and sister of another. There is the case of the brāhmaṇa Agastya similarly marrying in Cambodia. There are at least four other cases recorded in the inscriptions (see p. 211, *Hindu Colonies* by Dr. Ramesh Chandra Majumdar, Calcutta, 1963).

This evidently was also the case within India itself, in its far-flung Eastern Frontier. Traditions of brāhmaṇa settlements and brāhmaṇa adventurers going and establishing themselves in eastern India are there. As late as the thirteenth century, a brāhmaṇa of whom we have a record, Someswar Pathak, supposed to be from Kanauj, established himself and his family with the help of *sādhus* or wandering Hindu monks, among the Bodo-speaking population of Mymensingh district, and established the brāhmaṇa house of Susang State. There is also the story of five brāhmaṇas coming from Kanauj and settling in West Bengal and becoming the ancestors of the present Rādhiyā and Vārendra brāhmaṇas of Bengal.

This would be a fascinating subject of enquiry, and how the gradual inter-weaving of the Tibeto-Burman-speaking peoples with the Hindudom of Assam and Bengal in the easternmost areas of India was effected, would be a unique study of the story of the acculturation of peoples within the same cultural circle.

The economic and political urges, which can only be expected to have been operative behind these migrations of brāhmaṇa and kṣatriya torch bearers of Indian or Aryo-Dravidian-Austric culture in the outskirts of Aryandom and in the lands outside India, are not yet known. But the commercial enterprise of Indian merchants was certainly one great factor, as we see from early literary evidence; and after them the priest at teacher and the military adventurer who built political states could very well have followed suit. A fully documented study of this religio-cultural and politico-economic expansion and integration is a desideratum not only for the history of India but also for the migrations of men and cultures over a great part of Asia, under Indian tutelage.

This process which started probably 2,500 years ago, if not earlier, is still slowly at work, and finishing touches are being given to it even at the present day. The spirit of the *ṛṣi*s of the past, the sages and the brāhmaṇa scholars like Agastya and Kambu and Kauṇḍinya and the whole host of Brāhmanical and Buddhist teachers who passed into Burma and Malaya, Indo-China and Indonesia as worthy successors of the ancient *ṛṣi*s, requires to be told in its proper bearings.

And this tradition of integration of an important part of India into the field of Hindu cultures and religion has been carried on even down to our day by a number of selfless teachers and preachers who have largely remained anonymous. But in that context we can take note of the work of one great scholar and protagonist of Hindu culture who has sought to find a harmony between the basic spirit of Hindu culture and the culture and religion of an important people of Tibeto-Burman speech—the Meitei people of Manipur.

I have discussed the matter of the evolution of Meitei culture elsewhere, particularly in my monograph *The Kirata-Jana-Krti, or the Indo-Mongoloid and their Contribution to Indian History and Culture* (Asiatic Society, Calcutta, 1951). It is not necessary to describe it in all detail. But in the present context it is the bounden duty of Hindu India, whether in Manipur or outside Manipur, to pay its tribute of respect and affection to the memory of that great scholar who has been one of the greatest personalities in the cultural world of this country of India, although he had been working in his own corner of India saintly scholar and thought-leader, the late Panditaraja Atombapu Sharma. When we consider the great things he performed during his life extending over 74 years, we are forced to declare that Panditaraja Atombapu Sharma has been in the line of the ancient *ṛṣis*, and that he can be classed with a saint and sage of the past like Agastya Kauṇḍiya and Kambu, and similar other unnamed Indian brāhmaṇa scholars who went to Burma and Indo-China and Malaya, to Indonesia including Borneo, where they established or strengthened Vedic and Brāhmanical religion and way of life, without destroying or disturbing the earlier culture and ways of the people among whom they worked; and their work of integration was willingly taken up by the local rulers and the local peoples bringing in a new creation within the great Cultural Orbit of India.

(k) *The Purāṇas as the Expanding Repositories of an Ever-growing World of Hindu Cults, Customs and Legends: A Bible which Never became Sealed Book: A Vast Purāṇa Pariśiṣṭa or Apocrypha, in Sanskrit, in the Prakṛtic Dialects and in non-Aryan Speeches*

The Purāṇas form the repository of a huge mass of Indian lore—legendary, historical, didactic, ritualistic, legalistic, philosophical, scientific and what not. They are also the repository of a large mass of imaginative literature which was collected under Brāhmanical inspiration and was given a place in these huge collections. The Purāṇas represent only a part of that astonishingly large mass of literary output which was the glory of, and, at the same time, one of the most bewildering things in, Indian civilisation. Other similar masses of popular literature are found in similar collections brought together the Buddhists (in both Pāli and Buddhist Sanskrit) as well as the Jainas (in both the various Prākṛts and Apabhraṁśas, and in Sanskrit). The number of Purāṇas is accepted as eight, and an enumeration has been made of these eighteen standard Purāṇas. The following Sanskrit *śloka* gives the names of the accepted eighteen Purāṇas in their abbreviated forms:

> The two *bha*s (i.e. *Bhāgavata* and *Bhaviṣya*), the two *ma*-s (i.e. *Matsya* and *Mārkaṇḍeya*), the three *bra*-s (*Brahma*, *Brahmāṇḍa* and *Brahmavaivarta*) and the four *va*-s (*Viṣṇu, Vāyu, Vāmana* and *Varāha*), and *Agni, Nārada, Padma, Liṅga, Garuḍa, Kūrma* and *Skanda* these are declared to be the Purāṇas.

But this attempt to restrict the Purāṇas to a limited number (so that, as in the case of the Nigama or the Vedic literature, a generally accepted canon could be, established in these eighteen only) did not, succeed in the Brāhmanical worlds. The type of literature found in the Purāṇas went on accumulating, and the number grew, and newer additions or compilations became popular and began to have some authority or recognition. These were also collected as Upapurāṇas. Their number is also looked upon as eighteen, although they are not, so voluminous as the bigger Purāṇas. Then the *Mahābhārata* was there, which embodied in, itself, the saga of the Kauravas, and the Pāṇḍavas which were in all likelihood historical, going back, to the tenth century BC, but there was also quiet, a large mass of narrative, didactic, historical and romantic as well as philosophical and folkloristic materials which were embodied in it, and gave this book its unique character and made it almost like a Purāṇa. Then the supplementary addition to the *Mahābhārata*, the *Harivaṁśa*, was another great book in the Purāṇa tradition.

The orthodox Brāhmanical opinion, regarding these proper contents, of the Purāṇas were more or less accepted, and they, are said to consist primarily of the following matters:

(1) Creation of the universe (*sarga* or *visarga*); (2) Occasional dissolutions of the universe (*pratisarga*, or *vṛtti-rakṣa, somatha-hetu, apasraya*); (3) The genealogy of the gods, divine kings and sages (*vaṁśa*); epochs or different ages in the history of the world (*antara, manvantara*); and finally; (5) The deeds of the gods, kings and sages (*vaṁśānucarita* or *vamayānucarita*), etc.

But actually, we find, in the Purāṇas much more than the above topics, and excepting in some Purāṇas like the *Viṣṇu Purāṇa*, the subject-matter is not confined to these topics alone.

As a matter of fact, the Purāṇas are mostly a sort of huge collection of all popular lore as well as religious doctrines, dogmas and rituals, didactic and philosophical discussion, and above all, of stories, mostly moral and edifying, relating to the gods and men.

The Purāṇas as it could be easily seen, are not confined to the stories and traditions of the Aryan people only. With the development of the Hindus as a mixed people, whatever was current among the various component elements, which went to form the Hindu people—Aryan, Dravidian, Austric as well as Mongoloid—came to be known to the ever increasing Aryan-speaking Hindu population, both as an Aryan or as a non-

Aryan inheritance, and was taken over by the brāhmaṇas, and all this mass of materials of heterogeneous origin was accepted and put in Sanskrit. Sometimes, these stories were current in thc various Prākṛts, and were of a folk or popular character all through, and it was easy to render them into Sanskrit. But frequently in this process much of the old Prākṛt character of the language survived in the Sanskrit (which was the nature of a palimpsest). This was noted by the first Purāṇa investigators like F.E. Pargiter and others. When the original stories were in a non-Aryan "speech" it all depended upon the. extent to which the legends and stories current among these non-Aryan speakers were assimilated by the newly-formed Brāhmanical world, that these were early rendered into Sanskrit, or they were late in being adopted; and in many cases they have not been brought within the orbit of Sanskrit as yet. Whenever they were put into Sanskrit, their incorporation in one or other of the Purāṇas was easy. As a matter of fact, we can very well say that the heterogeneous and conflicting character of Purāṇas in their story material and their folklore elements is due to this basic fact, namely, that they represent whatever was current among the all-absorbing and ever-growing Hindu people of ancient and early medieval India. Whatever was not directly in opposition to the Brāhmanical synthesis, was allowed to find a place in the Purāṇas as there was no limit to this vast population of India, of diverse origin in race and originally having different languages and types of culture, and as there was the widest amount of accommodation, the Purāṇas came to be the true repository of the floating mass of popular literature in the departments of life, expressed in terms of the Sanskrit language.

Thus, from the very nature of the case, there was an unbounded and unrestrained scope for the Purāṇa to expand. Even some Brāhmanical scholars wanted to bring about some kind of literary discipline and tried to put on the brake by restricting the scope of the Purāṇa and defining its subject matter, but this was powerless to achieve the end. A Purāṇa canon was tacitly established, embracing the eighteen major

Purāṇas, as mentioned before. But then the Upapurāṇas had to be admitted after that. The Upapurāṇa are just in the same line, and we cannot call them "Purāṇa Apocrypha" in the strict sense of the term—they were just a continuation of the Purāṇa literature which obtained some kind of recognition fairly early, and they are virtually and admittedly part of the some class of compositions as the Purāṇas. But outside of the mass of literature which became available in Sanskrit as in the eighteen "Canonical" Purāṇas and the Upapurāṇas, the story-telling urge of the people of India has continued and has created other cycles of legends and stories. Sometimes, the myths and legends and stories of non-Aryan peoples who did not come within the fold of Hinduism in fairly ancient times have continued in the original languages, whether Austric or Dravidian or Sino-Tibetan. Even then there have been attempt occasionally to bring them within the pale of the Hindu Purāṇa. Local legends of the gods and goddesses and of kings and wise men are found all over India. Sometimes in the shape of Māhātmyas on "Glorious Tales" (like the medieval European. Aurea Legends or "the Golden Legends" of Christian saints and martyrs), they were rendered into Sanskrit and were docketed within the Purāṇas like, for example, the *Skanda Purāṇa* and *Padma Purāṇa*. Sometimes, they were not rendered into Sanskrit, although they were within the range of Hindu stories and as such they have remained outside the orbit of the All-India Purāṇa canon; and they are found in Tamil and Bengali, Hindi and Marathi and other languages. We have, for example, the whole series of Sthala Purāṇas which are found in the Tamil country which are really Purāṇas connected with particular holy places and with the gods presiding over them. We can mention in this context the Tamil Śaivite *Periya-Purāṇam*, compiled in the tenth-eleventh century by Chekkilar, a work which has acquired the high authority and popularity of the Sanskrit Purāṇas.

Here we have before us a whole mass of proper "Purāṇa Apocrypha" in languages other than Sanskrit. There are many stories which have a Parāṇa character, but which still remain outside of the Purāṇas only because there was no attempt at any time to render them into Sanskrit and include them in one of the well-known or canonical Purāṇas. Yet these stories are nevertheless current and are implicitly looked upon as genuine Purāṇa stories, although they are not in Sanskrit and are in the various modern Indian languages. In some cases, these may have been rendered into Sanskrit, but are for some reason or other outside of an all India Purāṇa canon. Thus, the story of Śāmba going outside India to Śaka-sthāna and bringing from there a new cult of the Sun-God is well known as a Purāṇa story, but the story of Vaṣiṣṭha going to China and bringing from there the cult of the Tāntric Goddess Tārā and introducing into India "the Ritual of the Chinese"—the Cīnācāra or Vāmācāra (or "the left-handed ritual") is not so well known, although it has been narrated in some of the Brāhmanical Tantras. Thus, there is quite a large mass of *Rāmāyaṇa* Apocrypha current in Bengali, which has been noted by the late Dr. Dinesh Chandra Sen. So also stories relating to the Goddess Manasā (including that fine Middle Bengali story of the wifely devotion of Bihula to her husband, young Laksmindhara); the stories relating to the Goddesss Caṇḍī and her devotees (the huntsman Kālaketu and his wife Phullara, and the merchant: Dhanapati and his two wives, Lahana and Khullana, and his son Srimanta), etc. are really of the same nature as Purāṇa stories. But they have not obtained a place in any canonical Purāṇa. We have in Bengal and in other parts of India quite a whole host of other stories relating to Rāma and Kṛṣṇa which show a development of the story element of the *Rāmāyaṇa* and the *Bhāgavata* Purāṇa right down to modern times. It can be elaborately shown how the Rādhā–Kṛṣṇa story went on developing from early centuries of the Christian era right down to the eighteenth century, and this development in its entirety has just escaped being recorded as proper Purāṇa only because they were not given All-India publicity through Sanskrit and added to Purāṇa canon, as these developments were late, and popular, and consequently came to be neglected by the brāhmaṇa scholars. They remained a vernacular Apocrypha, but of the greatest amount of popularity and interest. There are a number of folktales which could not be tagged on to the *Rāmāyaṇa* and the *Mahābhārata* and the Purāṇas, only because they escaped being rendered into Sanskrit and being taken in hand by the Brāhmanical Purāṇa reciters. The story of how Hanumān was responsible for the mango fruit coming to India; how the squirrel got the stripes on its back through the grace of Rāma; how according to a widely current Bengal legend, Kumāra or Kārttikeya, the son of Śiva, remained a confirmed bachelor; how in contrast to this version, Kumāra or Murugan in the Tamil land obtained a second wife in Valli; the daughter of mountain chieftain of the Korava people, over and above his first wife Devasen the daughter of Indra; how Śiva lived among the Koch women in North Bengal, and became the ancestor of a line of Koch kings; all these, and quite a number of other stories of this type, not yet adopted into Sanskrit, forms a veritable Purāṇa Apocrypha. The relations between Kṛṣṇa and Rādhā are of the nature of a late accretion to the Kṛṣṇa legend which, found in part a place even in the canonical Purāṇas. But considerable amount of other stories and legends have remained outside the canon, and are in all propriety to be labelled as Purāṇa Apocrypha.

When in ancient and medieval and even modern times, a non-Aryan speaking group was brought within the orbit of Brāhmanical Hinduism, its gods and godlings were identified with the great gods of Hinduism, so that the transition of the people from an *ādivāsī* or a pre-Aryan group into a Brāhmanical Hindu was facilitated, and absorption within the wider Hindu body-politic became easy and a matter of course. But sometimes this was not attended to, and the stories have not remained outside the orthodox or pan-Indian Hindu orbit. Not infrequently we have got a dual world—that of the pre-Aryan myths and legends which have mostly been tagged to the newly-introduced and usually eagerly accepted Brāhmanical Hindu myths and legends. And, even now, this old spirit of integration through compromise and cooperation appears to be quite active. In medieval times, it was in the nature of things that these stories would be the common property or groups of people who had not wholly forgotten their pre-Aryan heritage, although they did not have any historical or precise knowledge of it. The Brāhmanical spirit of accommodation and reinterpretation is nevertheless everywhere helping to bring about this kind of integration which we find in the Purāṇas.

(I) *Purāṇa Apocrypha derived from the Legends and Traditions of the Meitei or Manipuri People, a Veritable "Maṇipura-Purāṇa', Existing Side by Side with the Sanskrit Purāṇas*

Dr. Verrier Elwin has collected a number of folktales and legends from among the *ādivāsī* peoples of central and eastern India, and these form a true *Ādivāsī Purāṇa* for the areas. Similarly, in recent years there has been made a learned attempt by Panditaraja Atombapu Sharma of Manipur to harmonise the legends and traditions of the Meitei people with the Brāhmanical Purāṇa, including also the two Epics. This great scholar of Manipur and eastern India devoted his whole life to the teaching and propagation of the Sanskrit language, literature and sacred lore as the most respected religious leader of the Manipur people. He himself was a man of great faith in Vaiṣṇavism and his attempt at harmonising the world of the Meitei Maibas and Maibis or priests and priestesses with the Brāhmanical or Purāṇic world may be ingenious, but it is perfectly serious dsincere, and legitimate as being of tradition. The Meiteis had their old world of the gods with their Meitei names and their special stories and legends. After the Meiteis came within the fold of Brāhmanism which must have taken place at least 1,000 years ago followed by later phases of intensive Hindu campaign among them at subsequent epochs, these gods continued to be worshipped with the help of the Maibas and Maibis or priests and priestesses of the old Meitei religion continuing the old Meitei ritual. But it went on side by side with the new Hindu ritual entering round the worship of Visnu and Śiva and Durgā particularly of Viṣṇu in his incarnation of Kṛṣṇa. There was no clear margin between the two religions, but in Meitei society we have a definite attempt at translating things Meitei into terms of Sanskrit. Thus, e.g. the Shalais or clans of the Meiteis were connected with the *gotra*s of the brāhmaṇas. The result of this kind of harmonisation or integration, which has been going on, in India, ever since Aryans and pre-Aryans net on the soil of India and set about forming a single culture, and commingling to form a single people is still at work at Manipur, and it can be seen from the synthesis which has been arrived at and this synthesis or syncretised form of Hinduism is fully believed in by the larger number of Meitei People at the present day. This forms a proper *Maṇipura Purāṇa* and the nature of it will be apparent from a little resume which I am giving below of what is virtually ancient mass of Purāṇa Apocrypha which has been sought to be retold afresh. To start with, the Manipuri people themselves identified some of their own gods and goddesses with the divinities of the Hindu pantheon and in this way Mei has been identified with Brahmā, Ishing with Viṣṇu, and Nungshit with Śiva; so Shorarel with Indra, Marjing with Kubera, Khoriphaba with Varuṇa, Wangbrel with Yama, Irum with Agni and Taoroina with Ananta, the divine ruler of the Nāgas. The story goes that Śiva and Pārvatī came down from heaven and descended upon Manipur Valley. They were looking for a spot where they could perform their Rāsa dance in emulation of Kṛṣṇa and Rādhā's Rāsa dance at Vrindavana. They liked some of the hills in that area, and they first stood on the hill of Nongmaijing or Nilakantha Giri "the hill of the Blue-Throat or Śiva". These hills are considered to be sacred places, in Manipur; and thousands of pilgrims every year visit them. Śiva acquired a new name in Manipur, Poireiton, i.e. "He who came to a new spot"'. In Manipur (which Sri Atombapu Sharma identified with the ancient abode of the Aryans—the Pratnaukas, mentioned in Vedic literature), Śiva caused seven gods to descend from heaven which had seven mountain peaks in it. These seven gods were identified with the seven planets as they are known in Hindu mythology: (1) Nongmaijing or the Sun, (2) Ningthoukaba or the Moon, (3) Leipakpokpa or Mars,

(4) Yumsakeisa or Mercury, (5) Sagolsel or Jupiter, (6) Irai or Venus, and (7) Thanja or Saturn. These planetary deities in the Manipur scene were some of them, endowed with animal heads—Mars had the head of a buffalo, Mercury that of an elephant, Jupiter of a stag and Venus of a tiger.

After that Śiva, and Pārvatī went to the north-western direction of Manipur and took up their abode in the hill known as Koubru or Kumāra-Parvata. Manipur is now a predominantly Vaiṣṇava country; and naturally Viṣṇu, specially in his incarnation Kṛṣṇa, has a pre-eminence. According to this Manipur legend, when Kṛṣṇa was performing the Rāsa dance with the *gopis* or cow-herd maidens at Vrindavana, Śiva and Pārvatī were acting as guards at the entrance to the *maṇḍapa* or pavilion where the Rāsa dance was being held. From the outside, Pārvatī listened to the music and the revelry of this dance, and then she desired very much to see it. But Kṛṣṇa did not agree. Kṛṣṇa asked Śiva and Pārvatī to find out some other place where they themselves could hold the Rāsa dance. Pārvatī arrived in Manipur and took up their abode in Koubru hill was that they regarded this spot to be the most suitable to hold the great Rāsa dance. But the country was full of water because of numerous rivers in it, and Śiva asked Kṛṣṇa to make the country dry. Kṛṣṇa came down at Śiva's request, and then a certain area became dry, and this came to be known as Viṣṇupura. Ten gods namely Indra or Haoba Shorarel, Kubera or Marjing, Yama or Wangbrel, Varuṇa or Thorikaba, Agni or Irum Ningthou, Nirṛti (or the Aśvinī-Kumāras) or Thangjing, Isana or Chingkhei-Ningthou, Vāyu or Loiya Lakpa, and two others who have only the Meitei names, Nongsaba and Komba-Meiromba, came down to Manipur; and through the efforts of these gods, Manipur became a dry country, and the first eight of these ten gods became the eight Dikpālas, as in Brāhmanical mythology, only the last two shared with Indra the guardianship of the East. In Manipur, Śiva and Pārvatī found people of the Kirāta tribe in occupation.

When the country was properly cleared, the Rāsa or Mahārāsa dance by Śiva and Pārvatī was arranged, and the gods assembled with various musical instruments to participate in this dance undertaken by the Father and the Mother of the Universe. The serpent king "Ananta" came, and with the *maṇi* or jewel which was on his head, he filled up the whole of Manipur with light for seven days and nights, until the conclusion of the Rāsa dance by Śiva and Pārvatī. The gods were very happy, and they blessed the land of Manipur that it would always remain green and fertile and the people would always have devotion to Viṣṇu. The legend says that at first the country was called Śiva-nagara, but after this great Rāsa dance; when the country was illuminated by the light or *maṇi* or jewel of the Nāga king, the country came to be known as Maṇipura.

The gods had requested Śiva to continue to be the ruler of the country. But Śiva was unwilling, and made the Nāga king Ananta, the ruler. When Viṣṇu had assumed his boar incarnation, through the breath from the nostrils of this divine boar, a tunnel had been made at a spot in the soil of Manipur. And beside this tunnel, on the top of a hill, the capital city, with the throne of Ananta, was established. The images of Kārttikeya and Gaṇeśa were established on two sides of the main gate of Ananta's palace. Then, after setting up his kingdom, Ananta Nāga established the games and sports which are still very popular among the Manipur people. Boat races were started in which the gods and the *apasaras*es or heavenly nymphs also took part, and there was a kind of tug of war with a long pole rather than a rope. The god Kubera (Marjing) invented the game of Polo, and this pleased all the gods very much; and this is the reason, as the legend says, that whenever there is an epidemic in the country, the Manipuris offer polo-sticks and balls to the gods.

After ruling over Manipur for some time, Ananta went back this Nāga world down in the pātāla or the underworld. Because Ananta was the first king of Manipur, the Manipur rulers took up as their emblem the figure of a serpent with its body in a complicated coil, and with a crown on its head. Ananta Nāga was succeeded, according to this synthesised legend, by a *gandharva* named Citrabhānu.

There is, according to many Manipur Hindus, the story of the creation of man, and the story of genuine Meitei one. According to a native Manipur book in old Meitei on the legends of the gods which is still extant, the *Leithak-Leikharol*, Śiva first told this story to Gaṇeśa. This story of the creation of man runs like this:

> The Supreme Deity, Atiya-Guru-Shidaba, who lives in heaven (*Atiya* means "Sky or Heaven", Guru is the Sanskrit word, and *Shidaba* means "immortal") decided to create man. He produced a god named Kodin from his own body, and. Kodin was ordered to create such a being who would be subject to death just because of the fact that he was born. Kodin then created seven frogs and seven monkeys, and placed them before Guru Shidaba. But Shidaba did not like them because they did not have any intelligence and perception and no idea of right and wrong. He said to Kodin: "Here I stand; create some animal after my appearance or my shadow". Accordingly, Kodin created another creature, but he had no power to give it life. Guru Shidaba then put the breath of life into this creature, and in this way man was created. He made the frogs go into the water and the monkeys to the hills.
>
> After this Guru Shidaba created Numit or the Sun, and Toha or the Moon in the form of men; and the Sun received anew name Kojen-tu Thokpa and the Moon, Ashiba.Then Guru Shidaba vanished from the earth.
>
> Atiya Guru Shidaba had manifested himself on earth through the tunnel in the ground which was made by the breath of Viṣṇu in his boar incarnation. He was accompanied by seven goddesses or *asparas*es, each of whom has her own name in Manipuri. They were married to the seven planet gods, and each of these couples had one son. These seven sons of the gods

> were the ancestors of the seven Manipuri Shalais or clans, and these seven clans have been identified with the seven *gotras* of the brāhmaṇas. Thus we have the *shalais* or *gotras* as follows (1) Angom =Bharadvāja of Kauśika; (2) Ningthouja = Śāṇḍilya; (3) Luwang=Kaśyapa; (4) Khumal = Maudgalya, which has also been modified to Madhukulya; (5) Khaba-Ngangba = Naimiṣya or Bharadvāja; (6) Moirang = Ātreya; and (7) Chengloi = Bharadvāja.

This story is just a Manipuri version of the Purāṇa story of seven *ṛṣis* who were the sons of brāhmaṇas. According to another legend current in Manipur, the ancestors of these seven *shalais* or *gotras* were not the sons born of the seven gods and *apsaras*es as mentioned before, but rather they were born from the body of Guru Shidaba himself. This is like the creation from Brahma's person—from the Puruṣa, as in the *Ṛgveda* of the four caste, e.g. the brāhmaṇas from Puruṣa's mouth, the kṣatriyas from his two arms, the vaiśyas from his thighs and the śūdras from his feet. Similarly from the right eye and the left eye, from the right ear and the left ear, from the two nostrils and from the teeth came out the founders of these seven *shalais*.

In another legend which is found in the *Leithak-Leikharol*; we have a number of other stories which have not been brought in line with the extant Sanskriti Purāṇas. It is said that the two gods Pakhamba (alias Sentreng) and Shenamahi (alias Kuptreng), sons of Guru Shidaba, obtained permission from their father to descend on earth; and they came to Manipur. To test his sons, whether they could recognise him in a disguise, Guru Shidaba took up the form of a dead cow and began to float down the Vijaya River. The brothers recognise that it was their father who had taken this disguise and they dragged the dead cow on dry ground. Shidaba was pleased that they could recognise him, and gave to Sentreng the name of Pakhamba, i.e. "who knows the father". The two brothers then cut the dead cow into pieces and gave portions of the body to the seven ancestors of the *shalai*s. The place where the skin of the cow was dried came to be known as Kangla, which means "to dry". The seven ancestors then performed a *homa* sacrifice in a fire with the portions of the cow's body they had received. Here is thus a linking up of the Meitei legend with the Vedic ritual.

To test the intelligence of his two sons, Guru Shidaba declared that, he would give the rulership of the land to whichever of the two brothers would be able to make a circuit of the world and come back first Kuptreng (or Shenamahi) then started from Kanglato go round the world. But through the advice of another god, the other brother Pakhamba simply went round his father's throne seven times. At this, Guru Shidaba was pleased, because circumambulating round his father was equivalent to going round the world. The other brother returned after his journey round the world, and found that Pakhamba was already established as king, there is similar story current in Bengal about Gaṇeśa outwitting his brother Kārttikeya in the same manner by just going round the mother Pārvatī once, while Kārttikeya made a dash to fly round the world on his peacock. Out of anger, Shenamahi wanted to fight his brother Pakhamba. But Guru Shidaba came riding on Ananta, the Nāga King, and a compromise between the brothers was effected by which they were to rule in alternate years. It was also decided that during the year that he would be ruling, the brother waiting for his turn would get divine worship from the people of Manipur. The Goddess Leimaren-Shidabi who had been the patron of the unsuccessful brother now came and declared that Guru Shidaba was the supreme spirit.

It was after these two brothers that the gandharva Citrabhānu came to the scene. A pedigree has been found out for this Citrabhānu in the manner of typical Sanskrit Purāṇas. Thus we are told that Brahmā was born in the lotus which came out from the navel of Viṣṇu, and from the body of Brahmā came out the sage Marīci, and Marīci's son was the sage Kaśyapa, and Kaśyapa's son was Sūrya, the Sun-God, and sage Sāvarṇa was the son of Sūrya, and Sāvarṇa's son was Citraketu. Then we have after Citraketu his son Citradhvaja and his grandson Citrabīja, and Citrabīja's son Citrasarva, then came Citrarāja and finally Citrabhānu. Citrāṅgadā was the daughter of Citrabhānu, and then a connection was effected between the *Mahābhārata* and Manipur through the story of Arjuna coming to Manipur and marrying Citāṅgadā. This legend of Arjuna and Citrāṅgadā, which is very well known in India, became one might say, the pivot for linking up Manipur with the Brāhmanical Purāṇa tradition.

After this we have semi-history and early history of Manipur, in the shape of a succession list of the kings of Manipur. In this list of Manipur kings, we have names which are both Sanskrit and Meitei. But that need not detain us. Thus, the tragic story of the hero Khamba and the princess Thoibi, whom Khamba married after a series of heroic feats, but who was himself killed by Thoibi through an inadvertent mistake, is supposed to have taken place during the rule of the Manipur king Loyamba, whose name has been Sanskritised as Lavange Simha Loyamba is said to have ruled from 1127 to 1154. The story of Khamba and Thoibi, like many other romantic or heroic tales, has even been given religious value and therefore it could easily, become a story of the nature of a Purāṇa. Khamba and Thoibi came to be regarded as incarnations of Śiva and Umā. But it is one of the finest stories in literature produced by the Kirāta or Sino-Tibetan people in India. The popularity of the story can be gauged from the fact that, in addition to ballads which are sung by minstrels and priests (Maibas) to the accompaniment of the pena or Manipuri one-stringed instrument, in recent times a great poet of Manipur, the late Hijam Aṅganghal Singh (1892-1943) has composed a poem of 39,000 lines on the romantic tale of Khamba and Thoibi (the Khamba-Thoibi Sheireng). In this way, we have the legends and stories of the Meiteis which have been attempted to be re-told like a Purāṇa; and if these legends had been rendered into Sanskrit, say 500 or 1,000 or 1,500 years ago, they could easily have found place in some Sanskrit Purāṇa. Thus it is to be always remembered that in their nature the Purāṇas are largely of folk origin, and a mass of heterogeneous Pre-Aryan material has found a place within the bosom of Hinduism, which has never refused to accommodate the experiences and self-expression of any group of people which was itself tolerant and accommodating.

The approximation and syncretisation of the legends of Manipur with the Sanskrit Purāṇas had started early enough through the *Brahman* attitude of tolerance and acceptance. Panditaraja Atombapu Sharma brought in his Sanskrit learning and his faith in the philosophy and ritual of Hinduism to knit this syncretisation more closely, and even to bring in his own contribution to present a more complete Integration. Herein lay his great importance in the religious and cultural life of Manipur and of Hindudom—herein he acted like a true *ṛṣi* or *Brahman* Organiser and Integrator of old, who had helped to weld together diverse peoples into One Hindu People within a single cultural and religious orbit.

3
Progress of Aryan Culture in Eastern India

R.C. Majumdar

The immigration of the Aryans into India from the West marks an important stage in the history of India. So far at least as the upper-class Hindus are concerned, this event had long been regarded as the beginning of their history and culture. For, not long ago, it was usually held that the Hindu religion, literature, social conditions—in short everything that is comprised in culture—were the legacies of the Aryans, and were developed through many centuries, by normal process of change into the present state of Hindu religion and society.

Recent progress in Indological studies has demonstrated that this is an oversimplification of the evolution of Hindu culture which ignores certain important historical facts. The first of these is the existence in India of numerous groups of peoples in diverse stages of culture when the Aryans settled in India. Their history is mostly unknown, but there is no warrant for the popular belief that they all-played an insignificant part in the evolution of Indian history and culture. The discoveries at Mohenjo-Daṛo and Haṛappā first opened our eyes to the possibility of a flourishing culture in India before the Aryans came, and this has been confirmed by subsequent discoveries during the last half a century over widely spread regions in the western parts of north India. It is now generally recognised that the Aryans met with a highly civilised people in the Punjab, defeated them, and gradually imposed their language and culture upon them to such an extent, that their old culture lost its individuality and was practically absorbed into this new one. But the Aryan culture also was influenced by the old one, though the degree or extent of such influence is difficult to determine. As the Aryan gradually advanced from the Punjab towards the east, the same process was repeated till a large part of north India up to the River Sadānīrā (probably Gaṇḍakī) in the east was thoroughly Aryanised. It is evident from a legend in the *Śatapatha brāhmaṇa*[1] that for a long time the region to the east of this river was beyond the pale of Aryan culture. But by the time that this *brāhmaṇa* was composed, the Aryan culture was introduced by Mathava, the Videgha, in this land which came to be known after him as Videha (North Bihar). We are told that the brāhmaṇas did not cross the river in former times but "nowadays there are many brāhmaṇas to the east of it".

Videha seemed to have been the eastern frontier of Aryan culture for a long time, and the people living further east were looked down upon by the Aryans as uncultured. Thus, the *Aitareya Āraṇyaka* (101, 200) refers in contemptuous terms to Vanga-Vagadha which probably denotes Vanga and Magadha (south Bihar). The *Aitareya brāhmaṇa* (VII.13-18) also places the Puṇḍras (North Bengal) beyond the pale of Aryan culture.

The same spirit is displayed, even at a much later date, in the Dharmasūtras. The *Baudhāyana Dharmasūtra* (I.1.2.13-15) condemns the people of Aṅga and Magadha as Saṁkīrṇayoni which Buhler translates as "of mixed origin', but the commentator Govindasvami explains as "not following proper rules of conduct'. The Sūtra then prescribes a penance for those who visit, among other countries, Puṇḍra, Vaṅga and Kaliṅga. Thus while southern and Eastern Bihar were probably partially Aryanised, Bengal and Orissa were outside the pale of Aryan culture.

The Jaina Sūtras represent the people of Rāḍha (W. Bengal) as uncultured and almost savage. The *Ayaraṅga Sutta* contains a fine Prākṛt ballad, where it is related that Mahāvīra wandered for some time as a naked mendicant in Lāḍha of which Vajjabhūmi and Subbhabhūmi were apparently two divisions. Lāḍha is described as a pathless country (*duccara*). The rude natives of the place generally maltreated the ascetics. When they saw the ascetics, they called up their dogs by the cry of "Chucchu" and set them upon the *sāmanas*. It was difficult to travel in Lāḍha. It is said that many recluses lived in Vajjabhūmi where they were bitten by the dogs and cruelly treated in a hundred other ways. Some of the recluses carried bamboo staves in order to keep off the dogs (*Latthim gahaya naliyam*).[2]

But although the Aryans looked down upon the primitive peoples whom they met in India as uncultured or savage, the examples of Moheñjo-Daṛo, Haṛappā and many other sites in the Indus Valley leave no doubt that some of the peoples living in this region possessed a high degree of material culture, and may even be said to have excelled the Aryans in this respect. The same thing was probably also true of the people in eastern India.

This view is no longer a mere hypothesis but is supported by archaeological evidence. Recent excavations in the valleys of the Ajay, Kunur, Bakreśwar, Mayūrākṣī and Kopai rivers, in the districts of Burdwan and Birbhum, have revealed the actual remains of a pre-Aryan culture in this region.[3] Special reference may be made in this connection to the excavation of the mound known as 'Pāṇḍu Rājār Ḍhibī', to the south of the Ajay River in the Burdwan district, carried between 1962 and 1965 AD. The artifacts found there have been claimed to represent "the full-blooded chalcolithic culture" and even some type of culture earlier than that. The chalcolithic culture which is dated about 1000 BC is proved by the Ceramic type consisting of "bowls, shallow bowls, basins, channel-spouted bowls or basins (in black-and-red ware, often painted in the inside in white or cream), trumpet or tulip shaped vases often perforated at the bottom (in black-and-red ware), inverted helmet-shaped flower-pots or deep bowls with a flaring rim (also in black-and-redware), dishes-on-stand, bowls-on-stand (generally in red ware sometimes painted and sometimes in black-slipped ware), perforated vases or bowls, thick storage jars, ordinary jars and *loṭās* (generally in red ware), high-necked jars with a flaring rim and funnel-shaped narrow mouth (in black-and-redware and black-slipped wares), lids and dishes." There were also "innumerable fragments of pottery with painted decorations, complete red ware bowls with paintings inside and outside." The people used bangles, rings, and beads, all made in copper, as well as harpoons and arrowheads in bone. They also used silk-cotton textiles. Regarding house-plans of this period it may be observed that they lived in rectangular-to-square or round houses or huts framed with thick wooden or bamboo posts around which were put reeds plastered with mud both from inside and outside. Sometimes, the roof-tiles were made of terracotta. Floors of these huts or houses were either made of rammed *moorum* or lateritic pellets or of terracotta nodules or of clay mixed with cow dung (of central Indian sites) or were plastered with lime. The people of Pāṇḍu Rājār Ḍhibī probably ate rice, and the dietary seems to have included in some cases the meats of Nilgai, deer and pig (evidence from almost all the levels) besides fishes. The animals were also domesticated by the people. In all, thirteen burials of three different classes, viz. extended, fractional or secondary, and urn-burial, were found. Terracotta figurines, beads of semi-precious stones, scattered ovens, ash pits and clay-lined sullage-pits came in to use in a later period. At a still later period people lived in brick-built houses.

Of great historical interest is a round seal of black steatite found in the Pāṇḍu Rājār Ḍhibī. "The seal bears a row of engraved symbols like hieroglyphs in a compartment on the margin while three pictographs representing a wavy line, a fish shark) and a globular object in relief occur below successively." A young British archaeologist, Michael Ridley, claims to have deciphered script and has explained it as of Minoan origin. He draws from it a very important conclusion, viz., the possibility that the inhabitants of Crete found their way to India 3,500 years ago and traded with the people of Bengal. It is also claimed in the Archaeological Report of the Government of West Bengal, on which the above account is based, that "the seal and engraving conclusively reveal that there was once a method of writing of sharp linear pattern in the Ajay Valley somewhere in the second millennium, BC". According to the same report,

> a careful study of all these relics originally revealed that the chalcolithic habitation at Pāṇḍu Rājār Ḍhibī which might have begun in the latter half of the second millennium BC, continued to flourish in spite of recognisable changes down to the beginning of the first millennium BC. Recently, a Radio-Carbon analysis of an excavated charcoal sample from the Cemetery level of period II of Pāṇḍu Rājār Ḍhibī, as conducted by Shyamadas Chatterjee, Head of the Department of Physics, Jadavpur University, Calcutta, has confirmed the expectation by dating the chalcolithic phase to BC 1012+120. It is obvious that Period I belonged to earlier times.

Attention may also be drawn to other statements. The excavations at Pāṇḍu Rājār Ḍhibī have revealed the existence of a Copper Age Civilisation in eastern India which had once a close relation with chalcolithic civilisation of central India and Rajasthan as illuminated by the comparison of cultural assemblages of these regions.

> During the excavation of 1964 it was decisively proved that iron was known and probably smelted at this site side by side with the use of copper and microliths in Period III in a chronological horizon around 1000 BC.

It is too early yet to assess the validity of all these claims, as scholars competent to do so have not yet made a proper study of the excavations at Pāṇḍu Rājār Ḍhibī and expressed any definite views, on this subject.

While archaeological excavations have revealed the existence of civilised groups of people in Burdwan, long before the advent of the Aryans, literary, linguistic and anthropological evidences testify to the fact that primitive types, of people now represented by the Koḷs, Śabaras, Pulindas, Hadis, Ḍoms and Cāṇḍālas lived in all parts of Bengal before the Aryans settled in this country.

The possibility is that all these people with varying degrees of culture lived side by side all-over eastern India. But their culture was moulded by the gradually increasing contact with the Aryans. This gradual Aryanisation of eastern India forms the chief point of interest in its subsequent history. It is not possible to trace the progress of this Aryanisation stage by stage a general idea may be formed by the study of the Smpitis or Dharmaśāstras and the Purāṇas which, in spite of vague and sometimes even contradictory statements, leave no doubt that by the time they were composed the barriers between the Aryans and the peoples they found in eastern India gradually broke down, and the two were drawn closer together with the inevitable consequence that an admixture of culture took place, the lower being practically submerged in the higher. Though the *Rāmāyaṇa* and the Purāṇas contain only isolated references, they supply valuable information about eastern India. In the *Rāmāyaṇa* (II.10.37), Daśaratha enumerates a number of countries over which he holds sway, by way of illustrating that his kingdom was co-extensive with the whole world. But the only eastern countries meṇtioned are Vaṅga, Aṅga and Magadha. The long list of countries which the followers of Sugrīva were asked to visit in search of Sītā included Magadha, Aṅga, Videha, Puṇḍra, and Mandāra hill.

But there is nothing to indicate that the Aryan culture was established there. The Purāṇas show a fair acquaintance with eastern India beyond the Sadānīrā. In the stock list of peoples given in several Purāṇas, the easterners include people of Aṅga, Videha, Madguru, Monghyr), Antargiri-Vahirgiri, Suhma, Vaṅga, Puṇḍra, Prāgjyotiṣa and Tāmralipta. The *Bhāgavata* Purāṇa (II.4.18) describes the Suhmas as a sinful tribe, along with the Kirātas, Yavaṇas, Khasas, etc.

The Buddhist and Jaina literatures also indicate the gradual expansion of Aryan culture towards the east. While the Jaina *Ayaraṅga Sutta* describes the people of Rāḍha at the time of Mahāvīra as barbarous, the Jaina *Prajñāpanā* includes the Vaigas and Lāḍhas in the list of Aryan peoples.

We learn from the Hāthīgumphā inscription of Khāravela (first century AD) of Kaliṅga[4] that he brought back an image of the Jina which had been taken away from Kaliṅga by Nanda who ruled over both Magadha and Bengal. This proves the spread of Jainism in the fourth century BC in Magadha, Vaṅga and Kaliṅga, the three non-Aryan countries according to Brāhmanical literature.

The *Divyāvadāna* records a tradition which shows that the Nirgrantha of Jaina religion was established in Puṇḍra or North Bengal in the time of Aśoka. It is said that the lay followers (*upāsaka*) of Jainism in the city of Puṇḍravardhana (North Bengal) had painted a picture representing Buddha falling at the feet of Jina, and on hearing this Aśoka massacred 18,000 Ājīvikas of Puṇḍravardhana on a single day.[5] It is difficult to put much faith in such a story except as the echo of a tradition that Jainism flourished in Bengal at the time of Aśoka in the third century BC.

This view is strengthened by the statement in the *Kalpasūtra* that Godasa, a disciple of Bhadrabāhu, founded a school named after him Godāsa-gaṇa. In the course of time, it had four *śākha*s or branches, of which three were known as Tāmraliptika, Koṭivarsīya and Puṇḍravardhanīya, named after three very well-known places in ancient Bengal, viz., Tāmralipti (Tamluk in Western Bengal or Rāḍha), Koṭivarṣa and Puṇḍravardhana, both in Northern Bengal. The nomenclatures leave no doubt about strong Jaina influence in north, west and south Bengal. A Mathurā inscription of about second century AD refers to a Jaina monk of Rāḍha.[6] The story in *Divyāvadāna*, mentioned above, shows that Buddhism also was flourishing in Puṇḍra. According to some scholars, a Buddhist sect is named in the Mahāsthān (Bogra district) inscription in the third century BC.[7] The prevalence of Buddhism in North Bengal in second century BC is proved by two inscriptions at Sāñcī.[8] A list of prominent Buddhist countries found in an inscription at Nāgārjunakoṇḍda of about third century AD includes Vaṅga.[9]

The first definite evidence of the Aryan contact with the east is furnished by the *Mahābhārata*. The change in the cultural and political atmosphere is broadly indicated by the long account it gives of Magadha as a great power in India. This region was contemptibly referred to in the *Aitareya Āraṇyaka* as well as in the later *Baudhāyana Dharmasūtra*. But we find a detailed account of the power and prestige of this kingdom under Jarāsandha from which it appears that he was an Aryan king or at least had Aryan connection and culture.[10] He had defeated numerous kṣatriya rulers and many kṣatriyas, including the Yādavas and Bhojas, fled in terror from their homes towards the west. The Yavana ruler Bhagadatta was submissive, and Pauṇḍraka Vāsudeva, ruler of Vaṅga, Puṇḍra and Kirātas sought for his protection. He had two powerful lieutenants, Haṁsa and Dimvaka. These two names, the human sacrifice of Jarāsandha, and the miraculous story how the two queens of Bṛhadratha produced two halves of a child which, being united by a demonness (*rākṣsī*) named Jarā, formed the united body of a man who was accordingly named Jarāsandha, indicate some non-Aryan elements in the royal family. On the whole, the account of Jarāsandha in the Epic proves that Magadha was Aryanised to a larger extent than hinted at in the *Baudhāyana Dharmasūtra*, though the primitive non-Aryan elements were not altogether absent from its culture. It serves as an example of the early Aryanisation on a massive scale after the Videgha incident described in the *Śatapatha Brāhmaṇa* mentioned above.

Evidence of Aryan contact with countries further east is also furnished by the *Mahābhārata* in connection with

(1) the *Digvijayas* of the Pāṇḍava brothers (Sabhā-Parva 25.29) preparatory to the Rājasuya-yajña,
(2) the description of the yajña,
(3) the names of rulers participating in the Kurukṣetra war,
(4) description of holy places of pilgrimage (Vana-Parva, Tīrthayātrā section),
(5) the self-imposed exile of Arjuna (Ādi-Parva, 170), and
(6) the military campaigns of Arjuna in connection with the Aśvamedha sacrifice performed by Yudhiṣṭhira.

1. As regards the first, we are told that Bhīma, proceeding to the eastern regions, first subdued seven Kirāta rulers. Then, after having defeated King Vāsudeva of Pauṇḍra, and the ruler of Kausiki-Kachohha—both of whom were brave and powerful—he drove away the King of Vaṅga, He also defeated Kings Samudrasena and Candrasena and conquered Tāmralipta, Karvata, Suhma and the kingdoms of the Mlechhas who dwelt on the sea-coast as well as in the islands of the sea. Having exacted tributes, various kinds of jewels and precious articles, he proceeded as far as the Lauhitya or Brahmaputra River. Arjuna also conquered Prāgjyotiṣa by defeating after a severe fight its king Bhagadatta supported by the Chinese and Kirāta soldiers and also those living by sea-shore.
2. Among the rulers who attended the Rājasūya-yajña and made valuable presents, we find the names of Bhagadatta, ruler of Prāgjyotiṣa, of great fame, attended by the Mlechchhas living on the sea-coast and the kings of hilly region, and Pauṇḍraka Vasudeva of Vaṅga and Kaliṅga.
3. Sahadeva, King of Magadha and son of Jarāsandha, joined the Pāṇḍavas and was killed. King Bhagadatta who helped Duryodhana also shared the same fate.

4. As regards the places of pilgrimage the Gaṅgā-sāgara-Saṅgama, i.e. the estuary of the Ganges in south Bengal, is referred to both in connection with the legend of Bhagīratha, and the pilgrimage of Yudhiṣṭhira. Among the holy rivers are included the Lauhitya, the Karatoyā and the Ganges. It is said that in old days Lauhitya was made a sacred place through the influence of Rāma. Anyone who goes there gets large quantities of gold. Visit to the Karatoyā after three days' fast produces the same merit as an Aśvamedha sacrifice. One who bathes in the Ganges from its western bank after three days fast is freed from all sins.[11]
5. As regards the fifth, the most important episode for our present purpose is the marriage of Arjuna with Citrāṅgadā. The story, as recorded in different places in the *Mahābhārata*, may be summed up as follows: Arjuna, during his exile, came down from the Himalayas and proceeded to the eastern region. In the course of his journey, he visited the holy places, temples and hermitages in Aṅga, Vaṅga and Kaliṅga. He then passed by the Mahendra mountains to Manipur on the sea. After visiting the temples and holy places of this country he met its ruler Citravāhana, and married his daughter Citrāṅgadā. He stayed there three years and begot a son named Babhruvāhana, who became king of Manipur.
6. As regards the sixth, we are told that while protecting the horse, Arjuna had to fight strenuously for three days before he could defeat the great hero Vajradatta, son of Bhagadatta and ruler of Prāgjyotiṣa. Arjuna then followed the horse to the Sindhu and defeated the assembled chiefs or rulers (*rājānah*) who had seized the sacrificial horse, thus released, wandered about in different countries and then entered Manipur. This resulted in a fight between Arjuna and his son Babhruvāhana, in the course of which Arjuna was defeated and killed. But his life was restored by Ulūpī, the daughter of the Nāga king, whom Arjuna had

married just before he had married Citrāṅgadā, the mother of Babhruvāhana, as mentioned above.

The circumstantial narratives in the *Mahābhārata*, mentioned above, under the six different items, to which a few isolated references may be added, are all concerned with Magadha and Bengal with only two important exceptions, viz. the kingdoms of Prāgjyotiṣa and Manipur. Both of these have been located, outside Bengal, in Assam, the former being identified with Kāmrūpa on the Brahmaputra Valley, and the latter with the place where we meet today, still bearing the old name. But neither of these identifications is altogether free from doubt, and as this question assumes special importance, in view of the locality where this lecture is being delivered, I shall consider it in some details in my next lecture.

But whatever we might think of the location of the kingdoms of Prāgjyotiṣa and Manipur, the details culled above from the *Mahābhārata* establish a few important points.

- In the first place, the Aryans had a much more intimate knowledge of, and closer contact with, South Bihar, West Bengal and East Pakistan, than in the days of the Dharma-sūtras, and Aryan culture had made its influence felt throughout these regions. Mention of their peoples with respect and reverence shows a striking contrast to the contemptuous reference in earlier records.
- Second, there were powerful states in this area and their kings gave good accounts of themselves in their fights with the Aryan invaders from the west.
- Third, some localities in these regions were regarded as holy and contained religious sanctuaries venerated by the Aryans. Sometimes legends were invented to associate localities in these regions with sacred or memorial sites.
- Fourth, the progress of Aryanisation is indicated by inter-marriage and adoption of Aryan names.

Certain legends indicated the fusion of Aryan and non-Aryan blood in the royal families.

The most striking instance is the story of Ṛṣi Dīrghatamas who begot on the queen of *asura* king Bali five sons, named Aṅga, Vaṅga, Suhma, Puṇḍra and Kaliṅga, who founded the five States named after them.

The change of situation is also indicated by the fact that whereas the early Jaina literature describes the people of Rādhā as barbarians, the later Jaina *Prjñāpanā* includes the people of East and West Bengal in the list of Aryan peoples. Further, though the people of West Bengal rudely treated Mahāvīra, there were several important centres of Jainism in that very region in the early centuries of the Christian era. The lands of the despised, Puṇḍras and Vaṅgas were now not only the seats of powerful kings, but also flourishing centres of Buddhism and Brāhmanical religion.

All these significant changes must have been brought about between the ages represented by the *Baudhāyana Dharmasūtra* and the *Mahābhārata*. The date of the former may be put roughly about the fifth century BC. It is more difficult to assign any such precise date to the *Mahābhārata*, the text of which grew in volume by repeated additions extending over centuries. Nevertheless, there are good grounds to believe that the great Epic assumed its present form in or some time before the fourth century AD. It may, therefore, be reasonably assumed that the first stage of Aryanisation of eastern India took place between fourth century BC and fourth century AD.

The evidence of the *Manusmṛti* or *Mānava Dharmaśāstra* is very significant in this connection. While early Dharmasūtras and grammatical treatises confine the land of the Aryans to the upper Ganges Valley, the author of the *Manusmṛti* extends it from the western to the eastern sea. It should, however, be noted that the law-giver brands the Pauṇḍras as degraded kṣatriyas, and classes them with the Dravidians, Scythians, Chinese and other outlandish peoples.

If we remember that the composition of the *Manusmṛti* may be placed between 200 BC and 200 AD, it supports the above dating, representing, as it does, a halfway house between the ages of the *Baudhāyana Dharmasūtra* and the *Mahābhārata.*

It is interesting to note that while the Pāli *Vinaya Piṭaka* places the eastern frontier of Āryāvarta at Rajmahal, its later version, the Sanskrit *Vinaya Piṭaka*, locates it in the Puṇḍra country further east.

The conclusion based upon literary evidence is fully supported and supplemented by the authentic historical facts known to us.

The glowing account of Magadha under Jarāsandha in the *Mahābhārata* may be taken as a reflection of the great political power established in that region by the four royal families founded respectively by Bimbisāra, Śiśunāga, Mahāpadma Nanda, and Candragupta Maurya. From a small local kingdom under the first in the sixth century BC, Magadha became a mighty empire extending over a large part of north India under the Nandas in the fourth century BC. The mighty Maurya Empire embraced the whole of north and a large part of south India during the fourth and third centuries BC. A brāhmaṇa royal family, the Śuṅgas, also ruled over a large part of northern India from Pāṭaliputra (Patna), which was the capital of Magadha since the fifth century BC. So, whatever historical value we may attach to the account of Jarāsandha in the *Mahābhārata* and of his successors in the Purāṇas, there is no doubt that Magadha emerged as a great political power in the fifth century BC, i.e. almost immediately after the period of *Baudhāyana Dharmasūtra.*

It is a moot point whether the historical ruling families of Magadha were full-blooded Aryans or had a mixture of non-Aryan and Aryan blood. It is significant that according to the Purāṇas, Magadha was ruled by the descendants of Jarāsandha whose miraculous (and therefore doubtful) origin has been discussed above. Neither Śiśunāga nor Bimbisāra, whose descendants next ruled in Magadha, is known to have belonged to any ancient Aryan family. Mahapadma Nanda, who ruled next, is described as śūdra in the Purāṇas and called a barber by the Greeks. There is an ancient tradition that the mother of Candragupta Maurya was a śūdra woman. The Purāṇas make a general statement that Mahāpadma Nanda exterminated the kṣatriyas and thereafter all the kings were of śūdra origin, and state specifically that the far-famed kṣatriya families like Ikṣvākus, Pāñcālas, Haihayas, etc. passed away after the accession of Mahāpadma Nanda to power.[12]

It would thus be reasonable to conclude that while the first stage of the eastward expansion of Aryan culture from the Punjab ended with the settlement of Videgha in North Bihar, called Videgha after him, the second stage begins with the rise of Magadha into power. According to the story in the *Mahābhārata* referred to above, the political supremacy of Magadha was established by Jarāsandha, and while many kṣatriya rulers fled to the west, there were non-Aryan eastern potentates like Pauṇḍraka Vāsudeva of Bengal whose subjects included a number of Kirātas or primitive barbarians. Whether Jarāsandha, described in the great Epic, was a really historical person may be doubted, and it is very likely that he symbolised, and to some extent reflected, the rise of Magadha as a great political power from the fifth century BC down to the period when the Epic, or at least the portion relating to Jarāsandha, was composed. Even if we regard the story as authentic, the pure Aryan origin of Jarāsandha may be doubted, but the account in the *Mahābhārata* represents him as one who had imbibed Aryan culture, though still preserving some non-Aryan traits. That the Magadhas or people of Magadha were non-Aryan admits of no doubt. The name occurs for the first time in a hymn in the *Atharvaveda Saṁhitā* (V.22.14), where a wish is expressed that the fever might visit the Aṅgas and Magadhas. The same Saṁhitā associates the Magadhas with the outcaste Vrātyas (XV.2.1-4), who were a nomadic tribe, did not pursue either trade or agriculture, and went about in rough wagons with herds of goats, wearing turbans and wielding a particular kind of bow. That these peoples, though outside the pale of Aryan culture down to the time of *Baudhāyana Dharmasūtra*, had in the meanwhile imbibed many elements of Aryan culture, and possibly even Aryan blood, has been mentioned above. The organisation of such peoples into a powerful state under an Aryan, non-Aryan, or Aryanised leader was bound to have a great repercussion upon the march of Aryan culture towards the east. That such a development took place in or before the fifth century BC admits of no doubt, and the age of the *Mahābhārata* shows a larger degree of Aryanisation than that of the *Baudhāyana Dharmasūtra*.

The references in the *Mahābhārata* and other sacred literature mentioned above seem to indicate that the Aryan culture spread from Magadha to Puṇḍra or North Bengal, Bengal, Vaṅga (South), and Suhma (West Bengal). It appears that at the time of Alexander's invasion in the last quarter of the fourth century BC, Magadha had yielded its place of supremacy to Vaṅga. The Greek and Latin writers refer to two nations, the Prasioi and the Gangaridai (*var-Gandaridai*), who ruled over the whole of north India from the River Beas in the Punjab to the eastern frontier of India beyond the Ganges. The classical writers, however, did not possess a very accurate idea of the exact location of the Gangaridai and their relationship with the Prasioi who had their capital at Pāṭaliputra. Diodorus, for example, says in one passage that the "Ganges which is 30 stades broad, flows from north to south forming the boundary towards the east of the tribe of Gandaridae". This would imply that the Gandaridai were the inhabitants of Rāḍha. But according to other writers, such as Curtius, Plutarch and Solinus, the two nations, the Gaṅgāridae and Prasioi, dwelt on the further bank of the Ganges, i.e., the eastern bank. Diodorus himself in another passage says that the region where the Gandaridai lived "is separated from further India by the greatest river in these parts for it has a breadth of 30 stadia". These different statements have been reconciled by supposing that by the Ganges the classical writers meant the easternmost branch of the Ganges (the Padma) rather than the western-most (Bhāgīrathī or Hooghly). But the specific statement in the first passage that the river runs from north to south exactly describes the course of the second rather than the first. Evidently, the classical writers had a vague notion of the geography of this region, and we shall not be justified in concluding from their varying descriptions that the Gangaridai lived in Rāḍha. There is, however, no doubt that Bengal was the homeland of the Gangaridai.

Similar uncertainty prevails over the position of the Gangaridai *vis-à-vis* the Prasioi. The Greek writer Curtius, for example, refers to them as two nations under one king, but immediately after makes statements which would imply a united realm and not a dual monarchy. Diodorus also speaks of them as forming one nation whose king was Xandrames, and the people over whom he ruled is further on represented simply as the Gangaridai.

Although these confused statements cannot lead to any definite conclusion, it is certain that the Gangaridai were a very powerful nation and either formed a dual monarchy with the Prasioi, or were otherwise closely associated with them on equal terms, if not as the senior partner or more important member of the cooperative undertaking against Alexander. According to the classical writers the Prasioi-Gangaridai army, which assembled to resist Alexander, consisted of 2,00,000 infantry, 8,000 chariots and 80,000 horse, and Alexander's army had to beat retreat before this imposing array of force.[13]

Thus, the end of the fourth century BC marks a fixed point in the expansion of Aryan culture in eastern India. Aryanised Bengal and Bihar formed the strongest political power in the whole of India. The hegemony of completely and partly Aryanised kingdoms of northern India, first under Magadha (South Bihar) and then under both Magadha and Bengal, could not fail to Aryanise these eastern regions to a very considerable extent. That Bengal, like Magadha, had imbibed many elements of culture may hardly be doubted and may be demonstrated by positive evidence. An inscription written in Prākṛt in the Brāhmī alphabet of the third century BC has been found in the site of the old Puṇḍranagara now represented by the ruins at Mahāsthān in Bogra district (East Pakistan).[14] An image, found at Silua in the Noakhali district

(East Pakistan), also bears an inscription written, apparently in Prākṛt, in the Brāhmī script of about second century BC.[15] The discovery of a large number of coins,[16] both punch-marked and Kuṣāṇa, both in North and South Bengal, and of a single Kuṣāṇa coin in the Murshidabad district, show the continuity of the process of Aryanisation. The Susunia rock inscription[17] in Bankura district, West Bengal, written in Sanskrit and in Brāhmī letters of the fourth century AD refers to some donation to God Viṣṇu.

Thus, even before the establishment of Gupta supremacy, Bengal had already developed into a stronghold of Aryan culture. After the Gupta age there is abundant evidence to show that the whole of West Bengal and East Pakistan, excluding the hilly region in the north, had been completely Aryanised,—so much so that the problem now is to find out the pre-Aryan elements in the culture of this region.

Notes

1. First Kāṇḍa, 4th Adhyāya, 1st Brāhmaṇa, 14 ff. SBE vol. XII, p. 105.
2. Barua, B., *The Ājīvikas*.
3. The account of the excavations that follows is based upon the two following books by P.C. Das Gupta and published by the Directorate of Archaeology, Government of West Bengal:
   1. *The Excavations at Pāṇḍu Rājār Ḍhibī*, pp. 27-31.
   2. *Exploring Bengal's Past*, pp. 16-18.
4. *Epigraphia Indica* (henceforth referred to as *Ep. Ind.*), vol. XX, p. 71.
5. *Divyavadana*, edited by Cowell, p. 427. The account mixes up the Nirgranthas and Ājīvikas, but the name of the sect is uniformly given as Nirgranthas in the Chinese translation, Cf. Przyluski, *La legende de l'Empereur Aśoka*, p. 278.
6. R.D. Banerji, *Pālas of Bengal*, p. 72.
7. D.C. Sircar, *Select Inscriptions*, pp. 79-80, *Ep. Ind.*, XXI, p. 85; *Indian Historical Quarterly*, 1934, pp. 67ff.
8. *Ep. Ind.*, II, pp. 103, 380, Nos. 102. 217.
9. *Ep. Ind.*, XX, p. 22.
10. *Mahābhārata*, II. 13f.
11. Ibid., III. Ch. 33, vv. 2-5.

12. F.E. Pargiter, *The Purāna Text of the Dynasties of the Kali Age*, p. 69.
13. *History of Bengal*, edited by R.O. Majumdar, vol. I, pp. 41-44. For the account of the Classical writers mentioned in the text of R.C. Majumdar, *The Classical Accounts of India*,
14. Cf. References in footnote 8.
15. *Annual Report of the Archaeological Survey of India, 1930-34*, pp. 38-39.
16. R.D. Banerji, *Bānglār Itihāsa*, vol. 1, 2nd edn., pp. 32-33, 38-39.
17. *Ep. Ind.* XII, p. 317; *Ann. Report Arch. Survey*, 1927-28, p. 188.

4
Expansion of Aryanism beyond Bengal

R.C. Majumdar

The only region to the east of Bengal which is frequently mentioned in the Epics and Purāṇas and generally associated with Puṇḍra and Vaṅga, is named Prāgjyotiṣa. It denoted, generally speaking, upper Assam, but more particularly, the valley of the Brahmaputra after it enters India, and before it takes the southern bend beyond Dhubri. At a later period, the region was designated Kāmrūp, a name still applied to a district in Assam, to the north of the Brahmaputra.

Prāgjyotiṣa is mentioned in the *Rāmāyaṇa*, as one of the localities which Sugrīva directed his monkeys to visit in search of Sītā. As the list includes even distant regions beyond India, every country mentioned in it was not necessarily a region well known to the author, and it probably contained some whose name was only vaguely known to him as a mythical geographical name. This seems to be the case with Prāgjyotiṣa which is described as a "city of gold where dwells the wicked *dānava* king, Naraka".[1]

Naraka, as the name of the mythical progenitor of the kings of Prāgjyotiṣa, occurs not only in the Epics, Purāṇas and other literature, but in all the copper-plate grants of kings of

Assam from the seventh to the twelfth century AD. Various legends grew around his birth and career, the most detailed being that found in the *Kālikā* Purāṇa (Chs. 36-40). It may be summarised as follows:

> God Viṣṇu (or Nārāyaṇa), in his incarnation as Boar, rescued the Earth from the sea, and from the union of Viṣṇu and Earth was born an *asura* son named Naraka, who was brought up by Janaka, king of Mithilā (Videha). As the boy grew up, Viṣṇu came back to the earth, and proceeded with him to Prāgjyotiṣa. After defeating the Kirātas, who inhabited the land, and killing their king, Viṣṇu installed his son Naraka as king of the whole region extending up to the Karatoyā in the West, and settled the brāhmaṇas and other high-class Hindus in this area. After having instructed Naraka to lead the life of an orthodox Hindu and married him to a daughter of the king of Vidarbha (Berar), Viṣṇu left the earth. But Naraka became a friend of Bāṇa, son of *asura* Bali, king of Śonitapura, discarded Hindu religion and culture, and with his *asura* army under the command of Bāṇa defeated Indra, the king of gods, and Varuṇa. At this time, Viṣṇu had come to the earth again in his Kṛṣṇa incarnation, and Indra asked him to redress his grievances. Accordingly, Kṛṣṇa went to Prāgjyotiṣa, killed Naraka after a severe fight, and crowned His son Bhagadatta as king.

This curious legend, in spite of its mythical character, has preserved the memory of some historical facts which may be deduced from other sources also, namely:

1. That originally, the Brahmaputra Valley in Assam was peopled by non-Aryans, known by the generic name of the Kirātas and *asura*s.

2. That rich and powerful kingdoms arose under non-Aryan rulers who bravely defied and challenged the Aryans.
3. That Aryan culture gradually flowed into this region, and probably Videha (North Bihar), which was Aryanised before Magadha, as mentioned above, played a leading part in it. This may be deduced from the reference to Janaka, king of Videha, in connection with the birth of Naraka, and is rendered probable by the fact that the Karatoyā River which traditionally formed the western boundary of Prāgjyotiṣa and is known to be such even in historical time, was not very far from the eastern frontier of Videha.

It may be easily surmised that the expansion of Aryan culture to Assam followed two parallel lines, more or less about the same time; one from North Bihar through North Bengal, and the other from South Bihar through Central and East Bengal.

This conclusion gains some strength from the fact that the passages quoted above from the *Mahābhārata* clearly indicate that Aryan culture was not less dominant in Prāgjyotiṣa than in Bengal in the age of the great Epic. A passage in the Sabhā-Parvaa describing the fight between Arjuna and Bhagadatta is quite interesting from this point of view. After defeating a number of kings, Arjuna proceeded along with them and invaded the country of Prāgjyotiṣa. Bhagadatta had gathered round him a mighty army consisting of the Kirāta and Chinese soldiers as well as others living on the sea-coast. After the battle had lasted for eight days Bhagadatta told Arjuna in a jovial mood:

> "You are son of Indra and it is quite natural that you should show such valour and strength in battle. But I am a friend of Indra and am in no way inferior to him as a warrior. I am unable to continue the war. So, tell me what you desire and I will do it."

Arjuna said in reply:

> "Yudhiṣṭhira desires sovereignty of the world and wishes that you pay tribute to him. You are a friend of my father, and now there is friendship between us also. So, I do not command you to pay tribute but please do so out of love for me."

Bhagadatta said in reply:

> "You are dear to me and so is Yudhiṣṭhira. I shall pay tribute, what else do you want?"[2]

The whole account, and particularly the concluding talk is, of course, imaginary, but it is certain that when this passage was inserted in the *Mahābhārata*, Bhagadatta was held in the highest esteem by the Aryan world. If we remember that Naraka is described in the *Rāmāyaṇa* as a wicked *dānava*, and Purāṇic legends make him an enemy of *brāhmaṇas* and one who fought against Indra and Varuṇa, the contrast offered by his son Bhagadatta who is described in the *Mahābhārata* as a friend of Indra as well as of the Pāṇḍavas, is indeed very great. It may serve as a measure of the cultural changes that took place in Assam during the periods represented by Naraka and Bhagadatta. Though related as father and son, the interval between the two was very long, for Naraka was born in the Satya Yuga and Bhagadatta at the end of the Dvāpara Yuga. The legends thus preserve a memory of the historical truth that the Kirātas and other primitive peoples who dwelt in this region were being gradually Aryanised in the early centuries of the Christian era, if not earlier.

The legends also contain reminiscence of the means by which such transformation was achieved. According to the legend preserved in the *Kālikā* Purāṇa, Viṣṇu or Nārāyaṇa, after installing Naraka on the throne of Prāgjyotiṣa, settled brāhmaṇas and other high caste Hindus in the new kingdom. We may not believe the part played by Nārāyaṇa in the legend of Naraka, but we know from many sources that settlement of the orthodox Hindus in large number among primitive people was the principal means of Aryanizing them. It was not a case of conversion by violent means but of peaceful cultural evolution brought about by close association of the Aryans with the primitive peoples. It is likely that individual Aryans, mostly brāhmaṇas, kṣatriyas, vaiśyas, wandered about, either in a missionary spirit or urged by motives of founding kingdoms or carrying on trade in far distant lands, settled there in large number, married local women and thus established Hindu culture and a mixed breed of people. Concrete instances of the expansion of Aryan culture in Malay Peninsula and neighbouring regions by such means will be mentioned later. It is impossible to doubt that such peaceful penetration of Aryan culture also took place, nearer home, in the eastern regions of India. As a matter of fact, a critical study of Indian history leaves no doubt that this was the main process by which Aryan Vedic culture was established all over India from the first centre of Aryan settlement in the Punjab. That this process was deliberately followed in the case of Assam even in historical period is proved by epigraphic records. The most important among them is the Nidhanpur copper-plate of Bhāskaravarman,[3] a king of Prāgjyotiṣa at the beginning of the seventh century AD, and it is necessary to give a short account of it. The inscription begins with a reference to the birth of Naraka from Viṣṇu who rescued the earth in his Boar incarnation, and to Bhagadatta, the son of Naraka and friend of Indra, who fought with Arjuna—echoing the legends mentioned above whose antiquity, going back at least to the sixth century AD, is thus well established. Vajradatta, son of Bhagadatta, was also a favourite of Indra and his family, we are told, ruled for three thousand years, when a new royal dynasty was established by Puṣyavarman. His twelfth successor (in the eleventh generation) was Bhāskara-Varman who flourished early in the seventh century.

This record is of great historical value. In the first place, it introduces us to the first historical Aryan or Aryanised ruling dynasty in Assam. We may be reasonably certain that it was founded in the fourth century AD. This was the time when the famous Gupta dynasty was founded in North Bengal or South Bihar. Some sort of association between the two dynasties is indicated by the fact that the second king of this dynasty and his queen both bore the same names as the fourth king of the Gupta dynasty—the mighty emperor Samudragupta—and his queen Dattadevī. This can be hardly regarded as a curious coincidence and it has been suggested that Puṣyavarman, who founded the dynasty, was contemporary of Samudragupta, and having acknowledged his sovereignty named his son and daughter-in-law after the suzerain and his queen. As we know that Samudragupta certainly imposed his suzerainty over Kāmrūpa, it is also not unlikely that he removed the ruling king claiming descent from Naraka and installed in his place a friend or relation who showed his gratitude by naming his son and daughter-in-law after his sovereigns. But whatever may be the real explanation this royal family must have been either Aryan or thoroughly Aryanised. This is indicated by the royal names, the use of Sanskrit language in court, the beginning of the record with an obeisance to Śiva, and the performance of an Aśvamedha sacrifice by the eighth king, Bhūtivarman, presumably by way of asserting his independence after the decline of the Gupta power in the sixth century AD. His grandson Susthitavarman is said to have performed two Aśvamedha sacrifices. But the most interesting evidence of the Aryanisation of the people is furnished by the fact stated in there cord that king Bhūtivarman settled more than 205 brāhmaṇas in his kingdom by granting them lands. The name of each of these brāhmaṇas together with his *gotra*, the particular branch of the Vedas studied by him, and the share of the total amount of land assigned to him, are all recorded in the inscription. It is almost a unique record of a policy of mass settlement of brāhmaṇas among a population, either non-Aryan or only partly Aryanised. We have earlier examples of such mass settlement of Indians in non-Aryan lands far away from India. The Chinese chronicles record that in a certain locality of Malay Peninsula there were more than thousand brāhmaṇas of India, most of whom were permanently settled in the country. The local people, we are told, followed their religion and gave them their daughters in marriage.[4] We know that Malay Peninsula, Indo-China and Indonesia were visited by successive bands of Indians, who preached Hindu religion and established kingdoms. It was through them that

Indian culture was spread in those distant regions and the task was facilitated by the fact that they married local girls and permanently settled. What was done in these far-off lands must have been practised nearer home, and this very natural presumption is supported by the fact that in a much later age kings of Tripura and Coch-Behar invited orthodox Hindus from Bengal and settled them in their kingdoms.

In addition to Prāgjyotiṣa or Kāmrūpa there are several other states adjacent to Bengal, of whose Aryanisation we possess some definite and detailed information. Among these the most prominent are Tripura, Coch-Behar, Cachār and Manipur. In all these cases we find the same pattern. The legend of the founder-king whose non-Aryan origin is thinly veiled under miraculous or mythical stories of birth, the adoption of Brāhmanical culture-language, literature, religion, art, etc., and the development of all these by mass settlement of high-caste Hindus brought from outside.

The *Rājamālā*, a chronicle of the kings of Tripura composed in Medieval Age, traces the genealogy of the kings back to Yayāti through his son Druhya, who became ruler in Kirāta country. His son or descendant Tripura (called *daitya* king) had neither knowledge of the Vedas nor any regard for Brāhmanical religion, but followed the customs of the Kirātas. He was cruel and unrighteous but a very powerful king. Then by the grace of Śiva a righteous king Trilocana was born (according to some texts, procreated by Śiva). He was a contemporary of Yudhiṣṭhira and visited him.

After all these mythical tales we have an account of King Ratna-fa, who was the first to assume the title Māṇikya, which was henceforth adopted by the kings of Tripura. He lived in the court of Gauḍa and was quite unfamiliar with the manner and customs of civilised people. So, when he became king of Tripura, he asked for permission to settle Bengali families in his kingdom, and the Sultan of Gauda issued an order permitting ten thousand families to migrate from Bengal to Tripura. This may be assigned to the fourteenth or fifteenth century AD.

One of his ancestors, Dungur-fa, removed by about twenty generations from Ratna-fa, is said to have settled five brāhmaṇas in Sylhet by donating lands. The verses in a copper plate making the grant are quoted in *Rājamālā* (I.100), though the copper plate itself cannot be traced. Reference is made to this and another copper plate recording grant of land to brāhmaṇas in the official "Report on the progress of Historical Researches in Assam" (p. 12) published in 1897, and in Gait's *History of Assam*. The inscription is dated in year 51 of the Tripura era (AD 641). If this account be true then this settlement of brāhmaṇas by the king of Tripura took place about a century after the large-scale mass settlement of brāhmaṇas in Kāmrūpa by King Bhūti-varman. There are also many traditions of the performance of religious sacrifices by kings of Tripura and importation of brāhmaṇas on that account. It is very significant to note that according to the tradition which refers to the settlement of the brāhmaṇas in 641 AD, one of its consequences was that the Kukīs, a primitive people who lived in that locality, deserted it and went to the hills. The people in the plains derived their culture mostly from Bengal; Bengali was the language of the court and the people and Bengali literature flourished in Tripura.

Cooch-Behar is the modern form of Koch-Behar which contains the true appellation of the tribe or race to which the ruling dynasty founded by Bisu in the first half of the sixteenth century belonged. Even at this late date the old process of Aryanisation was still in evidence. A detailed account of this has been preserved in the *Vaṁśāvalī* or genealogical chronicle of the Darrang Rājās, a branch of the Koch royal family. It may be summed up as follows:

> Haria Maṇḍal was a leader of the Koch, or allied Mech, tribe, in Goalpara district in Assam. His son Bisu took advantage of the political confusion to defeat many local Bhuiyās or chiefs and established his authority over an extensive area from the Baṛnadī on the east to Karatoyā on the west. Having thus acquired a kingdom, he sought to raise his

> social prestige by adopting Hinduism and gathering brāhmaṇas around him to give him a high pedigree. This was not at all a difficult task for them. It was alleged that the Koch, Mech, and other allied tribes were really kṣatriyas, but when Paraśurāma was engaged in exterminating the kṣatriyas, the forefathers of these tribes saved themselves by throwing away their sacred threads and fleeing towards the east. Having thus given a high pedigree to the tribe, the brāhmaṇas placed its leader Bisu on a high pedestal by confident assertion that he was not really the son of Haria Maṇḍal, but of God Śiva who, in the guise of this man, beget him on his wife Hira, who was really an incarnation of Pārvatī. Armed with this pedigree Bisu assumed the title Bisva Singh, his brother Sisu became Śiv Singh, and the tribe, having discarded the old tribal name, began to call themselves Rājbaṁśīs, a well-known caste among the Hindus. King Bisva Singh now became an orthodox Hindu, worshipped Śiva but paid respect to Viṣṇu and honoured his disciples. He revived the worship of Kāmākhyā and rebuilt her temple. Hindu priests, astrologers, etc., were sure of generous gifts at his court, and Brāhmāṇas were imported by him not only from Bengal but also from such distant centres of orthodox Hinduism as Varanaśi and Kānyakubja. The Koch kings adopted Bengali as their language and Bengali literature flourished in the court and the kingdom.[5]

The Kachārīs who founded a kingdom in Assam and have given their name to one of its present districts, were members of a group of allied tribes to which the Koch and Mech also belonged. No early history of this tribe is available, but there is evidence to show that some time before the thirteenth century, before the Ahoms penetrated into India, the Cachārīs had built-up a powerful kingdom extending along the south bank of the Brahmaputra from the Dilkhuto the Kalang, and the valley of the Dhansīrī and at least the northern part of the present Cachār district were also included in it. They had developed a high degree of culture and civilisation, mainly through Bengali influence. This is indicated by the prevalence of Bengali as the spoken language of the people. The process of Hinduisation must have begun at a fairly early period, at least in the royal and aristocratic families. As is usual in such cases, a formal act of purification took place in 1790 when Rājā Kṛṣṇa Candra and his brother Govinda Candra passed through the body of a cow made of copper, and were proclaimed Hindus belonging to the kṣatriya caste. The brāhmaṇas had already prepared the way for this by constructing a genealogical table tracing the descent of the royal family from Bhīma of the Pāṇḍava dynasty and his wife Hiḍimbā.

Similarly, the royal family of Manipur is traced back to Babhruvāhana, the son of the Epic hero Arjuna and the local princess Citrāṅgadā, a detailed account of which has been mentioned above.

If we believe in these legends and the generally accepted identification of the localities mentioned in them, the expansion of Aryan culture practically all-over eastern India beyond Bengal, particularly in Prāgjyotiṣa, Manipur, Cachār and Tripura, must have taken place before the Epic *Mahābhārata* took its final shape in the early centuries of the Christian era.

But a critical study of the source materials raises grave doubts about the validity of such popular view of the Aryanisation of Assam. The case of each of the four individual states mentioned above may therefore be discussed separately in some detail.

We may begin with the least doubtful case, namely, the location of Prāgjyotiṣa. The theory about the Aryanisation of Assam is based on the presumption that Prāgjyotiṣa mentioned in the *Mahābhārata* is identical with Kāmrūpa or Brahmaputra Valley. But though this is the commonly accepted view, there are some grounds to doubt its authenticity. For the sake of historical truth these grounds should be considered in a dispassionate spirit, however much it might disturb our deep-rooted belief or even sentiments.

In the first place, we now know definitely the existence of a dynasty of Bhagadatta in the North-Western Frontier of India. An inscription found at Hatun in the North-Western Frontier, up the Gilgit River, refers to *Paramabhaṭṭāraka Mahārājādhirāja Parameśvara, Paṭoladeva Śāhī* born in the family of Bhagadatta (*Bhagadata-vaṁśasambhūta*).[6] On palaeographic evidence his reign may be placed in the sixth century AD and he was therefore a contemporary of Bhāskaravarman of Kāmrūpa, whose record contains the first epigraphic reference to Naraka and his son Bhagadatta. Second, some details mentioned in the *Rāmāyaṇa* and the *Mahābhārata* in connection with Prāgjyotiṣa is more in consonance with its situation in the north-western part of India than in the Eastern. In the *Rāmāyaṇa,* Sugrīva asked the search party going to the West to look for Sītā in Prāgjyotiṣa. As the direction was given with reference to Kiṣkindhā, this agrees more with the Gilgit area than with Assam. In the Digvijaya-Parva of the *Mahābhārata,* Arjuna is said to have reached Prāgjyotiṣa in the course of his northern expedition, but this kingdom is not mentioned in connection with the eastern expedition of Bhīma even though he is said to have reached the Lauhitya River. It is significant that even Kālidāsa, who identified Kāmrūpa with Prāgjyotiṣa, does not include its conquest in the eastern expedition of Raghu in the course of which he conquered Vaṅga and Suhma, but makes it a part of his northern expedition. After finishing his campaign in east, south and west India, Raghu proceeded north, defeated the Kambojas, Utsavasaṅketas in the Himalayas, and then descending from that mountain proceeded towards Kāmrūpa, and the king of Prāgjyotiṣa submitted to him.[7] Curiously enough, Kalhaṇa follows the same tradition while describing the *digvijaya* of Lalitāditya. This king, too, after conquering the rulers in three other directions "entered the very extensive area without path of the region of the north", and conquered the Tukharas, Bhauṭṭas, and Darads, sighted the town of

Prāgjyotiṣa, and then, passed through the *strīrājya* (kingdom of women) and the Uttarakurus he returned to Kashmir.[8] This description shows that Kalhaṇa, too, had a vague idea of Prāgjyotiṣa being situated in the Himalayas in the north rather than in the east.

As mentioned above, while guarding the horse of the Aśvamedha ceremony, Arjuna, after defeating the son of Bhagadatta, ruler of Prāgjyotiṣa, followed the horse to Sindhu. This is also more in consonance with the location of Prāgjyotiṣa in north-western India than in Assam.

As regards Cachār the marriage of Hiḍimbā, sister of the demon Hiḍimbā, with Bhīma; is described in the *Mahābhārata*, at first very briefly in two verses, but later in detail in five chapters.[9] But Hiḍimbā is not associated with any region, and the context shows that he inhabited a forest not very far from Vāraṇāvata or Hastināpura. Nevertheless, a territory in Assam, roughly corresponding to modern Cachār, has been traditionally associated with the legendary Hiḍimbā whose descendants are said to have ruled there. This locality is named Heḍamba in the *Rājamālā* which refers to intermarriage and political relations between the early legendary kings of Cachār and Tripura. Heḍamba is mentioned along with Manipur, Vārendra and Tāmralipta in the *Bhaviṣya Purāṇa* (Brahma Khanda 6/64) which also refers to the tutelary deity of this kingdom as Raṇacaṇḍī (*ibid.*, 22.41).The *Deśāvalī-vivṛti*, a geographical work composed in the eighteenth century, refers to the tradition that Ghaṭotkaca, son of Bhīma and Hiḍimbā, was the first king of Cachār, and after his death in the Kurukṣetra war in the hands of Droṇa, his son Barbarīka succeeded him.

Modern writers believe the Cachārīs to be the aborigines or earliest known inhabitants of the Brahmaputra Valley, and identical with the Mech tribe in Goalpāṛā and North Bengal. The Cachārīs call themselves Boḍo and were originally settled at the foot of the Himalayan hills to the north of the Brahmaputra.

As regards Manipur, its identification with the present state of Manipur has been rejected by many scholars. The following points deserve careful consideration in this connection:

I. The name is written as Maṇipura in some manuscripts of the *Mahābhārata* but Manalurin others. The critical edition accepts the reading Manalur in the Ādi-Parva (Ch. 207) but Maṇipura in the Aśvamedhik-Parva (Ch. 77-78), and notes the other variant reading in each case. So far, therefore, as the textual criticism of the *Mahābhārata* goes, there is nothing to choose between the two. But it is significant that the Purāṇas give the name as Maṇipura.

II. As regards the context in which the geographical name appears, there is no difference in the texts of the *Mahābhārata*.

As mentioned above, in connection with third episode, Arjuna first proceeded to Mahendra mountains (i.e. Eastern Ghāṭ) in Kaliṅga and then proceeded to Manipur on the sea.[10] This evidently locates Manipur in the Orissa coast, a view taken by a number of scholars.

But in the Aśvamedhik-Parva, the three countries where Arjuna had to fight for the horse are successively named Prāgjyotiṣa, Sindhu, and Manipur. Whether Manipur be identified with present Manipur in eastern India or located in Orissa, the mention of this place between Prāgjyotiṣa in Assam and Sindhu or Sindh, i.e. the two extreme limits of northern India seem to be an anomaly. It is not unlikely therefore that Sindhu is an interpolation, and in that case juxtaposition of Prāgjyotiṣa and Manipur certainly favours the identification of Manipur with the present state of that name in eastern India. But as against this we should remember what has been said above regarding the location of Prāgjyotiṣa in the north-west of India.

III. During his self-imposed exile Arjuna had married Ulūpī, the daughter of the Nāga king Kauravya of the

Elephant clan (*airāvata kula*) in the Netherlands (under the water of the Ganges). This episode and the marriage of Arjuna with Citrāṅgadā are mentioned in two successive chapters in the *Mahābhārata*. Again, when Babhruvāhana, king of Manipur or Manalur, refused to fight with his father Arjuna, it was Ulūpī who instigated him to fight and when Arjuna was killed, Ulūpī restored his life. When Babhruvāhana attended the Aśvamedha ceremony of Yudhiṣṭhira, he was accompanied by Citrāṅgadā and Ulūpī. Thus, the Nāga daughter and Citrāṅgadā are closely associated. In view of the present habitat of the Nāgas viz. the Nāga Hills, immediately to the north of Manipur, and famous for big elephants, the Nāga king Kauravya of the Elephant clan may be associated with this region.

IV. There is a living popular tradition in present Manipur that it represents the old kingdom mentioned in the *Mahābhārata* as the birthplace of Citrāṅgadā and Babhruvāhana. No such tradition exists in any part of Orissa, and no memory of a locality named Maṇalur has survived.

V. The antiquity of Manipur is proved not only by the variant reading in the *Mahābhārata* manuscripts but also by unambiguous references in the Purāṇas. Thus *Bhaviṣya Purāṇa* (Brahma Khaṇḍa) mentions it along with Lauhitya, Traipura (Tripura) and Jayanta (Jaintia Hills).[11]

As regards Tripura, there is no uncertainty about the location of the kingdom of which the history is dealt with in the *Rājamālā*, but the authenticity of the traditions contained in it may well be doubted. The present text of the *Rājamālā* is not very old and was probably composed in the nineteenth century. There is, of course, the tradition that this text as well as another in Sanskrit on which it was presumably based, was composed in much earlier times, and the Bengali text was revised from time to time in order to bring it up-to-date. According to tradition embodied in the existing text, the chronicle was first composed at the beginning of the fifteenth century AD by the orders of the king Dharmamāṇikya, but no copy of it has survived. It was revised successively towards the end of the sixteenth, seventeenth and eighteenth century, and finally it was revised in its present form in the nineteenth century.[12]

There is no authentic evidence that the chronicle *Rājamālā* was first composed in the fifteenth century. Nor is it true, as held by many eminent scholars, that it is a product of the nineteenth century. For, there is a manuscript of the *Rājamālā* distinctly older than the present text, in the Vangiya Sahitya Parishad, Calcutta, and there seems to be no doubt that the present text is not the original chronicle, but the final form it assumed after one or more revisions.

But even if we assume that the original text of *Rājamālā* was composed in the fifteenth century, of which there is no adequate proof, it must be clear to any impartial critic that very little historical value can be attached to the earlier portion relating the events in remote antiquity, or going back to any period before 1200 AD with which alone we are here concerned in a discussion of the expansion of Aryan culture. Its historical value consists mainly in an elaborated delineation of the views on this subject current in medieval age.

It would thus appear that while we have definite evidence of the Aryanisation of Bengal before the end of the fourth century BC, we possess no such evidence of its advance further towards the east before the fourth century AD.

There are, however, certain weighty reasons for pushing back this third stage of advance at least to the beginning of the Christian era.

In the first place, we know that the Aryan culture was carried to Indo-China and Indonesia by the first century AD at the latest. This shows that the process of Aryanisation was continued even after it had reached the eastern frontier of India, and advanced both by land and sea beyond it before the beginning of the Christian era. On general grounds, therefore, we may reasonably presume that eastern India beyond Bengal must have come under its influence at least some time before.

This presumption becomes almost a certainty when we remember that the prevalence of Aryan culture in Upper Burma in the first century AD is proved by the discovery of isolated letters of the Indian Brāhmī alphabet, and two gold plates containing inscriptions in characters which were in vogue in India in the first century AD.[13] According to the Chinese chronicle of the third century AD, a kingdom, called Lin-yang, which has been located in Central Burma, had an ardent Buddhist population of over 1,00,000 families, including several thousand monks. On the whole we shall be justified, on these grounds alone, in dating the Hindu colonisation in Burma certainly before, and probably long before, the beginning of Christian era.

Both traditions as well as general considerations lead to the conclusion that the Hindus must have reached this region by land-route.

This land-route must have passed through eastern India and it is difficult to believe that Aryan culture could have passed through this region without affecting it. We learn from the Chinese texts that at least as early as the second century BC there was a regular trade-route by land between Bengal and China through Upper Burma and Yunnan. Through this route, the Indians came and established their colonies not only in Burma, but also in the mountainous regions of the upper valleys of the Chindwin, the Irawadi, the Salween, the Mekong and the Red River as far as Yunnan, which was known by its Indian name Gāndhāra even as late as the thirteenth century AD. We know the Chinese names of several of these kingdoms. To the east of the hill ranges bordering Manipur and Assam there was the Hindu kingdom of Ta-tsin. About 150 miles further east, beyond the Chindwin River, was another Hindu kingdom just to the north of the town of Ngan-si. In Yunnan itself was the kingdom of Nan-chao or Tali and a local tradition regarded a son of the great Indian Emperor Aśoka as having founded the colony. The whole of Upper Burma was colonised by the Indians who established kingdoms at Prome,

Pagan, Tagaung and various other places, many of which still retain their old Indian names with slight alterations. There is evidence that similar Hindu kingdoms existed in Laos, in Central Indo-China.

It is inconceivable that these successive currents of Indian culture flowed through Assam to far distant lands without fertilising the intervening region by leaving sediments of culture. It is, therefore, a very reasonable hypothesis that the expansion of Aryan culture in eastern India beyond Bengal must have commenced at the beginning of the Christian era, if not long before it. That it did not make as thorough a conquest of these regions as Bengal even at the beginning of the Christian era, seems to be indicated by the references in the *Mahābhārata* mentioned above. As a matter of fact, the Aryanisation in these regions was never as thorough as in Bengal. This is shown by the existence, even today, of more numerous primitive peoples, only slightly Aryanised, within this area, than in Bengal. The geographical features are no doubt primarily responsible for it for the hills and jungles of Assam offered safe refuges to the primitive peoples such as did not exist in Bengal. But whatever the reasons, the fact has to be recognised.

On the other hand, the Aryan culture was more deep-rooted in the plains of eastern India than in more distant Hindu Colonies in Indo-China and Indonesia. This is proved by the fact that though a branch of the Thai tribes, the Ahoms, conquered the Aryanised Bramhaputra Valley they themselves were ultimately Aryanised, whereas when the same tribes conquered Siam, they imposed their language and some other traits of their primitive culture to a far greater extent upon the Aryanised people there and today there is a striking difference in respect of the degree and extent of Aryan culture between Assam and Siam (now called Thailand).

In conclusion, attention may be drawn to some general observations that may be reasonably made on the basis of what I have said in these two lectures.

In the first place, there is no historical basis for the popular belief that the peoples of India had no culture worth the name until the Aryans came and civilised them. Both in the Punjab and eastern India, as well as in other parts of this great subcontinent, many peoples are known to have possessed a highly developed material culture long before they came into contact with the Aryans, and this presupposes some degree of intellectual and moral attainments, though we do not yet possess sufficient materials for a proper estimate of these.

Second, no region in India may reasonably claim to be inherently superior in point of culture to any other, for its present culture is the product of Aryan influence, and we find the same process of Aryanisation advancing from the western to the eastern frontier of India. The process took a long time for full development, and so the Aryanisation took place later and later as it proceeded further and further to the east. But ultimately the same pattern prevailed all-over India, and this Aryan culture formed the only stable basis for the union or integration of the Indian peoples irrespective of their origin and primitive culture. An orthodox brāhmaṇa in the Punjab, Assam and Travancore offers the same pattern of culture.

Third, the process of Aryanisation in India is not yet complete, for there are localities where the primitive peoples are still almost unaffected by Aryan culture. This is specially characteristic of eastern India. The Nāgas, Kukīs, and other hill tribes of this region are even now almost outside the pale of Aryan culture. The failure of the Aryans to breakthrough their citadel of isolation may be due to lack of sufficient vigour or decadence of Aryan culture in later ages. The people of Free India must make a determined effort to resume the process of Aryanisation and make it a complete success all-over the country, not by force or compulsion, but by peaceful process, as in the days of old.

Notes

1. *Rāmāyana, Kiṣkindhā-Kāṇḍa*, Ch. 42, v. 31.
2. *Māhābhārata*, Critical Edition, II.28.
3. *Ep. Ind.* XII, p. 65; XIX, p. 115.
4. R.C. Majumdar, *Hindu Colonies in the Far East* (2nd Edition), p. 8.
5. Amanatulla, *History of Cochbehar* (in Bengali).
6. Cf. *Bhāratīya Vidyā* (Bombay), June, 1945, p. 112.
7. *Raghuvaṁśa*, IV.70-82.
8. *Rājataraṅgiṇī*, IV.163-76.
9. Ādi-Parva, Ch. 61, v.20; Chapters 162-66 (Calcutta Edition).
10. *Māhābhārata*, Critical Edition, Ch. 207.
11. The location of Manipur in the *Māhābhārata* is discussed in the two following works: 1. R.K. Jhalajit Singh, *Short History of Manipur*. 2. L.I. Singh, *Introduction to Manipur*.
12. Cf. Introduction to the *Rājamālā*, edited by Kaliprasanna Sen.
13. R.C. Majumdar, *Hindu Colonies in the Far East*, p. 228.

5
Cultural History of Arts and Crafts in India
(Lecture I)

N.K: Bose

I am deeply grateful to the authorities of the Atombapu Research Centre for this opportunity of paying my respect to Panditraj Atombapu Sharma. He was not only a great scholar who tried to develop the Meitei language and at the same time to introduce into Manipur the best that is in Sanskrit literature by means of translations, but he was also a nationalist to the core of his heart. Through his inspired writings Panditraj succeeded in arousing a deep sense of love and appreciation of what is best in Indian culture and added to it an understanding which was also of a rare quality. Suniti Kumar Chatterji has compared him to the Ṛṣi Agastya who was responsible for spreading the light of Aryan culture in the south of India. This comparison was indeed very well deserved by Panditraj Atombapu Sharma, and I feel happy in associating myself with Suniti Kumar Chatterji's judgement and sentiments in this respect.

In paying my tribute to Panditraj, my plan is to present before you an account of the cultural history of eastern India, and also incidentally to present some general views about regional civilisations and their interrelationship as they have developed in course of centuries in different parts of our country.

It is usual in anthropology to regard culture as the totality of the behaviour of human communities along with the material objects, social institutions, value-systems and world views which men build-up in course of collective living. I admit this is a rather clumsy definition of the term culture, but it would be possible to render the idea somewhat clearer if we take up some specific examples from the culture-history of our land.

Let us start with some items of the material equipment of man. We who live in eastern India use a kind of dress—*dhotī* and *cādara*—which is formed by unsewn pieces of clothing. In marriage or funerary observances, it is only unsewn pieces of cloth which can be worn, although in the towns and cities this custom is slowly wearing out. Up till the last generation, in Bihar, it was considered wrong for women to wear sewn garments while one was engaged in cooking in the kitchen. Among the Dahal Brāhmīns of eastern Nepal, it is even now the custom to take off sewn garments of any kind while one is at his meals, and put on unsewn clothing in their place for the time being.

It is interesting that the unsewn garment, and also the idea of ritual impurity of sewn garments, extends from Bihar and Bengal, Assam and Manipur or Tripura through Orissa, Andhra Pradesh, Tamil Nadu and even Kerala on the western coast of the Peninsula. As we travel from Bihar towards the west and north-west, sewn garments become more and more frequent, until one reaches Punjab, Himachal Pradesh, and then crosses over to Afghanistan. If we trace the distribution of unsewn clothing towards the east and south-east, we observe that in Burma, Java and the neighbouring countries, it is an unsewn skirt-like lower garment which is in use, and not so much sewn wear. Sewn garments are evidently of later introduction in these countries, introduced either by Moslem settlers who came in search of trade, or by Western people who came in much the same manner and eventually founded empires.

It would be interesting to find out whether ritual purity is associated with unsewn clothing in South-Eastern Asia as it is evidently done in eastern India.

There are two more items of material culture which seem to be of interest in this connexion. In some parts of east and south India shoes are not worn at all, these being considered impure. But in large sections of the country where they are worn, we can classify footwear into two broad kinds, namely, the slipper type and the shoe type. Shoes are those in which the foot is covered both in front and behind the heels, while in the slipper type, there is no cover or strap near the heels. The slipper type of footwear is present in Bengal, Assam, Orissa, Andhra Pradesh, Tamil Nadu, Kerala, while the shoe extends from Bihar to the farthest west as well as in central India.

It is interesting that Maharashtra has both slippers and shoes, but the shoe itself has its hind part near the heel pressed down, so that what is constructionally a shoe is worn like a slipper.

Oil is an important article of diet in many parts of India. In some places it is mustard oil, in others sesame or coconut. In Brāhmanical rites, what is offered is either clarified butter or *ghī* or whole seeds of sesame or coconut. It is interesting that in eastern India, at least, what is used in magical rites connected with the exorcisation of devils is mustard seed or mustard oil, never anything connected with milk or *ghī*. Perhaps Brāhmanical peoples and non-Brāhmanical communities offered different objects to their gods and goddesses; and if we had detailed information of a like nature from eastern and South-Eastern Asia on the one hand and Central Asia on the other, it would be possible to recover the history of the peoples and cultures which eventually confronted one another within our own land of India.

The cultivation of rice and wheat or millets, the nature of the plough, of husking implements, the way in which cereals are converted into food all hold interesting promises for the culture-historian. The Anthropological Survey of India carried out a survey of this nature over the whole of India in 1960, and collected a large amount of information in regard to the distribution of material traits. A preliminary report was published under the title of *Peasant Life in India* in 1961. Later on another more detailed report, but only on pottery, was also published by the Survey.

What is however significant from the culture-historian's point of view is this. Thanks to the work of Grierson, it is known that, in regard to language, India can be divided into a northern area of Indo-Aryan speeches and southern one of Dravidian speeches. The dividing line between the north and the south runs from east to west, at roughly the 16° Lat. N. But when we map the distribution of say, ploughs or rice or staple diet, the dividing line no longer runs east and west, but from north-east to southwest separating some portions of Bihar, large portions of Maharashtra, the south of the Peninsula on one side, from the rest of India on the other.

This discrepancy in the distribution zones of material arts and of language can be interpreted as follows. The Indo-Aryan languages evidently spread from the Indo-Gangetic Valley both eastwards and southwards. But in regard to material traits, the affiliation of eastern and southern India is more with south and south-eastern Asia, while that of western and north-western India is with Central Asia, across countries like Afghanistan and Iran. But there has been a considerable amount of infiltration across the hypothetical or indistinct boundary line within India itself. So that elements of one broad culture zone have penetrated into trait-complexes belonging to another, and these have given an immense richness to the kaleidoscopic variety of India's material culture.

My intention has been thus to indicate in very brief outline of how the arts and crafts of India have grown in their infinite variety. Changes are taking place by slow diffusion even now, as for example, the northern oil-press with a drain is gradually replacing the southern oil-press without a drain on account of the influences of the Khadi and Gramodyog Commission. In any case, as has been suggested above, a study of material culture, along with some of the ideas regarding their ritual purity or otherwise, does help us in the recovery of hitherto unknown or unsuspected lines of migration or affiliation of Indian culture at its base level.

The diversity of languages in India, of the food-habits and dress of the people, and of the nature of our villages and homes have all been sources of surprise and even discontent among many lovers of India. Many have patriotically desired that all India should have one language, one culture, so that we can become one unified and mighty nation. The fact that India was hardly ever bound together into one political unity has been emphasised again and again. It has been said that political unity appeared fitfully in the past and only in more stable form after British rule was established in India. These observations or complaints are indeed true. But let us look at other aspects of the culture of India a little more closely.

Caste is an institution which has been subjected to violent condemnation. It has however never been satisfactorily explained as to how caste has persisted in spite of revolts against orthodoxy over the last two millennia and more. What has often been overlooked is the economic substructure of the caste system which gave it a stability, particularly in times when political disturbances swept over the land.

Caste's economic organisation is based upon two important elements. It is a non-competitive mode of production based upon hereditary monopolistic guilds, each of which is supposed not to swerve from its ascribed occupation in any given area. Even if, during distress, a family cannot make its living by traditional means, its members can change their occupation to another after proper advice from colleges of brāhmaṇa which would prescribe for them number of possible alternative modes of living (*āpad dharma*) It was this productive organisation which gave Hindu society a stability which was not largely destroyed even under Muslim or British rule. The organisation whose central object lay in the suppression of competition in the subordination of individual enterprise to social, collective needs, proved so successful that even Muslims and Christians in rural areas succumbed to its charms.

Whether caste is good or bad, whether it should still be allowed to linger under the altered conditions today is a different question. But it cannot be denied that this organisation enveloped the whole of India from Sind to Assam and Manipur and from the Himalayan Mountains to Cape Comorin in the south. The details undoubtedly varied from one part of the country to another, and from one class to another within the same province. But the uniformity in the structure cannot be denied. Capitalism has prevailed in many countries in the world like Britain and Germany, Italy and Japan as well as in the United States of America. Its central theme based on the freedom of the individual to take to any occupation he chooses, and without much to political or social interference, its reliance upon encouraging competition, cannot be denied. Yet differences between England and Japan, between the United States of America and Germany have developed in course of time. Perhaps a similar phenomenon is becoming evident between the socialist countries of the world also. So that it should cause us no surprise that caste in, say, the Uttar Pradesh or the south differs from its counterpart in either Bengal or Assam, although the central ideas remain substantially the same.

In any case, all parts of India were thus knit together by the uniformity of their productive-cum-social organisation in the past. In a similar manner, the concept of property, except for small divergences, was also nearly the same. The whole of Hindu India is subject to the Law of Inheritances under Mitākṣarā or Dāyabhāga. And this also brought about a uniformity in Indian civilisation which cannot be overlooked just because there was no political unity in the past.

In religious matters again there is an element in Hindu civilisation which deserves a consideration at this point. When caste system was formed in part by the integration of various tribal or communal groups into one productive system, the leaders of Brāhmanical society thought that it would be right to allow each such group to continue the practice of its original socio-religious rites and ceremonies with the minimum amount of adjustment or change. One of the central ideas which thus ruled was that each culture is built round one core-idea; and as no culture sees Truth in its wholeness—i.e., every community sees Truth only in fragment—the religion of a community should not be interfered with as long as its members allow the same right of freedom to others also to follow their own.

As a result of this idea and corresponding attitude, in course of time, Brāhmanical religion became a confederation of cultures, and also of *dharmas*, rather than a single monolithic system like religious systems of Semitic origin. There was, however, a unifying factor, and this consisted of no more than the social practices prescribed by Brāhmanical priesthood, which sat very lightly on the multiplicity of practices prevalent among the constituent elements of Hindu society.

This idea about the multiplicity of fractional views of Truth was a dominant element in Hindu religious thought. And it is of significance that it spread from one corner of India to another, and even eventually pervaded some forms of non-Brāhmanical thought in the country in later times. In other words, this also brought about a uniformity in Indian civilisation as much as the productive organisation of caste and of property-relationships had done in other spheres of life.

When we view the whole of Indian civilisation in this manner, we observe that there was a greater diversity in the material aspects of life than in the details of the caste system. The difference was even less when it came to the higher aspects of life like religious beliefs and practices. So that an Indian from any part of India could go to any other part of the country and participate in religious rites and ceremonies without let or hindrance or without a feeling of strangeness. He could not do so in the economic life of another part of the country under the old regime, unless he settled down there and was recognised as one of the locally accepted *jātis*. In matters of food, and sometimes even of dress, his feelings would be very much like that of an alien. But according to accepted practice, he would be allowed to persist in them, more or less, as a closed group.

Indian unity might thus be characterised as a pyramidal structure in which the higher one rose in the level of life—from material arts to social structure to beliefs and sentiments—the gap became narrower and narrower. We can consider that at the apex lay the highest forms of world view which accepted multiplicity of forms, so long as there was unity in the central core, namely that the phenomenal aspects of life were built round fragmentary views of Truth—made up of Truth and non-Truth—and that when the highest point of Truth was reached, phenomenal distinctions became completely obliterated.

This is how we may view Indian civilisation in its totality and also appreciate from one point of view how Indians, in the highest flights of their thought and being, transcended the bounds of local temporisation, i.e. of culture, as it grew up due to the emergencies of a situation. It thus became ahistorical in the end.

6

Cultural History of Arts and Crafts in India

(Lecture II)

N.K. Bose

Yesterday, an endeavour was made to describe in broad outline the ruling ideas working behind Indian or Hindu civilisation. A productive organisation was built-up in which competition was discouraged. Monopolistic, hereditary guilds of farmers and craftsman, and even of soldiers, were built-up. Each such guild was encouraged to follow its own *dharma*, and it was by means of the complementary service of these *dharma*s that the life of the people as a whole was sustained. The regulatory power lay in the hands of the king; and it was his duty to see to it that each guild followed its own prescribed duties. He did so with the advice of the colleges of brāhmaṇas, which were either located in famous centres of learning or of pilgrimage. These centres might be in temples or *maṭha*s, or in *agrahāra*s or village settlements of brāhmaṇas, founded by the rulers of the land.

There is no doubt that such a social arrangement could only endure so long as there was no extraneous cause to bring about its dislocation. But such dislocations undoubtedly occurred due to growth of population, migration, the rise and fall of ruling dynasties, and external aggression to which the Indo-Gangetic plain was subjected again and again in the course of its long history. As a result, even the earliest law books prescribed a series of rules by means of which castes could take to alternative occupations when they failed to make their living by their original allocated ones.

There was, as we have already said, a superstructure guiding the religious and cultural life of the community as a whole. Each small component, called a *jāti*, was left free to pursue its own rites and ceremonies so long as it did not militate against the moral codes of Brāhmanical society. If a tribe absorbed into the Hindu social organisation originally practised human sacrifice, they were encouraged to give it up and replace by the sacrifice of a buffalo or a goat, or even that of a substance like a gourd. The *śraddhā* or respect of a *jāti* for its own religious beliefs was not to be uprooted, but only modified. And this is how, in course of a long history, Hinduism became a confederation of many beliefs and many practices. Each one was to live in accordance with his own faith, never tarry on the way of spiritual progress, but eventually reach a state when adherence to special local or temporary beliefs or practices was no longer necessary for him. From fragmentary truths he was to progress towards greater and greater truths until he was to reach the highest Truth, like an eagle soaring in the blue heavens from where all fragments of Truth by which men ordered their lives on earth below appeared to him, each to be true in its own context.

And this journey, according to Hindu belief, might spread over, not one, but many migrations of the individual soul, i.e., from one birth to another.

Moreover, the progress in spiritual matters was not to be in a linear direction, from one point to another, as is generally supposed in religions and civilisations which are ultimately of Semitic origin. Mahatma Gandhi gave a brilliant illustration of what spiritual growth was to be like. He once said to an interviewer "that when there was a feeling of expansion he was on the right track. But if there was a feeling of contraction, he was surely on the way, not towards life, but towards death". Explaining his views on Faith and Religion, Mahatma Gandhi once wrote:

> Religions are different roads converging to the same point. What does it matter that we take different roads so long as we reach the same goal? In reality, there are as many religions as there are individuals. (Bose, N.K.: *Selections from Gandhi*, 1968, p. 256)

In this statement, Gandhi was echoing the core of the teaching of Hinduism, a message which has been repeated again and again from the time of the Upaniṣads to those of Śaṅkarācārya, Ramakrishna or Ramaṇa Maharṣi.

It is now necessary for us to evaluate the central core of ideas in Hindu civilisation from a different point of view. We have so long defined and described it rather than try to find out its historical worth.

It will be obvious to any student that Hindu civilisation thus tried to synthesise, and not to replace one world view by another which was considered to be superior, it definitely believed, as has already been indicated in the first lecture, that all views of Truth enshrined in specific civilisations are fragments rather than whole. And once one reaches or realises what is whole, the need for a specific way of life—of a particular culture ceases to exist for him. He then understands all that is happening in time and in space as thing conditioned by specific situations; and he regards all of them as events of a transitory nature. Both Life and Death seem to be to him things which he cannot afford to evaluate or to choose. And then he transcends the bonds of culture and of the fragmentary views of Truth which each enshrines.

I am afraid that the picture of Indian civilisation and of the freedom of the individual seer, which it ultimately tried to encourage in every spiritual aspirant has become rather obscure or very much figurative in the above account. But I only draw your attention at this stage to the eleventh chapter of the *Bhagavad-Gītā* where a world view was opened up before Arjuna by Śrī Kṛṣṇa. That world view in which Arjuna say myriads of human beings swirling from one state to another *in a timeless universe* frightened him so much that he prayed to Śrī Kṛṣṇa to withdraw the scene so that the latter could once more be restored to His earlier relationship of Friend and Companion, and thus give him a haven which would sustain him, through an act of human feeling and devotion to God.

Through ages, Hinduism has tried to promote ideas and spiritual exercises designed to promote the growth of every individual soul in this direction. Individuals and communities have been encouraged to remain in their special worlds, with the result that, even if the economic and social organisation of caste have suppressed individualism at one level, Hindus have remained loyal to individualism of another kind, and never allowed themselves to be fused into one uniform mass.

Such a social or economic condition is predominantly an organisation of peace. It encourages the coexistence of many cultures, many separateness but it does not make a large community strong enough to wage war. It is natural that an organisation designed for peace will fail in the event of war. But on the other hand, it may also be true that an organisation of war may fall men when they have to live in peace with one another. And here, let us try to observe and understand the shape which European civilisation has been taking during the last century or two.

I must admit at once that my knowledge of European history and of its civilisation is of a very incomplete nature. And what I shall try to describe as the civilisation of Europe may be no more than a passing phase in the history of that continent.

Ever since the Reformation and the Rise of Protestantism, Europe seems to be passing through a phase which has given rise to an individualism of a new kind, and also to the needs of the subordination of that individualism to the demands of the state and the community on the other. European states and nations have been subject again and again to the demands a survival, whether they have been in the field of mercantile or industrial activity, or of a politically separate well defined national existence. And this has led the European nations, or those who have been guided by, its central ideas, into a perilous condition in the present age.

Even in Europe, there have been protests all through the past two centuries against the present state of affairs. Some have sought spiritual refuge in poetry or science, human service or mysticism. As the control over nature's material resources has gone on increasing, as large sections of the population have been saturated in plenty, men's minds have wandered away from this in search of something which would give them a solace and an anchor in a world which is engrossed in a fruitless search for satiety.

The human mind seems to be in revolt in Europe against its own creations.

It is at this stage that we should engage once more in a consideration of what is happening in India today. Our central task is not to try and evaluate Eastern and Western civilisations, if there are things which can be categorically distinguished in that way from one another. Our concern is principally with India, to the events which are occurring here, and find a meaning of the clash of cultures which has been taking place in our own land during the last century and a half.

When we see India in course of its long history of 2,000 years or so, we notice certain broad points of strength and weakness lying within it. Ever since the Afghan, Tatar and Mogul invaders professing Islam came to the land, it had been proved again and again that the political structure of India was useless in self-defence. In it, the defence of the state became the exclusive business of several castes and not of all the inhabitants of the state. Many cultures and religions existed side by side with one another; but the feeling of distinctness which was thus encouraged failed when there was need of combining the people into one "nation' for self-defence.

Perhaps this was indeed a source of weakness. All educated Indians are today conscious of this element of weakness in our social system, and those who wish to see in India the rise of a mighty nation, which can match its strength against that of any other nation, are impatient with every element in Indian civilisation which tends to weaken it from the military point of view. Caste has been held largely responsible for the absence of a sense of national unity. But what is overlooked is that caste was designed for one purpose, nationalism in Europe for another. The multiplicity of faiths in India, her variegated ways of life, with different kinds of food and dress, her many languages, have also been equally blamed for our lack of the sense of national unity. The fact that the spiritual quest for a transcendental view of Truth has, again and again, proved attractive to the highest individualism the land, has proved distressing to those who want to "secularise' and "modernise' India—an India which should, according to them, become as powerful a nation as any other in the modern world.

The weight of our poverty, the inequality between classes, all sit heavily upon us. And it is natural that an ardent and sincere desire has arisen among sensitive souls to find a way out of our present predicament. The examples of Russia, America or even China prove attractive. They seem to be blessed with all that we have not. And the tension thus grows in our ancient land of what history has left behind and what is desired by those who have drawn their inspiration from the successes of other lands.

This state of affairs is natural. The desire to cut away all the roots which hold us back to the achievements of Indian civilisation seem to be galling to those who are in earnest, and wish to see India emancipated as quickly as possible from its "bondage to the past'. The more earnest a soul is, the more intense becomes his suffering when he finds himself thwarted in his endeavour to destroy the past.

But let us not forget in this haste that Europe itself is not wholly satisfied with its own achievements. Undoubtedly her achievements are great. Undoubtedly the Religion of

Humanism and of the Freedom of Thought, namely, the faith she has lived by, are great assets to the whole of the human race. But let us not also forget that these have led her also into the morass of meaningless hedonism, and a desire to preserve its so-called higher standard of living by taking recourse to armaments which has brought the whole of humanity to the verge of suicide.

In our haste to enfranchise ourselves from one set of bondages let us not forge new fetters of our own making. In the broad history of humanity there is no East and no West. India tried to fashion a way of life in which many cultures, many individuals within the same culture, could thrive and progress towards a new kind of freedom. European civilisation took a different course, and suppressed many of the mystic ideas which it has shared in common with the East.

Through the accidents of history each one has marched along its own way; building up some mansion which it believed to be precious, lighting up a little lamp which it thought would illumine the whole universe.

Let us be more humble. Let us view each civilisation and its attainments in the perspective of history. And then we shall be able to realise that each little company of men has contributed its share to the common pool of human civilisation, to the total achievements of the human race. Stresses and strains have occurred when the shortcomings of each fragmental view of truth have been found wanting in certain respects. Let us not be unnaturally sensitive about the achievements or shortcomings of the particular civilisation with which we are concerned at the moment. Let us in humility admit that our vision is clouded or illumined by the demands of our immediate present. And then alone shall we be able to view the entire range of human history, and not be totally discouraged by our failures or intoxicated by our momentary success.

It is only a mind which can attain this freedom by strenuous endeavour that can liberate us from the hopes and despairs by which we are torn India today, and can help us in taking right decisions suitable to contingent circumstances without surrendering values which may be of eternal human utility.

7
Gandhiji as I Knew Him

Kakasaheb Kalelkar

I was already a seasoned national worker when I first met Mahatma Gandhi at Poet Rabindranath's institute—Shantiniketan in the year 1915. In politics, I belonged to the Tilak School. In social matters, I was a reformer. In religion, I was greatly influenced by the Vedantic teachings of Swami Vivekananda and other modern thinkers. A revolutionary at heart, I had devoted myself to National Education with the sole object of rebuilding and strengthening India for the struggle for Independence. Freeing India from the British yoke, was the main object of my life and activities. There was also, before me, the spiritual ideal of self-realisation.

When the British Government of India made my activities impossible, I retired to the Himalayas to practice my *sādhanā* and seek a new inspiration. On my return from the Himalayan solitude, I decided to work either in the Ramakrishna Mission or in Tagore's Shantiniketan.

I had already headed two or three important national schools before going to the Himalayas. I had also done some journalistic work in national Marathi papers and had therefore known about Karmavir Gandhi and his work in South Africa.

What is more, two of my old associates were intimately connected with Mahatmaji.

When Mahatmaji decided to return to India permanently, after his successful work in South Africa, he had sent his relatives and workers, known as the Phoenix party, to India in advance. They were staying at Shantiniketan, when I joined that institution temporarily. I had enthusiastically joined the staff of Shantiniketan in organising a grand reception to Gandhiji in right ancient style. So, it was no chance meeting when I first met Gandhiji in 1915, at Shantiniketan.

Let me here recount my first meeting with Mahatmaji.

> I frankly told Gandhiji that, I accept Truth and *ahiṁsā* as highest virtues. Having been brought up in the saintly traditions of Maharashtra, I do not need any persuasion for accepting either Truth or non-violence. I know and believe what the Upaniṣads have said that only through non-violence towards all beings can a man attain salvation.
>
> But I want you to convince me that *swarāj* can be wrested from the hands of the British, through non-violence. It was easy to secure the repeal of the three-pound tax in South Africa through a herculean movement of non-violence. But can the British give up the most valued jewel in their crown—namely India—through your non-violent methods? I do want *mokṣa*, but first and foremost, I want the *mokṣa* of India from the British Yoke; and I am prepared to go to hell ten times to achieve the salvation of India. Let me first free my mother from foreign domination. I shall then go to the Himalayas and practise *ahiṁsā*, *tapasyā* for my individual *mokṣa*.

When I asked him whether he could accept a man like me who was not pledged to his non-violence, he simply smiled and said,

> Do I not know that you belong to the majority? I, with my non-violence, am in a small minority.

> Whence shall I get workers if I reject people like you? I must patiently try to convince people that non-violence is a virtue of the brave. And, properly utilised, it can never fail to secure the salvation of the country. You come and work with me and study my methods. You are free to leave me the minute you are dissatisfied with my programme for *swarāj*. I am not going to clip your wings.

I wired to a Sindhi friend of mine, who was a professor in Bihar, to come and meet this extra-ordinary leader and strange revolutionary. He came. During our discussions with Mahatmaji, my friend said,

> Mr. Gandhi, I am a professor of history. There is not even single instance in the whole history of man, of a nation having secured independence through non-violence. What am I to teach my students?

Mahatmaji staggered us by quietly replying, "You are a teacher of history. I am trying to make new history". We immediately saw that we must accept this new leader as a maker of history and associate ourselves with him in the struggle for *swarāj*.

Within a few months I joined Mahatmaji in his newly-started *āśrama* at Ahmedabad. I discovered that here was a cent-per cent believer in non-violence who was also a consummate general. He had the faith, the energy and the tact of uniting the whole country. He had a consummate plan for national integration and more than that, I discovered that Gandhiji's plan was ultimately meant for universal integration of the whole of humanity. I was not surprised therefore when he wrote to a Westerner "My nationalism is intensest internationalism". I remember he once gave an assurance to the Chinese leader (Chiang Kai Shek) that India's struggle for independence will in no way harm China or any other country. India wanted freedom for all peoples of the world.

Gandhiji succeeded in achieving enthusiastic unity in the masses of the country for the achievement of Indian independence. It must be recognised, that during the few years that were given to him, Gandhiji succeeded in suppressing and overcoming our national weaknesses and fissiparous tendencies (he could not remove these age-old national weaknesses completely) but even on the strength of what he could achieve, he succeeded in securing the independence of the country. He displayed the highest tact, both as a nation-builder and as a general leading one movement after another for overthrowing the British Rule.

It was not lightly that a British Viceroy once said, "This Gandhi is strongest in his defeat". The Viceroy had realised, to his cost, that Gandhiji had the skill of turning even a defeat into a victory.

We have therefore, to study Gandhi not only as a saint, but as a leader of humanity both in the field of thought and action. We have to study him as a scientist and a consummate general and a nation-builder with a prophetic vision. Let us hope the present generation will be able to understand, appreciate and ultimately follow Gandhi. We need not confine ourselves only or wholly to the constructive programme which Gandhiji placed before the country before the advent of independence. But we have to work for cultural integration of a multi-racial, multi-lingual, multi-religious nation comprising of various degrees and types of culture, in this vast but compact country of Bharat. Gandhiji was like a great *ṛṣi* for our generation. His inspiration will have to be worked out during the coming thousand years. Gandhiji came into this world, to start a new civilisation and culture worthy of human evolution. Mankind will naturally take generations before it understands and appreciates the full implication of his words and policies. They will have to muster ultra-human courage to work out the details of the new social organisation which Gandhiji dreamt of.

Gandhiji was both a man of thought and a man of action. His philosophy and sociology ought therefore to go together.

Gandhiji started his experiments of a new social order very early in life in his own family. When he went to South Africa, he converted his family into an experimental *āśrama* where people of different religions and different cultures lived together and made experiments in inter-racial, intercultural corporate life.

The first thing which Gandhiji did when he returned to India after a successful career in South Africa was to start an *āśrama*. The *āśrama* was, one might say, the very breath of his life (he always said that the *āśrama* was his best creation and that he should be judged solely by the success or failure of his *āśrama*).

The *āśrama* represented, in a miniature form the new society Gandhiji wanted to build. Gandhiji experimented with his spiritual, social, political, and economical ideas, and ideals first and foremost through the *āśrama*.

In due time, Gandhiji plunged into the India's public life and he gradually carried on his various campaigns of *satyāgraha* (non-violent resistance) in many forms. Sometimes it was a direct non-violent resistance, sometimes it took the form of non-cooperation and ultimately being faithful to his principle of non-violence, he started his constructive programme in order to build a healthy peaceful society based entirely on non-governmental efforts.

A dozen or two movements which he started in the name of constructive programme were every one of them, conducive to rebuilding of society on the basis of *ahiṁsā* and *sarvodaya*.

When Gandhiji spoke of Truth and non-violence people did not understand the full implication of those words. Some thought it simply meant that he merely wanted to eschew the use of the bomb and other terroristic methods (that is why most of the Congress leaders promised to join him on condition that they be allowed to work for *swarāj* on the basis of non-violence not as a principle but only as a policy).

There were others who confused Gandhiji's non-violence with the vegetarianism of the Jainas and the Vaiṣṇavas. They were only partially correct and that is why they could not comprehend Gandhiji's thought and experiments of non-violence in their entirety.

The world has so far built a civilisation based upon competition, conflict, aggression, armed resistance, and universal exploitation of the backward by the more fortunate, more powerful and cleverer people. This civilisation believes in private property, competition and universal struggle for existence and domination.

Gandhiji wants to change the very basis of this human (?) civilisation evolved so far. He wants to destroy many old things but not in a violent way. He recognises the achievements of man in the past and he has infinite patience with the people when trying to inject into their minds and hearts human values of truth, non-violence, self-restraint and selfless service.

Can we call Gandhiji a pacifist? The answer is, Yes and No. That people should lead an honest peaceful, cooperative life without even a trace of exploitation is an ideal which is accepted both by the pacifists and Gandhiji. But the pacifist does not have any active and powerful method of resisting exploitation, aggression and injustice. They may, at the most, openly and boldly condemn aggression and injustice. They may resist forcible enlistment into the army by going to jail, but they have not any constructive non-violent way of successfully opposing aggression and injustice. Gandhiji evolved the technique of non-violent, moral resistance which can never fail. You do not kill others, you do not propose to harm them, but you also refuse to submit, even in an indirect way, to acts of injustice, repression or exploitation. You refuse to cooperate with the wrongdoer and you cheerfully accept the consequences of your step. Injustice you resist non-violently, even unto death. The non-violent man never accepts defeat. He has achieved cent-per cent success when he surrenders his body rather than surrender his principles. The effect of such moral and total resistance on society is wonderful. Gandhiji could invent and offer such an invincible weapon simply because of his belief in the soul.

Only those who believe in the power of the soul can cheerfully and whole-heartedly accept Gandhiji's weapon of *satyāgraha.*

One thing I want the present generation to realise is that Gandhiji was essentially a scientist and a good general. Gandhiji experimented not so much with the physical world as with men and society (his experiments with human diet maybe included both in "physical science" and humanities)! One great difference between Gandhiji and modern scientists was their approach to their search. The scientists start with a doubt. They distrust everything and then try to find out the Truth through experiments. Gandhiji, on the other hand, started with reverence for the achievements of humanity. He was prepared, therefore, to accept the teachings of the leaders of the past, but only provisionally. He would experiment on them and accept them, change them, or reject them only as a result of his own experiments.

It is very significant that Gandhiji called his autobiography *My Experiments with Truth.* With Gandhiji Truth was God, Truth was supreme. He would never compromise with Truth even for the benefit of his nation or for any worldly success. But he accepted truth finally only when it was proved to him by his patient and impartial experiments. That is why I call him the greatest scientist of our age. His constructive programme consisted of so many sociological experiments towards rebuilding of a non-violent human civilisation.

Let me end with a few personal anecdotes:
from my book *STRAY GLIMPSES OF BAPU*
SAṀNYĀSA AND SERVICE

One day, when we were still living at the Satyagraha Ashram, Swami Satyadev came to pay us a visit. He and I had already met in Almora, in 1911-12. He had then just lately returned from America, and soon after, taken *saṁnyāsa* (vow of renunciation) as a self-dedication to the attainment of Bharata's freedom.

He had written several books before he came to the *āśrama*. He had become famous as Satyadev Parivrājak (itinerant monk). As soon as he arrived, we started listening to his recitation of *Tulsī Rāmāyaṇa*, after evening prayers. Seeing his passion for Hindi, Bapu sent him to do Hindi propaganda in Madras. The first textbook to be published in connection with the propagation of Hindi in Madras was written by Satyadevji.

Later, we āśramites had left our rented bungalow in Kochrab and settled on our own land on the banks of the River Sābarmatī, when Swami Satyadevji, once visited us there also. He was simply delighted with the work that Bapu was doing for the freedom of the country. He was the guest of the *āśrama*, and we served him with a will. Special arrangements had to be made about his food, but it was a pleasure to us to make him comfortable.

One day, Satyadevji came to Bapu and said: "I desire to join your *āśrama* and live here as an āśramite."

Bapu said: "That is excellent! The *āśrama* is meant for people like you. But you will have to discard your *saṁnyāsī*'s ochre robe if you become an *āśramite*, you know!"

This was a great shock to Satyadevji. He was deeply annoyed, but, of course, he could not show his annoyance to Bapu. He contented himself with a mild protest: "How can that be? I am a *saṁnyāsī!*" Bapu retorted: "When have I asked you to leave your *saṁnyāsa*? Try to understand what I say." And then, very quietly, Bapu explained: You see, our countrymen have such a reverence for the ochre robe that the moment they see it they start worshipping its wearer and offering him their whole-hearted service. Now, we should make it a point not to accept service, but to give it. If you go clad in the *saṁnyāsī*'s robe, people will never take from you the service which we have made it our duty to offer them; on the contrary, they will fall over each other in their eagerness to serve you. So, you see, we cannot afford to retain anything which might act as an obstacle in the way of our prescribed acts of service. *Saṁnyāsa*, after all, is primarily an attitude of mind, a purpose and a resolve. What has it to do with outer vestments? Renouncing the ochre is by no means synonymous with the renouncing of *saṁnyāsa*. If, tomorrow, we go off into the villages and start cleaning the lavatories, do you suppose the people will let you move a finger as long as you have the *saṁnyāsī*'s ochre on your body?

Satyadevji understood, but could not agree to this. He came to me and said: "I simply cannot do this. I have donned this garb with a set purpose. I cannot now discard it.

Passion for English Literature

It must have been some time in 1916; Bapu sat writing one day, and I sat near him reading Fitzgerald's version of Omar Khayyam. I had often heard it praised, but had never read it. So, finding a chance to rectify this omission, I took up the poem, and began reading it with great enjoyment. I was nearly coming to the end of it when something drew Bapu's attention towards me. "What are you reading?" He asked. I showed him the book.

Since we had only lately become acquainted, Bapu probably did not feel like preaching to me right away. He heaved a deep sigh, instead, and said with a touch of pathos:

> I, too, used to be very fond of English poetry. But I gave it up thought to myself. I do not even know as much Sanskrit as I should. And if I have some time to spare, why should I not utilise it in trying to become a better writer in Gujarātī? My job today is to serve Bharat to the best of my ability, so I must dedicate all my time to developing my capacity for service.

After a pause he continued in the same simple, meditative fashion:

> If I can be said to have really renounced anything for the sake of national service, it is my passion for English literature. Money and career mattered so little to me that leaving them was no "renunciation"

at all. But oh, how I loved English literature! However, I decided that I must give it up, so I did.

I took the hint. I put Fitzgerald away.

I have not been able to give up English literature completely, but Fitzgerald has remained unfinished to this day. And I think I may add in a general way that I read no English book until I had attained a certain amount of proficiency in speaking and writing Gujarātī.

I never had to make any effort to learn Gujarātī, although it was not my mother tongue. I just absorbed it from the Gujarātī atmosphere around me, and reading Gandhiji's writings did the rest.

When I first started writing in Gujarātī, I found a very simple way of dealing with gaps in my Gujarātī vocabulary. When I could not find just the right Gujarātī word, I substituted for it a simple Sanskrit word. The result was that while my style remained simple and unpretentious, it acquired a Sanskrit tinge, and became as acceptable to the learned as it was suitable for the common people.

The greatest benefit that I derived from Bapu's significant remarks above was this that the energy which I used formerly to spend on finding out and learning all about the right English words, I now diverted to the proper study of the Gujarātī language.

Lokamanya and Bapu

After his return from deportation at Maṇḍalay, Lokamanya Tilak decided to re-join the Congress, and in the Belgaum Session of the Provincial Political Conference[1] he tried his best to persuade his party-members to do likewise. Acceding to my urgent request, and accepting Shri Gaṅgādharrao Deshpande's invitation, Bapu also attended that Conference.

We were followers of Lokamanya Tilak, but we had lost our hearts to the grandeur of Bapu's personality, to his patriotism, and to the flawless purity of his character. I had become completely his, and I was trying to win Gangadharrao over to Bapu, too.

Some of us believed that if Tilak and Gandhi could get to know each other, it would prove a great blessing for the whole country. We tried to bring about a private meeting between these two great men, but it could not be done where Lokamanya was staying. So Gaṅgādharrao took Lokamanya along to Bapu, and leaving them together, went off himself somewhere else. We never learnt what took place between the two leaders, but, as Lokamanya quitted Bapu's room, he said to Gangadharrao:

> This man is not one of us. He follows as different path altogether. But he is true in every inch of him, and no harm can ever come to Bharat through him. We must be careful to avoid any conflict with him—on the contrary, we must help him whenever we can.

All that Bapu said in his speech at that Conference was: "It is well that you gentlemen are rejoining the Congress. But I would ask you to come in as soldiers, not as lawyers."

Two or three days after this, Shri Belavi, a lawyer and leader of Belgaum, had occasion to visit the Collector on some matter of business. "Well", asked the Collector, "so, you invited Barrister Gandhi to your Conference, did you? And I have heard that the things he said to you all were far from pleasant! You must have been sorry that you invited him!" The "you poor fellows!" purr in the Collector's voice put Belaviji's back up. "Not at all!" he purred back sweetly. "Curious, isn't it, how little you English know of the Indian character? We have a deep reverence for Gandhiji. He has every right to give us advice and guidance. We listened most respectfully to what he had to say. You will have proofs of our sincere appreciation of him one day." The Collector fell silent.

"Forgive Him, Father..."

It was probably in 1917. The evening prayer was over and Bapu, propped up against a pillow, sat on his bed talking. It was rather chilly, so Bapu had folded a sheet and flung it over his back and shoulders. Bapu was deep in conversation with Shri

Ravjibhai Patel. As they talked, Ravjibhai's glance wandered to Bapu's shawl, and became fixed upon a curious blackline that was etched upon the white cloth. He leaned forward and looked at it intently—it was a great black snake that had crawled up Bapu's back right up to his shoulder! Having arrived at the edge of nothingness, it was now looking this way and that, seeking a way ahead. Bapu saw that Ravjibhai's attention had wandered, and his eyes were not upon him, but upon his shoulder. He asked: "What is it, Ravjibhai?"(Bapu himself was feeling a weight upon his shoulder.) Ravjibhai never lost his head in a tight place, and on this occasion, too, he kept cool and collected. He knew that if he spoke loudly, Bapu and all the others would be frightened, there would be hustling and bustling and running about, and then, the snake would be frightened in its turn. So, he just murmured gently: "Nothing particular, Bapu; merely a snake on your back. Keep quite still". "I shall keep quite still", said Bapu, "But what are you thinking of doing?" Ravjibhai replied: "I shall gather up the shawl by its four corners and remove it from your back, snake and all". The snake, feeling that something was up, had dived into the folds of the shawl and lay hidden there. Bapu said quietly: "I shall keep perfectly still: but take care of yourself".

> Ravjibhai gathered up the shawl and walked some distance with it, and the moment the snake crawled out of the shawl, he flung it far from him....
>
> (Ravjibhai has related this incident at length and with all the details, in his book. I have told the story as I remember it.)

The next day, the papers had a romantic tale of a cobra that reared itself up behind Bapu and spread its hood above his head. This meant, clearly, that Bapu was going to become an emperor. A friend said to me: "The cobra stopped at Bapu's shoulder. If it had climbed up to his head, there is no doubt at all that Bapu would have become King-Emperor of Bharat!"

This incident came to my mind once while I was talking to Bapu, and I asked "What did you feel, Bapu, what did you think, when that snake crawled up your body?" He said:

> I had one moment of pure terror—but only one! I recovered myself immediately, and then I felt nothing. I thought, if that snake bit me I would say to everyone, "That snake must not be killed. The moment you see a snake, your first impulse is to kill it; and so far, I have not prevented any of you from doing so. But the snake that has bitten me must have nothing to fear. It must be allowed to go free.'

Meet for Martyrdom

In Champaran, the prospect of Bapu's enquiry into the injustices and atrocities under which the people laboured was breathing a new life into that part of the country. And the schools which Bapu opened in many places[2] were also beginning to exercise an influence.

Everyone was feeling happier—because of this new hope—everyone, that is except the white planters!

Someone said to Bapu: "The planter of this place is the worst of the lot. He is bent upon murdering you. He has employed assassins."

When Bapu heard this, he went off alone, one night, to the bungalow of that planter and said: "I hear that you have employed assassins in order to kill me. That is why I have come alone and in secret to your house." The poor planter just stood there, as if turned to stone.

Homage to Lokamanya

It was 31 July 1920. Lokamanya's illness had taken a serious turn, I had gone to Bombay. I went to the Sardargriha to see Lokamanya. It was not easy, because those were practically his last moments, and people were not allowed to go in. However, I managed to get permission and went in. He was breathing very hard, and all the most prominent doctors of Bombay were gathered around his bed. I could not remain in that room for long. My feelings overcame me, and I went away and joined the Maharashtrian leaders who were sitting in silent grief in another room. Seeing my distress, Bapuji Aney called me to him, and started discussing the policy of non-cooperation.

I left by the evening train for Ahmedabad. All I said to Bapu was: "I have seen Lokamanya, now I am returning to the *āśrama*."

That same night Lokamanya quitted his earthly abode. The first words that Bapu uttered when he heard the news on the telephone were: "Oh, what a pity! I wish I had kept Kaka back".

After that he remained plunged in solemn thought. He spent the whole night, sitting on his cot, thinking. A lamp was burning by his side. He let it shine, and remained with his eyes fixed upon it, lost in thought.

Mahadevbhai awoke from sleep in the latter part of the night and saw Bapu sitting up motionless, in a very trance of thought. He went to Bapu, and Bapu spoke almost involuntarily, as it were: "To whom shall I go for advice now in moments of difficulty? And when the time comes to seek help from the whole of Maharashtra, to whom shall I turn?" He fell silent, then spoke again:

> I have been working for *swarāj* all along, but I have avoided uttering that word. But now it devolves upon me to keep Lokamanya's slogan alive and effective: it must not be allowed to sink into silence. And the banner of *swarāj* which this brave warrior had raised must not be lowered for a moment.

Bapu joined Lokamanya's funeral procession that day, and lent his shoulder to the bier. But he was grieved that the crowds were not as silent and serious as they should have been on that solemn occasion. He felt it very deeply. However, later on, he saw the thing from another angle and was comforted. When he returned to Ahmedabad and gave us his post-prayer talk, he said, describing the whole incident:

After all, that vast crowd had not gathered there to mourn. It was there to offer homage to its great leader. How then could we expect from it the solemn dignity of grief?

Principles beyond Purchase

This is an incident from 1921. The Gujarat Vidyapith had just been founded in Ahmedabad, but the constitution had yet to be finalised. I had much to do with this, and I was working like a demon, day and night, to get the thing going properly. One day we were having a meeting of our Senate, and Mr. Andrews, who was present by invitation, posed a question: "Will Harijans be allowed to attend the College, or won't they?" I answered promptly: "Of course, they will!" But there were many members of the Senate whose minds were not prepared for this drastic social reform. Amongst our affiliated institutions was a school called the Model School, the proprietor of which was one of the objectors. Some others also stated their difficulties if this rule were to be enforced. Finally, when we failed to reach any conclusion, we decided to drop the matter that day and refer it to Bapuji. I was quite happy. I knew what Bapu would say. And that was, in fact, exactly what he said: "The Vidyapith was to make no distinctions of any sort between human beings".

The news spread, and Gujarat began to buzz like a swarm of bees. Bombay awoke with a jerk and began to take notice. A few wealthy Vaiṣṇavas came to Bapu and said: "The work of national education is a truly religious one. We would be happy to give as much money as you need to further it, provided you can see your way to leave this Harijan-entry question alone." (Those Vaiṣṇavas had come prepared to give six or seven lacs on the spot.) Bapuji answered: "Leave alone the Vidyapith Fund; if somebody were to offer me even *swarāj* as a bribe towards keeping untouchability alive, I would not touch it with a pair of tongs."

Exit the Vaiṣṇava lords of wealth, definitely sadder, and, let us hope, wiser. It must have been a shock to them to realise that there were things in the world which their money could not buy.

Notes

1. This was in 1 May, 1916.
2. This was in late November 1917.

8
The Mission of Bhārata and Its Future

Kakasaheb Kalelkar

Friends,

I must thank you for the honour you have done me by inviting me to come to Manipur to deliver a lecture on a cultural subject, in honour of a great man of culture Atombapu who lived in your midst and influenced the life of this chosen land of God—Manipur.

Naturally I am reminded of the day I entered Manipur for the first time some thirty years back under humiliating conditions. Young citizens of India, who are born under freedom and who perhaps form a good part of my audience today, will be surprised to know that a "foreigner" like me could not then enter Manipur without securing a previous written permission of the British agent who then, dominated the kingdom of Manipur.

I do not remember the details now, the "kind" permission given to me was perhaps misdirected and I waited at the Telegraph Office of Dimapur for a telegraphic permission from the British agent, to enter a part of my own country, in order to meet my own people. I still remember the anxious hours I spent in the Telegraph Office before the permission came through, and then I was afraid of being stranded because most of the busses had left Dimapur by then. So you can imagine my joy that I have lived long enough to see the end of that British domination. Now, not only I am perfectly free to visit you but I am coming in response to an affectionate invitation, to share my thoughts with you. You have given me an opportunity of paying my tribute to the cultural services of a kindred soul, who, had we known each other then, would have welcomed me as a fellow student of the great culture which our country is evolving through the ages.

I find that you have so far invited great scholars like Suniti Kumar Chatterji and Ramesh Chandra Majumdar to give you the cream of their researches in Religious and Cultural integration of India and "the expansion of Aryan culture in eastern India". I have profited greatly by reading their lectures and their researches have strengthened my own views about the cultural growth of our country, as well as my faith in the mission of Bhāratavarṣa, assigned to us by the God of History.

My only sorrow is that I will not be able to give you a learned discourse that can come up to the level reached by these great scholars, although my love and reverence for the cultural mission of our motherland is in no way inferior to theirs.

You will permit me to recount here a little anecdote—Some of us, as young college students visited the great Lokmanya Tilak, the leader of Maharashtra and of India. We knew that he was hankering for the end of British rule and the attainment of full unrestricted *swarājya* for our Motherland. I shall give you a gist of what he told us in our own mother tongue.

> I know you are all college students, some of you must be brilliant scholars. I know you are proud of the history of Maharashtra and the struggle of our great Shivaji who fought Aurangazeb, the emperor of Delhi, and who was the first to dream of "Hindavī Swarāj".

> I know some of you will certainly add to the reputation of the great scholars of Maharashtra, who have written about our glorious past, about the religions, philosophy and arts of the country. Some of you may secure high places in government service.
>
> But who are there who will dedicate their whole lives to the wiping away of the black *tilaka* of slavery on the forehead of Bhārata Mātā? I want you, not only to forego lucrative careers in government service, I want you to forego even your scholarly careers and your deep study in various fields of human development.

And then with a voice trembling with emotion, he added

> You know Bhārata Mātā is not barren. She has produced great scholars in the past. Even under adverse circumstances today, she is still producing great scholars. The nation will not suffer or be poorer if you renounce your scholarly careers and reputation and dedicate the whole of your life for the attainment of *swarāj* and for enlightening the masses towards the same goal.

And then he gave us his own programme for national service, including of course, national education and revival of Indian Industries. He did not forget "prohibition of wine and intoxicant drugs".

I was one of those who took the vow in the presence of the great leader. And if I have made any study of Indian history and culture, it has been done only by stealth as it were and in spare hours of enforced leisure in the jails through the grace of the British government. You may not, therefore, expect from me a scholarly thesis like the two you were fortunate enough in securing from my predecessors.

All I can do is to place before you, the cream of my desultory study and earnest thinking for the attainment of *swarāj* and the full growth of our people as honoured members of a world family of Nations.

I had the highest good fortune and privilege of working under Mahatma Gandhi. A privilege which I know you all must be envy. Gandhi *jihād* all the noble elements of a nation-builder, and more than that, the prophetic elements of a leader of humanity. I can, therefore, place before you our vision of the future of our common motherland and invite you to dedicate your lives to helping Bhārata Mātā to fulfil the great mission which God has assigned to her.

And what is that mission?

There are a number of countries on this earth, where all the inhabitants belong to one race—they all speak one common language and they all belong to one common religion. They have evolved a common culture and they are thus contributing their share, big or small, to the universal culture which is going to bless humanity. These countries and these nations have not to worry about cultural clashes or religious differences. They do not find any linguistic difficulty in sharing with their fellow countrymen, their ideas, their experience and their ambitions for the future. Some may envy them the blessings of such a unity. But God says "My world is multiracial, multireligious, multilingual and multicultural". Its problem is how to bring about mutual adjustment, compromise, balance, synthesis and ultimate harmony amongst the various races, religions, literary traditions and cultural patterns?

God, therefore, said,

> I must have a laboratory for solving not intellectually, but through Life's rich experience, these great problems. I must have a spiritual and sociological laboratory where all noble experiments can be tried, tested, corrected and improved.

And God of History, in His wisdom and benevolence, chose Bhārata to be this divine laboratory, and he made our country multiracial, multilingual, multireligious and multicultural.

If you remember this central fact, you will be able to understand and interpret the whole history of India; our grand philosophical speculations, the great variety of our multiform *sāmājika sādhanā*; our conscious, deeply-planned sociology its brilliant success and miserable failures; our ancient leadership of the world and the later continuous humiliation of foreign domination, the birth of a galaxy of great men in every department of life and the vicissitudes through which we went from time to time, from age to age. All these stands well explained and truly interpreted when we discover how we are being trained to fulfil God's purpose in this country of evolving a multiform world-culture based upon spiritual ideals and neo-yogic *sādhanā*.

Even our pre-history is replead with cases of racial thesis, anti-thesis and synthesis, in this ancient land.

I make bold to say that God even changed the very configuration of our country in pre-historic times changing lakes into mountains and lifting seas up to provide us with land, to grow and cultivate. A Paraśurāma could demand, and get from the Western sea, a strip of land to make his sociological experiments, at the foot of the Sahyādri Mountain.

I am willing to believe that this beautiful valley of Manipur like that of Kashmir, was once a grand, extensive lake fostering marine-life. This lake was drained for your good and you are allowed to work out a synthesis here, between the prosperous culture of the plains and the sturdy culture of the hills. The Loktak Lake providing vast expanse of water for experimenting with aquatic elements of culture.

What interests me most is the fact that your Manipur is perhaps the only place where you successfully tried to fully introduce Hinduism in the life of the tribal people of this area and its surroundings.

Whether the Hindu colonists boldly identified themselves with the tribal people and their way of life, or whether it was the tribal people who accepted Hinduism thoroughly and became scholars in the Sanskrit-Hindu scriptures, is more than I know. But whatever the process and the initial source, it is most gratifying to learn that Hinduism became part and parcel of the life of the tribals here; and the tribals felt that they were Hindus from the very beginning. It is a great achievement and I have been quoting the name of Manipur in my lectures both in India and elsewhere, to show that such a thing is possible and the results are both outstanding and beneficial.

How I wish the people of surrounding countries could take their cue from the bold experiment of Manipur and follow it with grit, vigour, imagination and patient perseverance.

It is for this sociological and religious experiment that I value the cultural history of Manipur and I am anxious that research scholars try to find out the favourable circumstances that led to this most influential and happy experiment of cultural and spiritual synthesis. I should also like some scholars from Manipur to study in detail, the amount of give and take and the necessary modifications in each-other's cultures which led to this most paying and enriching synthesis. This would be a great lesson for people of other parts of India.

Sociology in India is a new study. It has not matured as yet, to the level of the intensive experiments of cultural synthesis that has gone on in the whole country ever since our Aryan ancestors cultivated this land and made it a home for their spiritual and cultural experiments.

I must admit and note that some of our experiments have not always been successful and equally profitable to both sides. The sense of racial or cultural superiority was there and every effort at cultural synthesis, in our country has been made and accepted only on the basis of a spiritual, cultural and racial hierarchy of superior and inferior types. But they were grand experiments on a colossal scale and they happened to succeed and prove satisfactory to all sides concerned. But I am not prepared to say that they were successful from the highest humanitarian standpoint which alone is the ultimate test of human development for the future.

It is high time we evolved a detailed plan for cultural synthesis in our country and placed it before the coming generations.

I recognise that it is not an easy thing. A new experiment demands that we know exactly, what are the essential things to be preserved and fostered for the future. We should also be able to decide what are the things which were once useful and satisfactory but today are handicaps and hindrances for the future progress of our people as well as of humanity as a whole.

Our racial mentality has learnt to worship the past. And whether we succeed in life or no, we try to be loyal to the ancient ideals. Even in a spirit of reform, we turn in favour of a revival of a golden age of the past.

Take the instance of the Arya Samaj. It put its finger accurately on many social evils and on some wrong and unhealthy socio-religious ideals. But it appealed to the people in the name of reviving the good old "Vedic days" when "everything was good and nothing harmful!" We may have succeeded in achieving certain reforms but the spirit of revival, the spirit of blind reverence for ancient wisdom, has come in the way of our onward progress, with the result that whereas the orthodox Sanātanīs swore by Sāyaṇācārya, the Arya Samaj started by swearing by Dayananda Saraswati and the habit of swearing by some great man persisted.

We still cling to the fond belief that the ancients were all-knowing that their wisdom was perfect for all times, and our loyalty demands that we follow them totally. Our only struggle being to remove the subsequent and later accretions!

Whereas what the history of all religions tells us is that "there is such a thing as evolution in understanding of God's revelations". The scriptures were all couched in a language and level which the people of those countries and those ages could understand. The scriptures are being interpreted and reinterpreted from time to time, not to find out exactly what the language yields, but with an idea to find how much of new and modern thinking and ideals could be loaded on the scriptures with impunity. That is why I always say that there is such a thing as evolution in understanding God's revelation. Sometimes I go further and try to persuade people that there is evolution in God's revelation itself. God, in His wisdom and mercy reveals not the whole Truth but only as much of it as the particular race and its times could stomach and utilise.

Of course, I do not, by this, mean to imply that prophets that come later in history are the better or the best conveyers of God's message. God has to suit His message to the understanding and level of the people. He wants to instruct and guide. If God can stand all the evils which His believers perpetrate in His name. He can certainly suit his revelation to the level of progress which those particular people and their historical evolution, can use profitably.

To my orthodox Sanātanī Hindu friends I say, "You must understand the word "Sanātana" a right. If you blindly revere the past and regret the changes brought about by later generations, you should call yourself "पुरातनी". The word "Sanātana" is a slight change from the word "सदातन" (Sadātana automatically becomes Sanātana in Sanskrit philology). Now Sadātana means that which is good for all times *sadā*, that which is ever fresh—नित्यनूतन. The growth and development of Hinduism fully justifies this interpretation. The days of the Upaniṣads are clearly an advance on the pristine Vedic times. Both the Śruti and the Smṛti were later greatly influenced by full-fledged Vedānta and Yoga. Read all the Smṛtis as they obtain today. They begin by paying lip reverence to Vedānta. Some of them end also, in the same way declaring that Vedānta is their ideal. But in between *vyavahāra* asserts itself and they accept the hierarchy of castes, *varṇa*s and *āśrama*s and ignore the teaching of equality of the *Gītā* by reminding us that पंडीताः समदर्शीनः should not be interpreted, to mean पंडीताः समयातिनः. They are free to look at all with eyes of equality. But in action they must differentiate between the powerful and the helpless, the learned and the ignorant, and are free to be unkind (and unjust) to "the lowliest and they lost" with the approval of religion. Then came the Purāṇas. They took up current stories, mythologies, folktales etc. and through them, popularised Hinduism. It is only through the Purāṇas that our religion reached the masses.

The ever-growing, ever-widening Sanātana Dharma has accepted and utilised even the later Āgamas and Tantras. Hinduism, therefore, is an all-absorbing, ever-growing religion of evolution, synthesis and up-to-date timely modifications. We have absorbed many races, many faiths and denominations and there is no limit set to this growth (नास्ति उंती बिस्तरस्य मे). Believers in this historic Hinduism should now study not only all the Śāstras—universal as well as local; they should collect the स्थल-पुराणानि and last of all, the customs, practices and practical ideals of the aborigines who have entered the Hindufold. (A good idea of these could be gathered from the very useful information collected by painstaking government officers who first edited the Gazetteers of India.)

Our scholars have done wonderful work in studying the philosophical ideas and metaphysical niceties of our forefathers. It is high time we studied the social ideals, manners and customs; disciplines and rituals of the various sections of our society and from them evolved a sociology of Hindu religious society.

We can then differentiate and declare what is consistent with our highest ideals and what is outmoded or unjustifiable.

Perhaps the contribution of Gandhiji towards reforming and revitalising Hinduism is the greatest in our times. In a gentle manner he has taught us to re-understand our religious and social ideals and bring them in line with the best development of humanity. His heroic struggle against untouchability has been unrivalled. His efforts for the uplift of the backward has improved the very basis of Hinduism. And we are now perhaps ripe to accept Gandhiji's ideal of *sarva-dharma-samabhāva* = equality of all religions. And establish in Bhārata "a loving familyhood of all religions". Our history shows that Bhārata has sent out many religious ideals and traditions that have influenced the world. Buddhism spread out from India and is holding sway over a great part of Asia. God sent Islam and Christianity to our country. These religions drew our attention to the great neglect we were guilty of, towards our backward people and towards the many races and castes we had ignored. We must now realise that religions which our own people have accepted and assimilated in their lives, are no longer foreign religions. They are all *swadeśi* so far as our common and composite culture goes. They have enriched our life and each one has re-emphasised some spiritual truth which we had ignored. Islam, for instance, declares equality of all believers and Christianity has placed before us brilliant examples of organised service of the masses both in the fields of medicine and of education.

One of the cardinal principles of Mahatmaji's *āśrama* life was the equality and familyhood of all religions. He therefore, welcomed intermarriages not only amongst all the Hindu castes without any exception; but he blessed interreligious marriages also.

Our country, at one time, influenced Asia as far away as the Russian dominions in Asia. Bhārata is now influencing the world with ideals of Vedānta and the technique of self-culture through Yoga. Vaiṣṇavism and Śāktism also, are attracting the attention of a wider world. But it should not be our effort to rival Islam and Christianity in getting converts for Hinduism from abroad. We should rather emphasise the familyhood of all religions and save ourselves and the world from the irreligious rivalries and suicidal antipathies between religions.

All this has a practical application for the social and political conditions of eastern India.

The whole atmosphere will change and change for the better, when we accept Jesus as an avatar of God and treat the Christians as fellow Vaiṣṇavas. We need not carry on a theological propaganda or controversy, thus rubbing people against their grain and rousing their prejudices. We should accept the Christians, the Muslims and all as our kith and kin. We should serve them and be solicitous for their well-being. We should not miss a single chance of being loving and helpful to them. Then alone shall we prove ourselves to be true Hindus in the highest sense. Our Śāstras interpret technical terms in two ways. One is *vyutpatti*—which follows the laws of grammar, philology and semantics. The other is *nirukti* (निरुक्ति), which catches the central meaning and import of a word and does not hesitate to draw the meaning out by artificially giving new meaning to each of the syllables of the term. Take for instance, the word—माँस (flesh). The word is made up of two syllables—माम्, and स:माम् = to me and स: (he). Now the *niruktikāra* declares that माँस भक्तयिता भक्क्षयितां मुत्र यस्य माँसं इहाद्मि अहम. (माँस = animal flesh). He (स:) (that animal) will eat me (माम्,) in the other world, whose flesh I am eating here. The message is—I am doing harm to the animal that I kill and eat, and I shall have to pay it back some time, in some way, through retribution. This is the message of the word माँस. In the same way we have found निरुक्ति (*nirukti*) for the word हिंदु. हिं means –हिंसा (*hiṁsā*); दू and means दूयते—"हिंसयादूयते चिक्तम् यस्य असौ हिंदुर् ईरित:".

"He is a Hindu whose mind is pained at the idea of using violence; (killing, harming, oppression, extermination, etc.)". Hindu culture, therefore, should always aim at removal of war, aggression, injustice, segregation and humiliation of any person, race, religion or culture. We should develop a family feeling towards all. This should be the sociology of our religion if we are to be truly Hindu.

Lovers and students of culture cannot afford to be mere historians and detached scholars when they deal with the culture of their own people and the well-being of their own country. We are first and foremost responsible for giving a new turn to the cultural life of our people. The religious heads are there because of their "orthodoxy". They are expected to support and defend the traditional culture. They are also expected to strengthen the hold of the scriptures and religious institutions inherited from previous generation. The social leaders, on the other hand, occupy their high position, these days, not always because they have, to their credit, substantial service of their people but often because they occupy a high place in government service or because they are rich enough to help financially people and institutions of their own community. The responsibility, therefore, lies with the scholars with a solid knowledge of culture. Real scholars are oftentimes the best well-wishers of humanity. They have got reverence for the spiritual ideals and aspirations of their country. Being conversant with history, they can't afford to be dogmatic or bigoted even in matters of religion. They can take a detached view and think of the good of the society as a whole, when controversies and bigotry divide society. And above all, they can educate the people continuously and bring up the level of society to a maturity which is all that is necessary for the harmony and progress which we long to achieve.

I would like, therefore, to place before this learned body a minimum programme calculated to secure cultural synthesis and national integration. The politician really hankers after national integration; even swears by it, but knows precious little as to how to achieve it. If mere wishes were horses, you may rest assured all the politicians would ride them.

As I said above, God has meant India to be the common home of many races, many religions, many languages and various degrees and types of culture; and even within India, "this checkered land of Prāgjyotiṣa is a sample laboratory-par-excellence even for Bhārata". Let us, therefore, begin with Mahatmaji's formula of सर्वधर्म समभाव (*sarva-dharma-samabhāva*) and cultivate equal reverence for all the religions accepted and followed by our people.

To begin with, let us decide to celebrate the festivals of other religions with the same reverence and enthusiasm that we feel for our own festivals.

Let me tell you, for your information that this idea has been taken up by a few Roman Catholics in Goa. They are celebrating our Diwālī (Festival of Lights) in their homes, inviting their Hindu friends to join them as guests. This inspired some Hindus in Goa to start celebrating Christmas in Hindu form. They wave the *āratī* before an image of Jesus and sing *bhajanas* in honour of Īśu Bhagavān; and Roman Catholic friends are invited to join the celebration.

You remember the great Śaṅkarācārya recommended to the Hindus that no worship of the *iṣṭadeva* could be regarded as complete, unless we worship the other four main *iṣṭadeva* of the Hindu pantheon. One must worship the five together—Śiva, Viṣṇu, Gaṇeśa, Sūryanārāyaṇa and Devī. One has the choice of placing one's own *iṣṭadeva* in the centre, but the five must be worshipped together. In Maharashtra this practice is recognised as पंचायतन पूजा (*pañcāyatana pūjā*). What we have to do now, is to enlarge the same practice and start *pañca dharma-pūjā*.

The main five religions being:

(1) *Sarva-samanvayakārī* Hinduism.
(2) Zoroastrianism of the Parsis. They emphasise the cultivation of good mind, good words and good deeds and insist on fostering the good and avoiding the evil.
(3) Islam which insist on recognising the unity of God and the absolute equality of all believers.
(4) Judaism which, like Hinduism respects all religions and insists upon reverence for traditions of the past, and;
(5) Christianity which, like Sikhism, sets great value on गुरुभक्ति (*gurubhakti*) and recommends to its followers the *sādhanā* of reaching God through the blessings of the *guru*. The Sikh places the *guru* above everything and the Christian worships his prophet and recognises him as the son of God.

There is a group amongst the Hindus, apart from the Sikhs, who also worship God as *guru*. They want to enlarge the *pañcāyatana* into *ṣaḍāyatana*.

Personally, I would not eschew the agnostic from our family of religions. He might have failed to discover and recognise God as we know and worship him, but he is a believer in Truth, Goodness, Harmony and selfless service of the neglected. "They may, in their ignorance, reject God but God has never thought of rejecting them."

"The second thing we must do is not to resist inter-caste and inter-religious marriages." Gandhiji, in his *āśrama*, definitely encouraged inter-caste marriages and blessed all the interreligious marriages that came to his notice.

Let me explain this position further.

Humanity has learnt intensely to cultivate some definite social virtues, aptitudes and qualifications by setting apart certain groups, castes and religious societies for specialising in them. During such a period of specialisation, the groups live apart and concentrate on their particular type of culture and sociological experiment. This is period of segregation for self-training. Hinduism has emphasised this element of progress for too long a time.

But this period must be followed by a period in which the different societies come together, help each other and cooperate in building a composite culture where people of different outlooks intermix and work for an all-absorbing integrated unity.

Hinduism, when it came of age, was wise enough to recognise inter-caste marriages and made way for them by dividing such marriages into अनुलोम and प्रतिलोम (*anuloma* and *pratiloma*). The *pratiloma* marriages were those that went against the grain of popular prejudice. The *anuloma* marriages although inter-caste, did not jar on the prejudices of those groups recognised by society as "upper caste". This distinction will lose its meaning as soon as we recognise the equality of all caste and all beings, in the spirit of the *Gītā* पंडीता: समदर्शिन:।

And now that we are accepting Gandhiji's formula of equality of all religions as the mission of India, we must accept interreligious marriages also, as perfectly agreeable to the wider sociology of Bhārata Mātā. In fact, we are recognising such marriages, if only informally. The lady who presides over the destiny of Bhārata today, chose a Parsi for her husband (the people of Manipur need to know that the Parsis living in western India are immigrants from Persia and they follow the Zoroastrian religion). Gandhiji not only blessed this marriage, but he also publicly declared that Hinduism would have no future if such marriages were not whole-heartedly recognised and respected.

I know that proselytising religions feel uneasy when asked to recognize the equality and familyhood of all religions. But they are gradually coming to recognise the justice and righteousness of such a reform.

One thing more, we should make it a social law that the benefit of all caste funds must be shared with people of other castes and religions—especially with those who are backward socially and educationally. No caste fund should be recognised and supported unless 50 per cent of its income is used for the benefit of other castes.

All this could easily be achieved if we train our hearts to recognise the equality of all castes and the familyhood of all religious groups.

I have given here just a minimum programme which is bound to grow if we recognise it in principle with our whole heart.

We are born in this present age to achieve this good object not only for ourselves but for the benefit of the whole of humanity.

Christians of India, for instance, will then be leaders of Christians of other lands and teach them to be true to the higher Christianity as evolved and perfected in India.

Muslims of India will likewise influence the whole Muslim world and Hindus can act as a leaven wherever they go.

Whatever is tested in a laboratory and found successful must be encouraged to spread and to work universally for the benefit of all.

9
Social Life in northern India during the Gupta and Post-Gupta Periods

D.C. Sirkar

Introduction

The era of the Imperial Guptas started from about 320 AD and the earliest genuine date of the era associated with the name of a Gupta monarch is furnished by the Mathura Pillar inscription[1] dated in the Gupta year 61 and in the year of the reign of Candragupta II (376-413 AD), which corresponds to 380-81 AD. It is usually believed that the era started from the accession of Candragupta I who was the grandfather of Candragupta II and the first emperor of the dynasty, his father Ghaṭotkaca and grandfather Gupta being petty chiefs.[2]

The latest known Gupta inscription is the fifth Damodarpur plate[3] which was discovered in the Dinajpur district of Bangladesh and had been issued in the Gupta year 224 corresponding to 543-44 AD, while the Sumandala plate,[4] discovered in the Gañjam district of Orissa was issued by King Pṛthivīgraha-bhaṭṭāraka in the Gupta year 250, i.e., 269-70 AD, when the Gupta-Rājya (Gupta empire) is stated to have been Vartamāna (flourishing). These records show that Gupta sovereignty was continuing in North Bengal in 543-44 AD and in coastal Orissa in 569-70 AD. At the same time, Īśānavarman of the Maukhari dynasty that originally owed allegiance to the Imperial Guptas was the first independent king of the family and his earliest record is the Haraha inscription[5] discovered in the Barabanki district of U.P. and dated in the Vikrama year 611, i.e., 553-54 AD. This shows that Gupta rule was ousted from U.P. considerably before 569-70 AD. Besides, we have two Jaina traditions, sometimes recorded in the same work, to the effect that the Guptas ruled for 231 or 255 years. Elsewhere we have tried to show that both these traditions are correct and that Gupta rule was extirpated from and parts of Bihar about the Gupta year 231 or 550-51 AD and from Orissa and parts of Bengal about the Gupta year 255 or 574-75 AD. Thus, the period 320-575 AD or roughly speaking 300-600 AD may be regarded as the age of the Imperial Guptas.

A Purāṇic statement refers to the dominions of the Guptas as comprising Prayāga (Allahabad district, U.P.) on the Ganges as well as Sāketa (Faizabad district, U.P.) and Magadha (Patna and Gayā districts, Bihar);[6] but Samudragupta (*c*.335-76 AD) conquered wide areas of northern India according to his Allahabad pillar inscription.[7] In the west, he temporarily supplanted Rudradeva (Śaka Rudrasena III) of Malwa and Gujarat and received tributes from such tribes or Rajasthan and the Punjab as the Madrakas (about Sialkot) and Malavas (about Uniyara and Tonk) while the Śaka-Kuṣāṇa rulers of the north-west, called Daiva-Sāī-putra-śahanśāhī-śaka-muruṇda, appear to have been his allies or subordinate allies. Likewise, in the east and north, Samtata (Tripura and Noakhali districts, Bangladesh), Davaka (Nowgong district, Assam), Kāmrūpa (Gauhati region, Assam) and Nepal bordered on his empire their kings probably being his subordinate allies. It appears that king Puṣyavarman of Kāmrūpa married a daughter of Samudragupta and that not only his son was named after his maternal grandfather, but even the latter's wife (Dattavati) was named after Samudragupta's queen (Dattadevī).

Thus Samudragupta's political influence spread over practically the whole of northern India. south India also felt the power of his arm since the Allahabad Pillar Inscription speaks of his victorious campaign in Dakṣiṇapatha as far as Kāñcīpura near Madras in the south. The extent of the east Indian kingdoms which came under Samudragupta's influence cannot be determined so that nothing can be said about the spread of Gupta influence in Manipur and its neighbourhood. The early history of Manipur is shrouded in obscurity because it is dependent on a chronicle entitled *Cheitharol Kumbaba* whose nature is like the Oriya chronicle *The Mādalā Pāñjī*. See our studies in the *Yuga Purāṇa* and other texts for an exposition of the unreliable nature of the Oriya chronicle, and the Purāṇic genealogy and chronology. The Manipuri chronicle gives a chronology in Śaka years from 33 AD which is dubious since the era is not expected in these parts before the twelfth century AD for the spread of the Śaka era, see our Indian Epigraphy. As regards the expansion of the Gupta empire after Samudragupta, his son Candragupta II permanently annexed the Śaka kingdom of western India and someone among Samudragupta's successors conquered Coastal Orissa. Candragupta II seems to have contacted matrimonial alliance with the Nāgas of central India, the Vākāṭakas of the Deccan and the Kadambas of Vanavāsī in Karnataka.

The biggest empire covering the ancient Madhyadeśa (roughly the present Uttar Pradesh) after the downfall of the Guptas in the sixth century AD was that of king Harṣavardhana (606-47 AD) of Thanesar and Kanauj, of King Yaśovarman (*c*.725-53 AD) of Kanauj and of the Gurjara-Pratihāras amongst whom the political influence of King Bhoja I (*c*.835-85 AD) and Mahendrapāla I (*c*.885-910 AD) who ruled from Kanauj, spread practically over the whole of north India. The inscriptions of Mahendrapāla I have been discovered in the Rājśāhī and Dinajpur districts of Bangladesh. The Gurjara-Pratihāra power declined with the rise of their erstwhile feudatories, the Candellas, in the second half of the tenth century AD. We may therefore regard (*c*. 600-1000 AD) as the post-Gupta period. The period that concerns us in these lectures is thus *c*.300-1000 AD.

Caste System

The division of the people into four *varṇa*s or social grades, viz. brāhmaṇa, kṣatriya, vaiśya and śūdra, was theoretical because a number of *jāti*s or castes were always included in each one of the *varna*s, and this was especially the case in the period under review. The word *varṇa* (colour) is found in the oldest literature of the Indo-Aryans to indicate the distinction both social and cultural, between the Aryans and non-Aryans though the expression *ārya-varṇa* (colour of the Aryans) and *dāsa-varṇa* (colour of the non-Aryans) must have originally pointed to the fair complexion of the Aryans and the dark or brown skin-colour of the aboriginal peoples of India.[8] In later times, the connotation of the term *varṇa* expanded so as to signify the four conventional grades of the Indian society mentioned above, in which Aryan and non-Aryan elements were gradually being mixed up. The units comprising the social grades called *varṇa* came to be known as *jāti*; but in later literature, this word is often also used in the sense of *varṇa* itself. The primary significance of the term *jāti* is "birth"; but the early *cāturvarṇa* division of the Brāhmanical society was not really dependent on birth. The word *jāti* appears therefore to have originally indicated tribal groups whose membership is depended strictly on birth. Numerous non-Aryan tribes of different grades of civilisation were gradually imbibing, in various degrees, not only the blood but also the culture of the Aryans; but most of them usually retained, at least for a considerable period of time, their tribal names and also certain social customs and prejudices. These elements of the mixed society of the Aryan and non-Aryan peoples had many characteristics dependent on birth and were *jāti*s in the real sense of the term. The incorporation of these tribes in the Brāhmanical social system seems to have popularised the word *jāti* in the sense of a caste and later also of a *varṇa*. It should also be noticed that the intermediate grades of complexion resulting from an admixture of the original white and dark skin-colour of the people, may have had something to do with the developing of the conception of four *varṇa*s out of the original two.[9]

The formation of castes from tribal groups is a characteristic of the social life in all periods of Indian history and the period under survey is by no means an exception to that.[10] We know how the *Manusmṛti* (which in its present form is, in our opinion, not much earlier than 300 AD) and other works on law are eager to include all Aryan, non-Aryan and foreign tribes and communities of various grades of culture into the theoretical scheme of the *cāturvarṇa*. The attempt was mainly to represent a tribe or class of non-Aryan or foreign origin and even professional groups, as a *vrātya* or degraded class of brāhmaṇa, kṣatriya or vaiśya or as originated from an admixture of the blood of two or more of the four conventional *varṇa*s. This was usually done with due regard to the primary occupation, position in the contemporary Brāhmanical society and the degree of Aryanisation or particular tribes of groups. There is general agreement on this arbitrary scheme amongst authorities on law, though there is difference in many particulars. The Māhiṣyas, a tribal people apparently deriving their name from the land called Mahiṣa after the Mahiṣa people, are not recognised in the *Manusmṛti*; but they find a place in the social scheme of later writers like Yājñavalkya[11] (about the fourth century AD). The Yavanas (Greeks) and Śakas (Scythians) who came to India and settled in this country are regarded by Patañjali, author of the *Mahābhāṣya*, (pure) śūdra; but they are included by Manu (X.42-43) in the list of degraded kṣatriya along with such non-Aryan peoples of foreign and indigenous origin as the Cīnas, Licchavis and Draviḍas while Gautama (IV.21) regards the Yavanas as the product of the union of kṣatriya male and śūdra female. Of course, the social position of the "pure śūdra" of the degraded "kṣatriya" and the offspring of the śūdra wife of a kṣatriya mother is called *mūrdhavāsikta* by some and kṣatriya by others[12] the second view being supported by several inscriptions. During the period under survey, a number of foreign tribes including the Hūṇas and Gurjaras were absorbed in Indian society. The

Hūṇas became ultimately recognised as one of the thirty-six respectable Rājpūt clans.[13] A number of other important Rājpūt clans such as the Paramāra, Pratihāra, Cāhamāna, Cāḷukya (Solaṅkī), Kalacuri, etc. may have also been of foreign origin. The Pratihāras were very probably a branch of the Gurjara people. The Kalacuris, whose name is supposed to have derived from the Turkish title Kulchur, appear to have been of Turkish origin. The case of these peoples was similar to that of the Greeks, Scythians and Parthians (Parthians) of an earlier age. As they were fighting and ruling races, it was natural for them to claim, after Indianisation, the status of the kṣatriya and ultimately, they came to be called Rājpūt which is a word derived from Sanskrit *rājaputra* (literally "a prince", but later "a cavalier") and was applied to indicate a member usually of the foreign ruling clans settled in western India although a few aboriginal tribes and other Indian clans also swelled their ranks. The word *rājaputra* is also found in the modified form a Rāval which is a title of noblemen. The change in the meaning of the word is comparable to that of the Rāval derived from Sanskrit *Rājakula* which originally meant the king's family, then a member of the royal family, and later also a title of noblemen.

A tradition in the Cand Raisa and other late records groups together four Rājpūt clans, viz. Paramāra, Pratihāra, Cāhamāna and Cāḷukya, as the Agnikulas since they are said to have originated from a sacrificial pit on Mount Abu in the Sirohi district, Rajasthan. This folk tale has been accepted by some historians who think that the Agnikula tradition refers to a rite of Purgation by fire whereby the impurity of the foreigners was removed and they became fit for entering into the Brāhmanical caste system.[14] We have, however, shown elsewhere[15] that such views are totally wrong. In the first place, all the four clans were not foreigners, the Cāḷukyas being Dravidians and the Paramāras descendants of the Mālavas of ancient India. Second, no fire-rite was required by the Indianised foreigners and the Aryanised non-Aryans for a place in the Brāhmanical social system.

> "When a foreign tribe became Hinduised, its members claimed the status generally of the kṣatriya, though the orthodox Brāhmanists were inclined to assign the position of degraded kṣatriya at least to the people of the ruling classes, while the rank and file, when developed into a caste, could have been characterised as śūdra in spite of their own claim to be kṣatriya. It was easy for the ruling classes to sustain their social status as they had no difficulty in contracting matrimonial alliance with other Indian ruling families since... in ancient India communal consideration played little part in that matter. We have numerous instances of such marriages as between the Mauryas of Pāṭaliputra and the Seleucid Greeks of Western Asia, between the Ikṣvākus or Vijayapurī and the Śakas of Ujjayinī, between the brāhmaṇa Vākāṭakas and the non-brāhmaṇa Guptas, between the Dravidian Sātavāhanas claiming the brāhmaṇa status and the Śakas of Ujjayinī, etc., etc. The process of Aryanised non-Aryans being accepted as members of any of the four conventional classes of the *cāturvarṇa* is similar."

An interesting fact is that, during the medieval period, many Indian ruling families are known to have tried to enhance their social prestige by claiming a fictitious descent from the solar, lunar, Yādava or Nāga lineage. The fabricated nature of the claim is, however, sometimes clearly demonstrated by the conflicting claims. Thus, the Guhilas of Mewar usually represent their houseas belonging to the solar race; but sometimes the Guhila dynasty is stated to have sprung from the lunar race as well.[16] It has also to be noted that the earlier records of the family clearly represent the Guhilas as brāhmaṇas, although the founder of one of the branch lines of the house is compared to Paraśurāma (who was a brāhmaṇa's son from a kṣatriya girl) and is called brāhma-kṣatrāṇvitā which is the same brāhma-Kṣatrāṇvaya showing that Guhilas or at least some of them claimed to be brāhma-kṣatriyas. As we had occasion to point out elsewhere[17] the real meaning of brāhma-kṣatriya is often misunderstood though there is clear evidence to show that the brāhma-kṣatriyas claimed both the brāhmaṇa and kṣatriya blood in their veins and could pose either as brāhmaṇa or as kṣatriya. At least a branch of the Guhilas, who appear to have belonged to the Nāgara brāhmaṇa community of Gujarat, thus claimed to have sprung from a union of persons one of whom belonged to the brāhmaṇa and another to the kṣatriya community.

The formation of castes out of professional communities is known from the *Manusmṛti* and many other earlier works; references may be made to an interesting historical instance of the period under review. The office of the Kāyastha (accountant-scribe) is first noticed in a Mathura inscription[18] of the Kuṣāṇa age; but it became popular in Indian administration during the Gupta period. In the Gupta and post-Gupta ages, the Kāyasthas served kings, feudatory chiefs, petty landlords, rulers of provinces and districts judges, etc., in various capacities such as scribe, secretary accountant and collector of revenue. An official, who usually sat beside his master and was often the chief intermediary between his master and the latter's clients or subjects, may have been naturally called *kāya-stha* in the sense "as if staying in the person of his master" by reason of his intimacy with or influence on the master, his position often next to that of his master and of his seat beside that of his master at least when the latter was a petty landlord or the like.[19] This like some other professions, was not restricted to any particular *varṇa* and could be followed by people of different *varṇa*s including the brāhmaṇas. But references such as that of the Valabha-Kāyastha-Vaṁśa (the vaṁśa of the Kāyasthas of Valabha) in Gujarat in the Sanjan plates of 871 AD[20] and certain other evidences appear to suggest that the Kāyasthas were gradually losing their original official, and professional character and becoming a social class or community before the end of the period under survey at least in some parts of the country. The crystallisation of the community into a caste at least in parts of the country may have been influenced by the adoption of the clerical profession by most members of an old tribe called Karaṇa,[21] just as the organisation of the professional community of the *vaidya*s or physicians of Bengal at a later date seems to have been influenced by their association with a tribal people called the Ambasthas who came to Bengal from the Far South.[22]

Noticing Brāhmanical personal names with a large number of modern Bengali Kāyastha cognomens (e.g., Datta, Ghoṣa, Soma and the like) in the Gupta and post-Gupta epigraphs discovered in the Bengal-speaking areas, it has been suggested by some scholars that there is a considerable brāhmaṇa element in the present-day Kāyastha population of Bengali.[23] In this connection, the evidence of the Nidhanpur (Sylhet district, Bangladesh) inscription[24] of Bhāskaravarman (*c*.600-50 A.D) is very interesting. In this record, persons belonging to the same *gotra* under a particular *śākhā* of a Veda have usually the same name-ending which, moreover, are now found usually as cognomens among the Bengali Kāyasthas. It may be pointed out that cognomens, unknown in the earlier period of Indian history, gradually developed in many cases in the period under review. A large number of the cognomens now prevalent among the upper caste Hindus of Bengal is derived from the name-endings of the ancestors of the members of particular families stereotyped at a certain date prior to the late medieval period. This process of a name-ending becoming a cognomen began to operate in the early centuries of the Christian era; but the process was not complete even in eastern India till much later times. The first known king of the Gupta dynasty of Magadha was Gupta whose son was Ghaṭotkaca; but when the latter's son Candragupta founded an empire, his descendants always stuck to the name-ending Gupta and soon the family came to be known as the Gupta dynasty. In the early part of the eighth century, there was in Bengal a person named Dayitaviṣṇu whose son was Vāpyata; but when the latter's son Gopāla founded an empire, his descendants continued to use of the name-ending Palla and soon the family became known as the Pāla dynasty.

The Kāyasthas as well as the Śreṣṭhins (bankers), Sārthavāhas (merchants) and Kulikaṣ (artisans) were the most important classes in the population of North Bengal in the Gupta period and the headmen or representatives of these classes were often the leading members of the administrative boards of the Pancayat type which helped the governors of the districts and subdivisions especially in the sale of government land (often fallow land) to parties willing to create rent free holdings in favour of gods and *Brahman*.[25] Another important class of people mentioned in the epigraphic records was that of the Kutumbins or agriculturist householders. The classification of the population based on profession as suggested by these east Indian records of the Gupta age reminds one of a similar classification known to Megasthenes and a few Arab travellers[26] and is possibly an indication of the conventional and theoretical character of the traditional division of the Indian people only into four *varṇa*s.

According to later writers of the *smṛti-nibandha*s (believed to have been written before the end of the tenth century) such as Yama and Satapapa,[27] the names of brāhmaṇas should end in words like *śarman* or *deva*, those of the kṣatriyas in Varman, Trātr, etc. those of the vaiśyas in Gupta, Datta, Bhūti, etc. and those of the śūdras in dāsa; A tendency towards such specification can be clearly traced even in the *Manusmṛti* (II.32), although in actual practice, we find that the rule was not rigidly followed even down to the end of the period of our survey. To cite only one late instance, we may refer to the family of the brāhmaṇa Pitavāsagupta Śarman who was the son of Sumaṅgalagupta, grandson of Varāhagupta and great-grandson of Makkaḍagupta and received a gift from king Śrīcandra of Bengal in the tenth century.[28]

The son usually adopted the profession of his father; but the conventional prescription of different professions for the four *varṇas* were often not followed in practice. The Smṛtis speak of Brāhmaṇas following non-Brāhmanical callings, and inscriptions testify to the existence of Brāhmaṇas who were agriculturist householders, traders, architects and government servants.[29] But the number of brāhmaṇas devoted to religious and literary pursuits was not small. They were highly respected by the kings and commoners. Their position at the head of the society was fully established. The Chinese pilgrim Hiuen-tsang, who visited India in the seventh century AD, speaks of the great honour commanded by the large number of learned men at the courts and with the public. He says,

> "Hence men can force themselves to a thorough acquisition of knowledge. Forgetting fatigue, they expatiate in the arts and sciences seeking for wisdom while relying on perfect virtue they count not 1000 li (about 165 miles) a long journey. Though their family be in affluent circumstances, such men make up their minds to be like the vagrants, and get their food by begging as they go about. With them there is honour in knowing truth (i.e., in having wisdom) and there is no disgrace in being destitute."[30]

There were also many brāhmaṇas who adopted military career and made themselves rulers of kingdoms.

The kṣatriyas were also a respectable class, although they sometimes took to the profession of vaiśyas. Acalavarman and Bhṛkuṇṭhasiṁha of an inscription at Indore in Uttar Pradesh were kṣatriyas, but are described as *vaṇika* (merchant) following the traditional profession of the vaiśyas.[31] The kṣatriyas were however, enjoying the status of the *dvija* or twice born. There was no doubt many caste groups in the brāhmaṇa and Kṣatriya communities even in earlier times. We have reason to believe that in many cases non-Aryan priests claimed the status of the brāhmaṇa just as non-Aryan rulers claimed to be kṣatriyas.[32] However, the characteristic of caste-formation was more remarkable among the vaiśyas and śūdras who formed the majority of the population. Such communities as the smiths, cattle-rearers, carpenters, oil-mongers, weavers, garland-makers and others became full-fledged caste groups. In some areas, some of these castes may have still enjoyed the status of the *dvija* as vaiśya; but in many regions they were gradually falling in line with the śūdras. The members of such caste-groups usually took interest only in their own caste and not in the wider social group to which they belonged. Occasionally they could have changed their profession. A section of the silk-weavers of the Lata country in Gujarat, after settling at Dasapura in West Malwa adopted various professions like that of an archer, a story-teller, and exponent of religious problems, and astrologer, a warrior and an ascetic.[33]

An important feature of the caste system in the period under review was the gradual elevation of the social position of the śūdras, although the process seems to have begun in far earlier times. The Smṛtis no doubt objected to taking meals with a śūdras; but an exception was made in regard to one's farmer, barber, milkman and family friend.[34] Some writers like Yājñavalkya, moreover, permit the śūdras to become traders and agriculturists.[35] Hiuen-tsang[36] refers to the śūdras as an agriculturist class in the seventh century while, in the eleventh century, Al-Biruni[37] found no great difference between the vaiśya and śūdra. According to this eleventh century authority, members of the four *varṇa*s lived "together in the same towns and villages, mixed together in the same houses and lodgings" but commensality was not allowed. The low-caste peoples were in our period called *antya* or *antyaja* who represented the impure fifth social grade outside the *cāturvarṇa* and followed various kinds of despised professions.[38] Their social position was much lower than that of the śūdras. They had often to love away from the area inhabited by the upper caste peoples. The Chinese pilgrim Fa-hien, who visited India early in the fifth century, says that the *cāṇḍāla*s lived apart from other villagers.[39] When they entered a city or market place, they struck a piece of wood to make themselves known so that men may avoid coming into their contact. Hiuen-tsang says,

> Butchers, fishermen, public performers, executioners and scavengers have their habitations marked by a distinguishing sign. They are forced to live outside the city and they sneak along on the left when going about in the hamlets.[40]

According to Al-Biruni, the Hindus of north-western India regarded for foreigners (meaning the Musalmans especially) as impure.[41] In his words,

> all their (i.e., the Hindus) fanaticism is directed against those who do not belong to them against all foreigners. They call them Mleccha, i.e., impure, and forbid having any connection with them, be it by intermarriage or by any other kind of relationship, or by sitting, eating and drinking with them, thereby, they think, they would be polluted. They consider as impure anything which touches the fire (of the oven) and the water of a foreigner... Besides, they never desire that a thing which once has been polluted should be purified and thus recovered, as under ordinary circumstances; if anybody or anything has become unclean, he or it would strive to regain the state of purity. They are not allowed to receive anybody who does not belong to them, even if he wished it, or was inclined to their religion... in all manners and usages, they differ from us to such a degree as to frighten their children with us, with our dress and our ways and customs, and as to declare us to be devil's breed, and our doings as the very opposite of all that is good and proper.[42]

The doctrine of impurity of the foreigners was no doubt very old; but as we have seen, many foreign peoples were regarded as members of the Indian social system shortly after they settled in the country. On the whole, the attitude of the Indians towards foreigners was never extremely hostile. This is further suggested by the treatment accorded to the Chinese pilgrims. There is also evidence to show that the Musalmans were favourably received in some parts of India. We know that there were some Arab Musalmans among the provincial governors under the Rāṣṭrakūṭa kings especially in western India.[43] While there were mosques for the Arab Muslim residents of Cambay and Prabhās Patan during the reign of the Cālukyas and Vaghelas of Gujarat. There is an interesting story how an Arab Musalman of Cambay received justice from king Jayasiṁha Siddharāja.[44] The strong feeling of the Hindus of north-western India against Musalmans, as evidenced by Al-Biruni was very probably the result of the atrocities perpetrated by the latter. This seems to be admitted by the servant when, after describing the banishment of the Buddhists from the dominions of Persia by the Zoroastrians and the conquests of Muhamad Ibn Qasim and the conversion of the Hindus to Islam, he observes, "All these events planted a deeply rooted hatred in their hearts".[45] After mentioning the variety and self-conceit of the Hindus, he further says, "if they travelled and mixed with other nations, they would soon change their mind, for their ancestors were not as narrow minded as the present generation is".[46]

Slavery always existed in Indian society; but the social positions of the slaves appear to have been better than that of the *antya* or *antyaja*, i.e., the despised castes. They were not regarded as a social grade as in some other parts of the world. Prisoners of war, debtors unable to pay their debts and gamblers unable to pay off their stakes were often reduced to slavery. Poor persons sometimes sold themselves to the rich for maintenance during famines. The children of slaves were also slaves. The debtor-slaves could regain their liberty by getting their dues paid either by themselves or by somebody else, while a prisoner of war had to supply a substitute for himself. A slave saving his master's life not only became free, but was also entitled to get a share of the latter's property. A female slave bearing a child to her master also attained freedom. Nārada deals with the question of slaves elaborately and also refers to the procedure of emancipating a slave.[47] The master took a jar from the shoulder of the slave and smashed it. He then sprinkled over the slave's head water containing grains and flowers and thrice declared him a free man.

The influence of the theory of *cāturvarṇa* on the minds of the people was immense. The kings of the periods not excluding those who professed the Buddhist faith, claimed to have been engaged in settling the system of *varṇa* and *āśramas* (although the *vānaprastha* and *saṁnyāsa āśramas* were losing their popularity and coming to be regarded as *kali-varjya* or prescribed for the Kali age and in "keeping the *varṇas* confined to their respective spheres of duty". But this was an ideal never fully realised. As in the outlying provinces of the country even today, there appear to have been principally only two social grades, besides the despised peoples, in many parts of the land at least about the end of our period, viz. the brāhmaṇa and śūdra, the number of those recognised as kṣatriya and vaiśya becoming gradually smaller. The word *dvija* was coming to mean mainly "a brāhmaṇa".

Among foreigner's accounts of the castes in Indian society, there is an interesting notice by the Arab travellers Ibn Khurdadba (844-48 AD) followed by Idrisi (1154 AD).[48] The former says,

> There are seven classes of Hindus, viz. the 1st, Sabkufria, among whom are men of high caste, and from among whom kings are chosen. The people of the other six classes do the men of this class homage, and them only. The 2nd Brahmā who totally abstain from wine and fermented liquors. The 3rd Katarfa who drink not more than three cups of wine; the daughters of the class of Brahmā are not given in marriage to the sons of this class but the Brahmās take their daughters. The 4th Sudaria who are by profession husbandmen. The fifth Baisura, are artificers and domestics. The sixth, Sandalia who perform menial offices. The seventh Lahud; their women are fond of adorning themselves, and men are fond of amusements and games of skill.[49]

The same castes are mentioned by Idris as (1) Sakriya (2) Brahman, (3) Kastariya, (4) Shardya, (5) Basya, (6) Sabdaliya or Sandaliya and (7) Zakya.[50] As regards the people of the first class, Idrisi says "these are the most noble. All the other castes pay homage to them; but they render homage to no one." The second group is called "the religious class":

> They dress in skins of tigers and other animals. Sometimes one of them, taking a staff in his hand, will assemble a crowd around him and will stand from morn till eve speaking to his auditors of the glory and power of God and explaining to them the events which brought destruction upon the ancient people that is, upon the brāhmaṇas, they never drink wine nor fermented liquors. They worship idols (whom they consider to be) able to intercede with the Most High. "About people of the third class, we are told that they could drink upto three *ratrs* (pounds Troy) of wire, "but not more lest they should lose their reason"; this caste may marry brāhmaṇa women; but the brāhmaṇas cannot take their women to wife." While people of the fourth class were labourers and agriculturists those of the fifth and sixth classes were respectively artisans and mechanics and singers, the women of the latter class being noted for their beauty. The people of the last class were jugglers, tremblers and players of various instruments. The correct reading of the name of the seventh class is believed to be Dhunbiyya.[51]

There are some discrepancies between the two accounts and apparently some errors also. The kṣatriya community has been divided into two classes, viz. the ruling (class I) and ordinary (class III), the social status of the brāhmaṇa (class II) being taken to lie between those of the said two. Another interesting fact is that the śūdra (class IV) has been given a higher social position than the vaiśya (class V). The *cāṇḍāla* (class VI) and *ḍomba* (class VII) represented two of the foremost *antyaja* communities.

This partly confused account reminds us of a similar notice of the Indian caste system reproduced from the Greek Ambassador Megasthenes (who was at the court of

Candragupta Maurya about the close of the fourth century BC) by Strabo (*c*.54 BC - 24 AD), Diodorus Sicalus (*c*.44 BC) and Arrian (*c*.96-180 AD). The Greek account also speaks of the seven castes (1) Philosophers or sophists, (2) Husbandmen, (3) Shepherds and cowherds or hunters, (4) Artificers, merchants and boatmen, (5) Warriors, (6) Inspectors, and (7) Councillors and assessors.[52] The description of the first caste[53] may be taken by one to suggest the brāhmaṇa caste; but this is not really the case. While pointing out that the Indian custom prohibits a person from exercising two professions or from changing from one caste to another, Arrian says, "It is permitted that the sophist only be from any caste for the life of the sophist is not an easy one, but the hardest of all". Really therefore the ascetics of all the castes formed this group.

The second caste which consists of the tillers of the soil and formed the most numerous classes of the population are the vaiśya.[54] According to Arrian, the third caste consisted of the "herdsmen, both shepherds and neat herds" who were nomadic people living in hills but not in cities and villages.[55] They were probably the Aṭavikas or forest-dwellers of early Indian literature as well as the *antyaja* tribes like Vadha. According to the same authority the fourth caste consisted of handicrafts men and retail-dealers[56] and appears to have the vaiśya representing the artisans. Thus, while the Arabs divided the kṣatriya into two castes, the Greeks divided the vaiśya into two classes, viz., the cultivators and the artisans. The fifth caste, corresponding to the kṣatriya consisted of warriors who were second to the husbandmen in point of number and led a life of supreme freedom and enjoyment having only military duties to perform.[57] The profession of the sixth caste is stated by Arrian to be spying out "what goes on in the country and town and report everything to the king where the people have a king, and to the magistrates where the people are self-governed".[58] Likewise the people of the seventh caste are stated to have advised "the king or the magistrates in the self-governed states, in the management of public affairs".[59] It may be conjectured that officials in the administration of the country were divided into two groups regarded as castes, the lower officers forming the sixth and the higher officers the seventh caste, though it is better to think that the seventh caste, consisted of the brāhmaṇas. It will be seen that, although the number of castes is the same in both the Arab and Greek accounts, there is considerable difference between the two.

Notes

1. Sircar, *Select Inscriptions*, 2nd edn., pp. 277-79.
2. Cf. *Ibid.*, p. 277, note 1.
3. *Ibid.*, pp. 346 ff.
4. *Ibid.*, pp. 490 ff.
5. *Ibid.*, pp. 385 ff.
6. Cf. Pargiter, *The* Purāṇa *Text*, etc., p. 53.
7. *Sel. In., op.cit.*, p. 262 ff.
8. See Sircar, *Stud. Soc. Adm, Anc. Med. Ind.*, p.104; cf. Vedic *Index*, s.v. varṇa (2) and Dāsa.
9. See Sircar, *loc.cit.*
10. *Ibid.*, p. 105; cf. Risley, *People of India*, pp. 72 ff.
11. I.92, cf. Gautama, IV.20.
12. Cf. *Manu*, X.6 and commentaries thereon, also Sircar, *op.cit.*, pp. 48-49, 101-02.
13. Sircar, *op. cit.*, p. 105, note.
14. Crooke in *J.R. Anth. Inst.*, 1911, p. 42 Smith, *EHI* 1924 p. 428; Tripathi, *Hist. Kan.*, p. 221; etc.
15. See Sircar, *The Guhilas of Kishkindha*, p. 18. *Note how the aboriginal rulers of Chota Nagpur became Nāgavamsi Rājpūt* (*Ibid.*, p. 9).
16. *Ibid.*, p. 5; also, *Bhavnagar Inscriptions*, p. 141, text lines 33-36.
17. *The Guhilas of Kishkindha*, *loc. cit*; also pp. 6 ff.
18. See *Ep. Ind.*, vol. XXXVII, p. 152, text line 3. It is an inscription or the time of King Vāsudeva, dated in the year 93 (171 AD).
19. Sircar, *Stud. Soc. Adm. Med. Ind.*, vol. I, pp. 156ff, *Bhar. Vid.*, vol. X, pp. 280-84. Some scholars believe that the word *kavastha* is the Sanskritised form of a non-Aryan word, while others take the word *kava* in this case as indicating "a department administration". See *N. Ind. Ant.*, vol. I, pp. 740-03; vol. VI, pp. 160-62; cf also, p. 49.

20. *Ep. Ind.*, vol. XVIII, p. 251, text line 77 cf. the Śrīvāstavya-kulodbhūta-kāyastha mentioned in the records of the Gāhaḍavālas of a later date.
21. Sircar, *Stud. Soc. Adm. Anc. Med. Ind., op. cit.,* pp. 158-59.
22. *Ibid.*, pp.106 ff.
23. Sircar, *Indian Epigraphy*, p. 424
24. Bhattacharya, *Kāmrūpasasanavali*, pp. 1 ff.
25. Cf. *Sel. Ins., op. cit.*, pp. 290 ff. See Sircar, *Ind.Ep.*, p.114.
26. R.C. Majumder, *The Classical Accounts of India*, pp. 224 ff. 236 ff.k 263ff., also below.
27. Cf. Sircar, *Suc. Sat.*, pp. 197, 211.
28. N.G. Majumdar, *Ins. Beng.*, vol. III, p. 5, text 27 ff.
29. For the agriculturist brāhmaṇas, cf. the name of Māghaśarman, etc., in the list of the Kuṭumbins in *Sel. Ins. op. cit.,* p. 353, text lines 5 ff.
30. Watters, *On Yuan Chwang's Travels in India,* vol. I, p. 161.
31. *Sel. Ins.*, *op. cit.,* pp. 318 ff.
32. For a list of degraded brāhmaṇa communities, See *Manu* X.21. In the period in question, there was a tendency among rulers, even of aboriginal or foreign communities to claim the status of the kṣatriya and to trace descent from celebrated epic hero as we have said above.
33. See the Mandasor inscription of 473 AD; *Sel. Ins.*, *op. cit.*, pp. 299 ff.
34. Cf. *Yaj.* I.166.
35. I.20.
36. Watters, *op. cit.*, vol. I, p. 168.
37. Sachau, *Alb. Ind.*, vol. I, p. 101.
38. Cf. *Manu*, VIII.68, XI.59, etc.; *Yājñavalkya*, I.148, II.294. Sometimes, the words have been taken to mean śūdra though in many cases the said class has been separately mentioned.
39. Legge, *The Travels of Fa-hien*, p. 43.
40. Watters, *op. cit.*, vol. I, p. 147.
41. Sachau, *op. cit.*, vol. I, pp. 19-20.
42. He also says, "... we must confess in order to be just, among us and the Hindus, but is common to all nations towards each other" (*Ibid.*, p. 20).
43. *Ep. Ind.*, vol. XXXII, pp. 45 ff.
44. *Ibid.*, p. 146.
45. *Ibid.,* p. 21. After referring to Sultan Mahmud's activities, Al-Biruni says how his Hindu enemies cherished "the most inveterate

aversion to all Muslims" and how Hindu sciences retired from the conquered territory to Kashmir, Benares and other places: "And there the antagonism between them and all foreigners received more and more nourishment both from political and religious sources" (*Ibid.*, p. 22).

46. *Ibid.*, p. 23. He adds that, in former times, the Hindus used to acknowledge, the great progress of science due to the Greeks (*loc. cit.*).
47. See *Vyavahárapada* V, verses 25 ff. The *CHI*, vol. I, p. 279, assigns Nārada to the fifth century AD.
48. Cf. Nainar, *Arab Geographer's knowledge of southern India*, pp. 12, 17, 129 ff.
49. Elliot and Dowson, *History of India as told by its Own Historians*, vol. I, pp. 16-17.
50. *Ibid.*, p. 76.
51. Nainar, *op. cit.*, p. 132.
52. Cf. Elliot and Dowson, *op. cit.*, p. 17, note 1.
53. See Arrian's account in R.C. Majumdar's, *The Classical Account of India* pp. 224-25. Thus, Arrian says, "Among these are the Sophists who are not so numerous as the others, but hold the supreme place of dignity and honour; for they are under no necessity of doing any bodily labour at all, or of contributing from the produce of their labour anything to the common stock, nor indeed is any duty absolutely binding on them except to perform the sacrifices offered to the gods on behalf of the state. If anyone again has a private sacrifice to offer, one of these sophists shows him the proper mode as if he could not otherwise make an acceptable offering to the gods. To this class the knowledge of divination among the Indians is exclusively restricted and none but a sophist is allowed to practice that art. They predict about such matters as the seasons of the year, and any calamity which may befall the state; but the private fortunes of individuals they do not care to predict,—either because divination does not concern itself with trifling matters, or because to take any trouble about such is deemed unbecoming. But if any one fails thrice to predict truly, he incurs, it is said no further penalty than being obliged to be silent for the future, and there is no power on earth able to compel that man to speak, who has once been condemned to silence. These sages go naked, living during summer, when the heat is too powerful, in meadows and low grounds under large trees, the shadow whereof, Nearchers says extends to five plethora in circuit, adding that even ten thousand men could be covered

by the shadow of a single tree. They live upon the fruits which each season produces, and on the bark of trees, the bark being no less sweet and nutritious than the fruit of the date-palm.

54. Arrian says, "They are neither furnished with arms nor have any military duties to perform; but they cultivate the soil and pay tribute to the kings and the independent cities. In times of civil war, the soldiers are not allowed to molest the husbandmen or ravage their lands; hence while the former are fighting and killing each other as they can, works, perhaps ploughing, or gathering in their crops, pruning the trees, or reaping the harvest." See Majumdar, *op. cit.*, p. 225.
55. "They too are subject to tribute, and this they pay in cattle. They scour the country in pursuit of fowl, and wild beasts" (*op. cit.*).
56. "They have to perform gratuitously certain public services, and to pay tribute from the products of their labour. An exception, however, is made in favour of those who fabricate the weapons of war, ... and not only so, but they even draw pay from the state. In this class are included ship-builders, and the sailors employed in the navigation of the rivers" (*loc. cit.*).
57. "Others make their arms, and others supply them with horses, and they have others to attend on them in the camp, who take care of their horses, clean their arms, drive their elephants, prepare their chariots, and act as their charioteers. As long as they are required to fight, they fight; and when peace returns, they abandon themselves to enjoyment, the pay which they receive from the state being so liberal that they can with ease maintain themselves and others besides" (*Ibid.,* pp. 225-26). The mention of pay received by the soldiers from the state goes against the theory regarding the prevalence of the feudal system in ancient India.
58. "It is against use and wont for these to give in a false report; but indeed, no Indian is accused of lying" (*Ibid.*, p. 226.)
59. In point of numbers, this is a small class; but it is distinguished by superior wisdom and justice, and hence enjoys the prerogative of choosing governors, chiefs of provinces, deputy governors, superintendents of the treasury, generals of the army, admirals of the navy, controllers and commissioners who superintendents agricultures.

10

Marriage and Family

Social Life in Northern India during the Gupta and Post-Gupta Periods

D.C. Sirkar

The ideal form of marriage was that between the bride and bridegroom of the same caste, although it was rather in accurately called *savarṇa* marriage; but a *savarṇa* and inter caste marriages were also known especially in the royal families. It must, however, be remembered that early works on law appear to have recognised marriage as including various conditions of sexual intercourse between man and woman leading the latter giving birth to children.The old eight kinds of marriage were accepted generally by the writers on law during the period under review, e.g., Yājñavalkya (I.58). These were:

(1) *Brāhma* in which the bride's father invited and offered his daughter to a learned man,
(2) *Daiva* involving the offer of the girl to a priest officiating in a sacrifice as a part of dakṣiṇā,
(3) *Ārṣa* allowing the offer of a maiden after taking from the bridegroom one or two pairs of cows and bulls,
(4) *Prājāpatya* prescribing the offer of the bride with the stipulation that the couple should jointly perform their religious duty, probably as long as both of them live,

(5) *Āsura* in which one marries a girl after paying bride-price to herself and her relations,
(6) *Gāndharva* involving the union of the bride and the bridegroom at their own will,
(7) *Rākṣasa* allowing the forcible abduction of the unwilling bride by the bridegroom from her people, and
(8) *Paiśāca* resulting from the rape of a girl when she is asleep intoxicated or unconscious.[1]

It will be seen that, although the importance of *sampradāna* or the ceremonial offering of the bride in marriage was gradually increasing, such forms of marriage as *āsura*, *gāndharva* and *rākṣasa* could hardly have the said ceremony under ordinary circumstances while *Paiśāca* which was really no marriage at all, was recognised merely for safeguarding right of the son that might have been born as a result of raping a girl. It is thus intelligible why some of the practices, prescribed in early works, gradually came to be obsolete and were ultimately called *kali-varjya*, "not permissible in the kali age", in the post-Gupta period.[2]

The *Manusmṛti* (X.6 ff.) rather reluctantly admits the validity of marriages between a man of the higher *varṇa* and woman of the lower, technically known as *anuloma*, while the *Yājñavalkyasmṛti* (I.93) does not regard even *pratiloma* marriage (those between the woman of a higher *varṇa* and the man of a lower as entirely invalid). Marriage with a śūdra girl is recognised, but condemned. *Manu* (IX.151; cf. *Yāj.*, I.56), however, allows the son of a śūdra woman to inherit the property of his brāhmaṇa father, although Bṛhaspati[3] (VI.42-43) recognises the right only in the case of movable property, but not in regard to land. The Smṛtis[4] permit the wife of a lower *varṇa* to participate in religious ceremonies only if the husband had no wife of his own *varṇa*. The Tippera (Bangladesh) plate[5] of Lokanātha, dated 665 AD however shows that brāhmaṇa's marriage with a śūdra girl was not condemned in Bengal as late as the seventh century AD. According to this record, the brāhmaṇa Keśava, son of Vīra, was called Parāsava (issue of the śūdra wife of a brāhmaṇa husband); but Keśava's daughter was given in marriage to a pure brāhmaṇa of the Bharadvāja *gotra*. The social status of the chief (*sāmanta*). Lokanāṭha, born of the said Keśava's daughter, was by means low as, in that case, he would have never disclosed the history of his origin in the record.

It is clear from the attitude of the writers on law that inter caste marriages often took place in the society, although they were disliked by the orthodox. The case seems to be analogous with that of the *punarbhū* (remarried woman) to be discussed below. There is no doubt that marriage within one's community had become the social ideal and that the tendency towards it led to legal union outside one's communal circle being obsolete. The description of the search of a merchant's son for his bride in the Gomini story of the *Daśakumāracarita* suggests that the common people hardly thought of marrying a girl who did not belong to his own community, technically called his *savarṇa*. Thus, there is reason to believe that, at least amongst the ordinary people, *anuloma* and *pratiloma* marriages were not much more than legalised concubinage even in the early part of the period under survey.

However, there are many instances of inter caste marriages of both the *anuloma* and *pratiloma* types in royal family. Thus, we may refer to the marriage of a daughter of Kākusthavarman of brāhmaṇa or brāhma-kṣatriya[6] Kadamba family with a bridegroom of the non-Brāhmanical Gupta family and to that of the Gupta princes Prabhāvatīgupta with Vākāṭaka Rudrasena II who was a brāhmaṇa of the Viṣṇuvṛddha *gotra*. Prabhāvatī became the chief queen of her husband; but it is interesting to note that she still retained her father's family and *gotra* names as is indicated by her name Prabhāvatī gupta and her epithet *dhāraṇa-sagotra*. This shows that there was no *sampradāna* and the consequent *gotrāntara* (change of the wife's *gotra* to that of her husband) in her marriage with the Vākāṭaka king. The marriage therefore could not have been of the *brāhma, daiva, ārṣa* or *prājāpatya* categories, but was apparently one among the other four types, although the *asura* form seems to be possible in the present case. Prabhāvatī's mother Kubera-nāga who was born in the Nāga family, also retained her father's family name even after her marriage in the Gupta dynasty. But marriages, which were not based on *sampradāna* and did not involve *gotrāntara*, became gradually out of use at least amongst the ordinary people.[7] As a matter of fact, caste was no consideration in the marriage contacts of royal families, and Indian rulers often married even girls belonging to foreign clans.[8]

The system of *niyoga* approved of by early writers like Manu (IX.51) became gradually extinct from the society. Yājñavalkya (I.68) and Nārada were not opposed to *niyoga* but Bṛhaspati and others were not in its favour. This is because India is a vast subcontinent and the customs varied in different areas of this land. The remarriage of widows is another case of the same type. It was looked upon with disfavour; but its prevalence in the society had to be admitted by Yājñavalkya (I.67) and other writers.

Nārada and Parāśara (between the seventh and tenth century) permit remarriage of a widow when the husband was *naṣṭa* (lost), *mṛta* (dead), *parivrājaka* (became an ascetic), *klība* (impotent) and *patita* (ostracised).[9] It is thus possible to think that the areas where these Smṛtis were compiled viewed at widows" remarriage more liberally and were opposed to statements like that of Manu (IX. 65) that "nowhere in the injunction on marriage is the marriage of a widow mentioned". Nārada also says that a woman of any of the four *varṇa*s, whose husband is absent for a long imputed to her. It should, however, be noticed that the same Nārada speaks of the three classes of *punarbhū* together with the four classes of *svairiṇī*[10] (a woman who lives with another man during the lifetime of her husband) while Parāśara is significantly eloquent about widows who live the life of a *brahmacāriṇī* or commit *satī* (i.e., die on the husband's death preferably by burning herself on the latter's funeral pile). Some authors like Vasiṣṭha make a distinction between a woman whose marriage was consummated and another whose marriage remained unconsummated and prescribe remarriage only in the case of the latter. But both *niyoga* and remarriage of a married girl ultimately came to be regarded as *kali-varjya.* According to the story of Viśākhadatta's drama entitled *Devīcandragupta*, Dhruvādevī or Dhruvāsvaminṇī, chief queen of Candragupta II Vikramāditya (376-413 AD), was the widow of his deceased elder brother Rāmagupta.[11] Whatever be the historicity of this tradition, such marriages were apparently not regarded as abnormal in the days of the author of this work, who seems to have flourished about the close of the sixth century. A story in the *Mahāvastu*, redacted in the Gupta age likewise reminds us of the epic legend of Damayantī's second *svayaṁvara* when there was at least no evidence that her husband Nala was dead. The *Mahāvastu* story tells us how when Siddhārtha became a recluse, his step-brother and cousin approached his wife Yaśodharā with proposals of remarriage which the latter refused.[12] The above cases show that the attempts of orthodox authors to interpret the stanza in the works of Nārada and Parāśara in different ways must be regarded as nonsensical. But the position of the remarried widow; called *punarbhū*, in the society of some parts of the country at least seems to clear from Vātsyāyana's *Kāmasūtra*, which in its present form, probably belongs to the Gupta age. This work seems to suggest that there was no regular marriage for widow or a married girl deserted by her husband, but that there was no bar for a woman without husband to ally herself to a man of her choice. The position of a *punarbhū* in such cases was apparently nearer to that of a mistress than that of a wedded wife. The same work suggests that, in the royal harem, where separate quarters were allotted to different types of women, the *punarbhū*s occupied a position midway between that of the *devī*s or queens, who lived in the innermost apartments, and that of the *gaṇikā*s or courtesans who were quartered in the outermost. This seems to be supported by Hiuen-tsang who says in the seventh century AD that in India "a woman never contracts a second marriage".[13] While the widows, who did not marry again, lived an ascetic life, the custom of *satī* was quite well known. The

Kāmasūtra (IV.2.53) refer to *anumaraṇa*, i.e., burning of the widow with the dead husband and the Eraṇ (Saugor district, M.P.) inscription[14] of 510 AD records a specific case but the custom wạs not popular during our period as in the later days.

The inferior position of the *punarbhū* is also indicated by that of her son. Even *Nārada* (XIII.45-47) regards one's son born of a *punarbhū* as only a kinsman of the father and as inferior to one's sons including those begotten on one's wife by others (call *kṣetraja* under various circumstances as well as the *putrikā-putra* (son of an appointed daughter), who are all both kinsmen and heirs of their father. A *punarbhū*'s son could inherit his father's property only in the absence of the superior sons according to the same authority (XIII.50).

The types of marriages and the categories of sons recognised by the Smṛtis show that public opinion was not particularly fastidious, at least in the earlier part of our period, about the establishment of sexual relation between man and woman. Such works as the Cchakatika show how a *gaṇikā* or courtesan could become an honoured mistress of a brāhmaṇa. But the social position of the *gaṇikā*, like that of the *punarbhū*, was no doubt normally lower than that of a wedded wife, although in many cases they may have wielded considerably more influence on the husband.

As, however, already indicated above, India is a wide country and it is possible that social customs were not everywhere exactly the same. We cannot also forget that changes may have taken place as time passed by. Such differences due to time and place are sometimes noticeable in the works on law compiled in different parts of the country and in different ages. This has to be remembered specially when one thinks of the social position of women. The degree of freedom in their movements was probably different in different parts of the country and in different ages and also different with different classes of the people. The upper-class women enjoyed less freedom. Vātsyāyana's *Kāmasūtra* depicts the life or a *nāgaraka*'s wife as a round of duties in an atmosphere control and restraint,[15] while queen Kumāradevī, whose name is found on some coins along with that of her husband, may have exercised some power in the administration of the Gupta empire during the reign of Candragupta I, we have evidence even of queens reigning by their own right in Orissa and Kashmir. The Bhauma-Kara queen Tribhuvanamahādevī is said to have ruled Orissa during the minority of her son just as an ancient queen named Gosvāminī. King Śubhakara IV of the same family was followed on the throne by his queen Gaurī, then by his daughter Daṇḍīmahādevī (first quarter of the eleventh century) then by his other queen Vakulamahādevī and then by a queen of his elder brother.[16] In the history of Kashmir, the period of about half a century from 958 to 1003 AD was dominated by the outstanding personality of queen Diddā. She first exerted her influence on the administration of her husband Kṣemagupta (950-58 AD), then ruled the country as guardian of her son Abhimanyu (958-72 AD) and her grandsons Nandīgupta (972-73 AD), Tribhuvana (973-75 AD) and Bhīmagupta (975-81 AD) and finally ruled as the queen of Kashmir (981-1003).[17] The Gupta Princess Prabhāvatīgupta ruled the Vākāṭaka kingdom at least for about 13 years as "the mother of the Yuvarāja".[18] Rājyaśrī is known from Chinese sources to have administered the government in conjunction with her brother, king Harṣavardhana (606-47 AD).[19] Girls, at least of the noble families, were expected to master some of the 64 *kalā*s or arts and thus appear to have received a more or less education. Vātsyāyana says that women did not ordinarily get education in the "Śāstras, but that the daughters of kings and nobles as also the *gaṇikā*s had their intelligence trained and sharpened by the "sastras".[20] Manu (X.11), if not also Vātsyāyana (III. 1.32, etc.), probably refers to middle class families when he suggests that the "husband usually appointed the wife to receive and spend money, to keep daily accounts and to pay the servants' wages, and such duties not doubt required some amount of education. In some cases, they also received training in various art. Among poetesses and learned ladies belonging to the age and area in question, prominent mention should be made of Avantīsundarī (beginning of the tenth century AD) who was born in the Cāhamana kṣatriya family and whose views are thrice quoted by her brāhmaṇa husband Rājaśekhara in the latter's *Kāvayamīmāṁsā*. Rājaśekhara's Prākṛt drama entitled *Karpūramañjarī* is stated to have been first staged at her request while three of her Prākṛt stanzas are quoted by Hemacandra (1088-1172 AD) in his *Deśīnāmamālā* for illustrating the meanings of certain expressions.[21]

Bhavabhūti's *Mālatīmādhava* (eighth century AD) envisages a state of society in which a woman (Kāmandakī) could learn at the feet of the same teacher along with male students (Bhūrivasu and Devarāṭa) who later became high officers of state. Women could have *upanayana* according to Hārīta and Yama; but Manu (II.66-67) does not support practice of olden times. The *Bhāgavata* Purāṇa (I.4.25), often assigned to the ninth century AD disallows Vedic studies for the women, the śūdras and the degraded *dvija*s.

The theoretical nature of many of the injunction of the Smṛtis seems to be demonstrated by their approach to the questions relating to marriage. As regards the marriageable age of girls, their post-puberty marriage was general in earlier times, pre-puberty marriages also sometimes took place. The *Manusmṛti* is not in favour of post-puberty marriage of girls (IX.94), although it permits (IX.89) a person to keep his daughter unmarried up to any age in case a suitable bridegroom was not available. Later writers gradually offered stricter prescriptions in the matter. Several Gṛhyasūtras prescribe a nagnika bride (i.e. a girl at the pre-puberty stage) while most of them prescribe at the same time the rite called *caturthī-karman* (cohabitation on the fourth night after marriage).[22] This suggests some kind of a conflict between the customs as well as the fact that both pre-puberty and post-puberty marriages were prevalent in the society in different areas and age so Yājñavalkya is against post-puberty marriage, and about the close of the period of our survey, the marriage of a girl when she was between 8 and 10 years of age was gaining ground.[23] But this related more or less to the high class brāhmaṇas. Bāṇa's *Harsacarita* (ch. IV), written about the beginning of the seventh century AD mentions Rājyaśrī as a quite grown-up girl at the time of her marriage and also speaks of the consummation of the marriage in the first night. Before her marriage, Rājyaśrī *yauvanam aruroha*, i.e., became a *yuvatī* after her *bālā* stage. The father of Rājyaśrī is represented as saying to her mother, Devī, *taruṇibhūt vatsa rājyaśrīḥ; hṛdavan=andhakarayati me payodhar-onnatir=asyāḥ*, i.e., the princess was then *taruṇī* (the same as *yuvatī*) and her breasts were *unnata* (developed). According to medieval theory a girl was called *taruṇī* when she was between sixteen and thirty years of age,[24] though the idea was more or less theoretical so that the actual age of Rājyaśrī at the time her marriage cannot be determined with any amount of certainty.

Glimpses of the People's Life

Hiuen-tsang gives us an idea of the cities and houses of India in the seventh century AD even though the description may not be correct for the whole country. According to his, the quadrangular walls of the cities were broad and high but the thorough fares were narrow tortuous passages. Most of the city walls were built of bricks, while the walls of houses and enclosures were wattled bamboo or wood. The halls and terraces belvederes had wooden flat-roofed rooms and were coated with lime and covered with burnt and unburnt tiles. They were of extraordinary height. The houses thatched with coarse or common grass were of bricks or boards; their walls were ornamented with lime and the floor was cleansed with cow dung and strewn with flowers of the season.[25]

Vātsyāyana's *Kāmasūtra* gives a picture of the life of a Nāgaraka or city-bred wealthy man of fashion.[26] He lived in a *harmya* or *prāsāda* with a pleasure-garden attached to it. Various kinds of flowers and vegetables were grown in the garden under the care of the wife. The house contained a *samudra-gṛha* or summer house surrounded by water and also rooms having secret passages for water in the walls in order to take away heat. In inner apartment of the house was occupied by the ladies of the family, the Nāgaraka passing most of his time in the outer chambers. In Nāgaraka's room, there were two couches with sofa and white beds low in the middle and having rests forehead and feet at the two ends. At the head of the bed was the *kūrca-sthāna* for placing the image of the deity he worshipped. There was also a shelf for keeping articles of toilet such as sandal paste, flower garlands, sweet perfumes, sking of the citron fruit for perfuming the mouth and betel-leaf preparation with spices. On the floor was a spittoon and on brackets on the wall a vina which the Nāgaraka played, and a casket containing a poetical work, requisites for painting flowers, etc. On the floor was spread a carpet on which there were cushions as well as boards for playing chess and dice. Outside the room were hung birds for game and sport. There was a room where the Nāgaraka amused himself by working at the lathe or the chisel. Some works speak of a *nidrā-kalaśa* in the bed chamber,[27] about which much is not known.

The Nāgaraka got up early in the morning, attended to his morning duties including cleansing his mouth and teeth and then proceeded to his toilet. He rubbed a moderate quantity of sandal-wood or other sweet-smelling paste on his person, scented his clothes with the smoke of incense and wore a garland on his head of neck. He applied collyrium to his eyes and a red dye to his lips which were then rubbed over with wax. Then he chewed betel, attended his hair and went to his business. He wore rings on his fingers and other ornaments and generally two garments, a *vāsas* or *vastra* and an *uttarīya* which was properly scented. After attending to his morning business, the Nāgaraka took his bath. Occasionally he got his limbs massaged and also cleaned with a soap-like substance called *phenaka*. He shaved his beard every fourth day and dressed his nails specially, particularly those of the left hand. He often carried a *karpaṭa* or napkin for removing perspiration. He took meals, one in the forenoon and the other in the afternoon. Among his articles of diet there were rice, wheat, barley, pulses, a large number of vegetables, milk and its preparations like ghee, meat, sweets including molasses, sugar and sweetmeats, salt and oil. Meat boiled as soup as well as dry or roasted was taken. Fish was not taken in the area where the *Kāmasūtra* was composed and even meat was not favoured by all. The Nāgarakas included, besides water and milk, fresh juice or fruits, extracts of meat, rice-gruel, sherbats and stronger drinks like *surā, madhu, maireya* and *āsava* which were taken from a vessel of wood or metal and were often mixed with sweets and savouries in order to impart a relish.

As regards to food of the Indians, Hiuen-tsang says,

> Milk, ghee, granulated sugar, sugar-candy, cakes and parched grain with mustard-seed oil are the common food, and fish, mutton and venision are occasional dainties. The flesh of oxen, asses, elephants, horses, pigs, dogs, foxes, wolves, lions, monkeys, apes is forbidden and those who eat such food become Pariahs. "Onions and garlic are little used and people who eat them are ostracised."[28] About wines and other beverages, the Chinese traveler says that the kṣatriyas drink wines made by fermenting grapes and sugarcane, the vaiśyas a strong distilled spirit and the brāhmaṇas and Buddhist monks' juice or grapes and sugar cane, while the low mixed castes had no distinguishing drink.[29]

After midday meal, Vātsyāyana's Nāgaraka enjoyed his siesta and viewed fights between cocks, quails or rams or was engaged in some artistic amusement. He kept cuckoos, peacocks, and monkeys for this purpose, though at the king's palace, there were also lions and tigers in cages. In the afternoon, the Nāgaraka attended the gosthi or special gathering where he engaged himself in intellectual diversions with his friends and in tests of skill in arts. At night he enjoyed, in his own room, vocal and instrumental music often accompanied by dance.

The above picture of the life of a wealthy and cultured citizen is no doubt artificial to a considerable extent; but it certainly gives us a general idea which may be regarded as more or less true for the whole of our period. Vātsyāyana also refers to several kinds of occasional festivities. There was gathering on the occasion of festivals connected with the worship of different deities (*samāja*, *yātrā*, and *ghaṭa*) often attended with processions. There were *goṣṭhī*s or social gatherings of both sexes, *samapanaka*s or drinking parties and *udyāna-vihāra* or garden parties including picnic and water sports. In such gatherings, often many persons took part in *samasyā-krīḍā* or solution of puzzles, viz. *kāvya-samasyā* (literary puzzles) and *kāla-samasyā* (puzzles relating to various arts). The *kāvya-samasyā* included literary arts such as extempore composition of verses, completion of a stanza of which only a part was given, expounding passages written in a secret code and the like, while *kāla-samasyā* offered the Nāgarakas opportunity to show their skill in painting, singing, instrumental music, etc., and also in such practical arts as the making of garlands, etc. *Samāja*s were occasionally held in honour of deities like the Goddess Sarasvatī and were accompanied by the performances of musicians, dancers and other artistes (e.g., wrestlers) who were often permanently appointed for periodical performance. Sometimes, itinerant parties of artistes were also employed to show their skill in the samajas. Masude says that the Indians often hear, says and musical performances and have various kinds of instruments which produce on men all shades of impressions between laughīng and crying.[30]

The cultured people of the Gupta age, when the *Kāmasūtra* of Vātsyāyana seems to have been recast, appear to have spoken a language that was a mixture of Sanskrit and Prākṛt. *Goṣṭhī* was also held by women in the *antaḥpura* and sometimes by persons with a view to doing mischief to others. The *gaṇikā*s or courtesans often played an important part in *goṣṭhī*s which were mostly held in their homes or in gambling houses. The *sambhūya-krīḍā* or sports in which many people took part was organised on the occasion of festivals like the Yakṣarātri (Dvipānvitā), Kaumidījāgara (modern Kojagari), Holākā (modern Holī), Navapatrikā (probably associated with Durgā's worship), Madanotsava (vernal festival), Suvasantaka (Madana Trayodaṣī), Alola-caturthī (Hindol held in Śrāvaṇa) and various other festivals like Sahakārabhañjikā, Abhyusakhadikā, Viśākhadikā, Udakakasvadikā, Pañcālanuyana, Ekaśālmali, Yavacaturthī, Madanabhañjikā, Aśokottaṁśikā, Puṣpavācayikā, Ikṣubhanhikā and Kadambayuddha. Vātsyāyana also mentions Hallisikā which was similar to the Rāsa-Krīḍā described in the *Bhāgavata Purāṇa*.[31] Besides the lute, *ḍamaru*, *mṛdaṅga*, *udaka-vādya* (playing on cups filled with water in varying proportions), concert, etc. were popular. Dramatically performances by trained men and women were also extremely popular.

According to Vātsyāyana, playing with dolls and games of chance with dice and cards, games like odd-and-even, close-fist, hide and seek, blindman's buff, etc., were popular among girls. Wrestling and hunting were popular with a section of the males. Games with balls were popular with children and women. Gambling in public with dice, which was well known, required authorisation from the king.[32] The master of the gambling hour arranged for *dyūta*, i.e., gambling with dice, small slices of leather, little staves of ivory, etc. and for *samaḥvāya* or betting on birds employed in fighting, and paid the stakes which were won. Manu[33] regarded gambling as open theft and advised the king to suppress it; but Yājñavalkya[34] and others allowed it under state supervision. The Mitākṣarā[35] says that such games included chess and races of elephants, horses, chariots, etc. and that the birds were cocks, pigeons and others although wrestlers, rams, buffaloes, etc., were also engaged in similar fighting. Bṛhaspati adds deer to the list of animals and says that gambling was prohibited by Manu, but was permitted by other legislators in order to allow the king a share of the stakes, and that, in a prize fight between two animals, the amount at stake had to be paid by the owner of the defeated animal. The keeper of the gaming house, according to the same authority received the stakes and paid the shares of the victorious gambler and the king.[36] The profit of a conductor of games amounted to 10 per cent according to Nārada.[37] No gambler was allowed to enter into another gambling house before payment of his stake to the master of the gaming house. Gamblers could also play elsewhere in public; but they had to pay to the king the share due to him.

As regards eating of meat and drinking of wine, the attitude of the society seems to have been gradually stiffening. Sulayman says that the people of Hind do not drink wine or vinegar which they include in the category liquors.[38] This, however, may not be quite correct.

Water clocks were used by wealthy persons, government offices and religious establishments to ascertain time. A bowl with a small hole at the bottom was kept floating in a larger vessel filled with water so that it was filled by water coming into it through the hole in 24 minutes. Attendants were necessary to empty the bowl out and float it again the moment it was filled and drowned and to indicate the time by striking a gong.

The Nāgaraka's dress, referred to above on the authority of Vātsyāyana's *Kāmasūtra* was in general use among gentlemen in northern India; but the kings often used coats and trousers introduced by foreigners. The Gupta emperors, as known from their coins, used both the traditional as well as the foreign dress. The Arab writer Istakhri speaks of the 'trousers and tunic that were worn by the kings of Hind'.[39] Turbans and shoes (rarely worn, according to Hiuen-tsang) were also often used.[40] In the north-western part of the country, the people adopted the dress introduced by foreign settlers. With reference to the cold regions of north India, Hiuen-tsang says, "closely fitting jackets are worn somewhat like those of the Tartars;" although generally speaking,

> "The inner clothing and outward attire of the people have no tailoring as to colour, a fresh white is esteemed and motely is of no account. The men wind a strip of cloth round the waist and up to the arm-pits and leave the right shoulder bare. The women wear a long robe which covers both shoulders and falls down loose."[41]

This also seems to refer to the north-western districts of India. Al-Biruni says,

> "They use turbans for trousers. Those who want little dress content to dress in a rag of two fingers" breadth, which they bind over their loins with two cords; but those who like much dress, wear trousers kind with so much cotton as would suffice to make a number of counterpanes and saddle rugs. These trousers have no (visible) openings, and they are so huge that the feet are not visible. The string by which the trousers are fastened is at the back. Their *sidar* (a piece of dress covering the head and the upper part of breast and neck) is similar to the trousers, being also fastened to the back by buttons. The lappets of the *kurtaka*s (short shirts for females from the shoulders to the middle of the body with sleeves) have slashes both on the right and left sides."[42]

The dress of women were not exactly the same in different parts of the country. In some areas and amongst certain classes, petticoat and *sāṛī* were used, although the *sāṛī* alone was popular elsewhere. The use of bodice under the *sāṛī* in order to cover the bust was known and becoming gradually popular; but the practice of keeping the bust uncovered was widely prevalent in earlier times. Foreigners introduced the use of jackets, blouses and frocks which were acquiring popularity gradually, although some sections, e.g., the dancing girls, appear to have adopted them quite early. Cotton garments were generally used; but silk was popular with the ladies of the fashionable and wealthy classes.[43]

Women dressed their hair in a large number of graceful fashions. The use of false hair to increase the volume of the braid was well known. Regarding the people of both sexes, Hiuen-tsang says,

> "The hair on the crown of the head is made into a coil, all the rest of the hair hanging down. Some

> men clip their moustaches or have other fantastic fashions. Garlands are worn on the head and necklaces on the body."[44]

Sulayman also speaks of the India's beard and moustaches, the former sometimes as long as three cubits.[45] Both men and women were fond of wearing various sorts of ornaments. Rings, bangles, armlets, anklets, girdles, necklaces and earrings were the most popular ornaments, all of which had a great variety of designs. Necklaces with a number of strings covering parts of the bust were often used by the rich. A similar ornament was occasionally used to adorn the thighs. The nose-ring was not in use. It was introduced by the Muslims during the medieval period. Precious stones of various colours were embedded in the golden ornaments worn by rich people. The poorer section of the population remained satisfied with ornaments made of cheap metals such as silver, brass or lead. According to Hiuen-tsang,

> "The dress and ornaments of the kings and grandees are very extraordinary. Garlands and tiaras with precious stones are their head-adornments and their bodies are adorned with rings, bracelets and necklaces. Wealthy mercantile people have only bracelets."[46]

Education and General Characteristics

The kings and the high officials as well as the cultured and wealthy citizens usually patronised literary men.[47] The styles of Sanskrit poetical composition, known as Vaidarbhī and Gauḍī must have developed under the patronage of the rulers of Berar and West Bengal some time before the seventh century. Pāṭaliputra and Ujjayinī were great centers of learning in the Gupta age.[48] Kanauj and Valabhī became famous at a later date.[49] Some holy places like Varanasi were also regarded as centres of learning. The celebrated Arab astronomer Abu Ma'shar of Balkh who died in 885 AD is said to have studied for ten years at Varanasi.[50] Buddhist monasteries like the *vihāras* of Nālandā in the Patna district and Vikramaśilā (popularly called Vikramashila) near Colgong in the Bhagalpur district, both in Bihar, were also famous centres of education and attracted students from distant countries like China.[51] Private teachers who trained students in exchange for a small honorarium lived in cities and towns as well as villages. Learned brāhmaṇas received gifts for their maintenance from the kings and wealthy persons. The brāhmaṇas of some localities, such as those of Tarkari in Śrāvastī, appear to have been famous for their learning throughout the country. As we have seen above, Hiuen-tsang says that in India there is honour in having wisdom and no disgrace in being destitute but learned. About teaching, the pilgrim says,

> "These teachers explain the general meaning to their disciples and teach them the minutes; they rouse them to activity and skilfully with them to progress; they instruct the inert and sharpen the dull. When the disciples, intelligent and acute, are addicted to idle shirking, the teachers doggedly persevere repeating instruction until their training in finished. When the disciples are thirty years old, their minds being settled and their education finished, they go into office and the first thing they do then is to reward the kindness of their teachers."[52]

Of all subjects of higher education, the study of scriptures was the most popular, and most of the highly educated persons were brāhmaṇas. The study of logic and philosophy was also esteemed. The advice of persons proficient in the sacred lore was sought by the people on ceremonial occasions. But all students of Sanskrit learnt grammar which was considered the "gate" of Sanskrit learning. The Buddhists and Jainas, who originally preferred to write respectively in Pāli and Apabhraṁśa, now wrote in Sanskrit. Among the sciences that were studied, the most popular appear to have been that of medicine and astrology with astronomy. The number of professional astrologers, astronomers and physicians in all parts of the country must have been high. The *Aṣṭāṅgahṛdaya* of Vāgbhaṭa (sixth-seventh century) and the *Rāgviniścaya* of Mādhavakara (eighth-ninth century) were composed during the period under review. The study of political science was popular with the nobility. A notable contribution to this branch of study was Kāmandaka's *Nītisāra*. For the primary education of ordinary people there must have been a large number of smaller educational institutions, not probably always under a teacher of the brāhmaṇa community, throughout the country. The Kāyasthas or clerks, who were employed by the rulers and merchants, learnt how to keep accounts and to draw up documents apparently in such primary schools. People of different communities including the brāhmaṇas and Karaṇas adopted the profession of the scribe, though about the close of our period, the Kāyasthas were being organised as a caste. Teachers or primary schools, sometimes called *lipiśālā*, were usually known as *dārakācārya*. The alphabets were learnt by writing them by fingers on the ground covered by sand or fine dust. Children of rich men often used to write on wooden boards with some kind of coloured pencil. As already pointed out above Vātsyāyana's *Kāmasūtra* suggest a fairly high standard of general education at least amongst the wealthy men and women of the city. Wealthy and cultured families often employed special tutors for the education of boys as well as girls.[53]

Since most of the professions had become hereditary, technical education was usually imparted in the family. Sometimes, however, young students attached themselves as apprentices to master artisans for an agreed sum of money and an agreed number of years. According to Nārada,[54] apprentices, after learning particular arts and crafts, had to work gratis for some years for the master.

The life of the people, at least of the upper classes, was dominated by ceremonies, important and un-important; but the ideal of moral standard was high. It was believed that, unlike the contemporary Iron Age (Kali Yuga) which was regarded as full of sin, there had been a Golden Age (Kṛta or Satya Yuga) in olden times when there was no sin on earth, and the kings are often described as making particular efforts to restore the moral standard or the Golden Age. The Smṛti writers such as Yājñavalkya[55] prescribed the following virtues to be observed by all classes of the people: non-injury to living beings, truthfulness, non-stealing, purity, restraint of senses, charity, self-control, kindness and forgiveness. Unfortunately, this was actually an ideal and it was admitted that the percentages of sin and virtue among the people of the Iron Age were respectively 75 per cent and 25 per cent. It should, however, be admitted that the people were conscious of the ideals. Kings are often found to have granted lands to brāhmaṇa householders to help them in performing the five daily *mahāyajñas*[56] which were:

(1) lecturing on sacred knowledge,
(2) presenting libations of water to the deceased ancestors,
(3) offering oblations to gods by throwing clarified butter into the consecrated fire,
(4) offering a portion of the daily meal to all creatures, and
(5) reception of guest.[57]

But the standard of sexual morality does not appear to have been high at least in the earlier part of the period under survey. The character of Indians is generally praised by the foreigners. According to Hiuen-tsang,

> "They (the Indians) are of hasty and irresolute temperaments, but of pure moral principles. They will not take anything wrongfully, and they yield more than fairness requires. They fear the retribution for sins in other lives and make light of what conduct produces in this life. They do not practice deceit and they keep their sworn obligations."[58]

Idrisi says that

> "The Indians are naturally inclined to justice, and

> never depart from it in their actions. Their well faith, honesty, and fidelity to their engagements are well known, and they are so renowned for these qualities that people flock to their country from every side. Hence, the country is flourishing and the condition of the people is prosperous. Among other typical instances of their love of truth and horror of vice, the following is related: when a man has a right to demand anything of another, and he happens to meet him, he has only to draw a circular line upon the ground, and make his debtor enter it, which the latter without satisfying his creditor or obtaining the remission of the debt."[59]

Pilgrimage to holy places such as Prayāga, Gaṅgāsāgara-saṅgama, Varāhakṣetra (on the Kauśikī in Nepal), Gayā, Varanasi, Prabhāsa (in Kathiawar, Gujarat), Puṣkara (near Ajmer), Kedāra (in the Himalayas) and other became popular.[60] Sometimes persons (usually those suffering from incurable diseases or from extreme old age) voluntarily immolated themselves in the holy waters of a tirtha.[61] *Śrāddha* of the departed ancestors was considered more affective if it was performed at a holy place, particularly at Gayā.[62] Gifts were regarded as more meritorious if made on auspicious occasions such as the solar or lunar eclipse, vernal or autumnal equinox, and the sun's entry into a zodiac.[63] The conception of the auspiciousness of particular days for the performance of ceremonies gradually gained great popularity. The importance of auspicious moments in marriage was in favour as early as the days of the Gṛhyasūtras; but its growing popularity in later times is testified by Vātsyāyana and Varāhamihira. Vātsyāyana favoured marriage when signs, portents and *upaśruti*s (supernatural ocular voices heard as a result of mystic invocations of gods or miraculous utterances heard especially at night) were favourable.[64] Varāhamihira gives details of a developed Śakunaśāstra or "the science of omens" compiled from the work of King Dravyavardhana of Avantī.[65] Signs observed at the time of *varaṇa* or the selection of the bride were considered important for the selection or rejection of a girl. Yājñavalkya speaks for the first time of *graha-śānti* and Gaṇapati-Pūjā for *karma-vighna-siddhi*.[66] Some of the *vratas*, such as the Ekādaśī-Vrata, seem to have become popular with the upper classes of the people.[67] Such popular ceremonies, which are mostly of non-Aryan origin and were gradually adopted by the upper classes of the society, were coming to be dominant factor in the socio-religious life of the people. Some of the early festivals referred to by Vātsyāyana have been mentioned before. The autumnal worship of Durgā, which was originally a non-Aryan cult and is mentioned by Hiuen-tsang, Al-Biruni and Sandhyākaranandin, was becoming popular with the upper classes of the society.[68]

Grants of land were made by kings in favour of gods and brāhmaṇas for the sake of merit.[69] Granting lands and protecting the gifts made by former rulers were regarded as equally or even more meritorious.[70] Confiscation of the gift lands by a later ruler of the country was regarded as especially unworthy of king.[71] Chapters of the post-Gupta period often make mention that a king made a particular grant on realizing the transitoriness of life and prosperity.[72]

Notes

1. The Nāgara-Khaṇḍa section of the *Skanda Purāṇa*, which was apparently composed in the Gujarat region during the late medieval period, gives a list of ten forms of marriage by adding *pratibhā* and *ghaṭanā* (said to have been prevalent among the pure śūdras) to the above eight. See chap. 241, verses 33 ff. also Sircar, "The ten forms of marriage", in *Ind.Mus. Bul.*, vol. V, 1970, pp. 7-8. Kings generally had more wives than one and the nobility and rich men emulated them.
2. The *kali-varjya* idea began to develop before the ninth century when Medhātithi (on *Manu*, X.112; cf. I.85) refers to authorities regarding *niyoga* (allowing a widow to get a son preferably from her husband's brother; *Manu*, IX.59) etc., (cf. *Ap. Dharm. Sut*, II.6.14. 6-10; 10.27. 2-6) as *kali-varjya*. By the beginning of the

twelfth century, it was fairly well established at least in some parts of the country since Aparārka (*c*.1115-30 AD) speaks of *niyoga*, the secondary sons, the marriage of widows and several other practices as *kali-varjya* on the authority of Bṛhaspati, Śaunaka, the *Brahma Purāṇa*, etc. Vijñāneśvara's *Mitāksarā* (about the end of the eleventh century), also regards *niyoga* as a *kali-varjva*. See Kane, *Hist. Dharm*, vol. III, pp. 926-30.

3. He is assigned roughly to the sixth century AD.
4. Cf. *Yāj*, I. 88.
5. *Ep. Ind.*, vol. XV, pp. 301 ff.
6. Brāhma-kṣatriya was one who claimed the blood of both the brāhmaṇa and the kṣatriya in his veins. See Sircar, *The Guhilas of Kiskindha*, pp. 6 ff.
7. For various other cases of ancient Indian marriage without *gotrāntara* and therefore without *sampradāna*. see Sircar, in *Proc. IHC Amamalaināgar*, 1945, pp. 48-52; also, *Stud. Soc. Adm. Anc. Med. Ind.*, vol. I, pp. 204 ff. In our previous writings referred to above, we have cited a mass of epigraphic and literary evidence. Recently, T.R. Trautman has said, "If Indo-Aryan society, ancient or contemporary, were so exclusively patrilineal as is sometimes made out, there would be no reason to pay any attention to a mother's natal lineage when choosing a bride, or ascertaining the status of her children. A man could then marry a woman any variety whatever, and her status would be wholly determined by his, erasing any antecedent status she may have possessed. But the historian must not be misled by the categorical idiom of the law books and the ritual of marriage, for the legal and ritual affiliation of women taken as a whole is, as we have seen, ambiguous. Furthermore, this ambiguity is not accidental, and overlooked contradiction in an otherwise logical system, but rather is inherent in the system itself. It is not in spite of the strong patrilineal emphasis, but as a direct result of it that the wife never fully relinquishes her affiliation to her patrilineage even though she has been initiated by marriage into her husbands, and that the mother's patrilineage constitutes the complement of the father's in descent." See *JRAS*, 1972, p. 15. The above is followed by the conclusion: "We could perhaps rationalise this state of affairs by saying that the wife's *gotra* and lineage is that of her husband while the daughter's and mother's *gotra* and lineage is that of her father. That is to say, the *gotra* and lineage affiliation of a woman is perceived to have depended upon the role which she plays within the legal context in which she is viewed" (*loc.*

cit.). We are sorry to feel that all this is entirely imaginary and against the fairly clear evidence on the subject offered by our epigraphic and literary records thoroughly discussed by us in our writings cited above. Thus, while one of the Andhan inscriptions mentions Jasodatta of the Sainika *gotra* not only as the daughter of Siṁhadatta but also as the wife of Madana of the Aupasati *gotra*, the *Garuḍa Purāṇa* (II.26. 21-22) categorically states: *brahmādiṣu vivahesu va vadhur= iha saṁskṛta| bhartṛ-gotreṇa partatyas= tasyaḥ piṇḍodaka-kriyāḥ|| asur-adivitahesuya vyudha kāmyaka bhavet | tasyas= ṭupitr-gotreṇa kuryāt piṇḍodaka-kriyām||* We find it difficult to accept a twentieth-century guess in reference to early or medieval evidence.

8. *JAIH*, vol. I. p. 87 ff.
9. Cf *Nāraaa*, XII.45-48, 97, 101; *Parāśara*, IV.27 ff.
10. *Yājñavalkya* (I.67) regards *punarbhū* (both *kṣata-yoni* and *akṣata-yoni* as a remarried wife and *svairiṇī* as an unmarried concubine.
11. See Sircar, *Ancient Malwa, and the Vikramaditya Tradition*, pp. 136 ff.
12. *JAIH*, vol. VI, pp. 179-80.
13. Watters, *op. cit.*, vol. I, 168.
14. Sircar, *Sel.Ins.*, *op. cit.*, pp. 345-46.
15. See III.1; also Chakladar, *op. cit.*, pp. 353 ff. also P. Peterson to *Journ.Anth. Soc. Bomb.*, 1892, pp. 459 ff.
16. Sircar, *Stud. Soc. Adm. Anc. Med. Ind.*, I, pp. 238 ff.
17. *Ibid.*, pp. 243 ff.
18. *Sel. Ins., op. cit.*, pp. 435 ff.
19. *Stud. Soc. Adm. Anc. Med. Ind.*, p. 231.
20. See I.3.12. For the 64 arts enumerated by Vātsyāyana, including *pustaka-vacana* (recitation or reading of books) and *Kāvy-samasyā-purāṇa* cf. I.3.16.
21. Cf. *Stud. Soc. Adm. Anc. Med. Ind.*, pp. 264 ff., for this and some other cases.
22. Kane, *op. cit.*; vol. III, pp. 440 ff.
23. *Ibid*, p. 445; *Śabdakalpdruma* s.v. *kanyakā aṣṭavarṣa bhaved = gaurī navavarṣatu rohiṇī daśame kanyakā proktā ata ūrdhvam rajasvalā.*
24. Attention may be drawn to a girls age of maturity. According to the *Kauṭilīya Arthaśāstra* (III.3), *dvādaśa-varṣa strī-prāpta-vyavahāra bhavaresodar-varṣaḥ pumān*, "a boy attains maturity at 16 and a girl at 12". The later specification must be regarded as dubious in regard to the girl; Cf. *aṣoḍaśad= bhaved=bālā taruṇī triṁśata mata pañcapañcaśatah prauḍha vṛddha bhavati*

tat-param|| See also a *ṣoḍaśad=bhaved=bālās taruṇas=tata ucyate*| *vṛddhan syāt sapter=ūrdhvam varṣiyānnavateḥ param*|| See *Śabdakalpadruma* s.v. *yavati, yuvati*; also, *yava*.

25. Watters, *op. cit.*, vol. I, p. 147. The Chinese traveller says, "For seats all use corded benches. The royal family, the grandees, officials and gentry adorn their benches in different ways; but all have the same style of seat. The sovereign's dais is exceedingly wide and high, and it is dotted with small pearls. What is called the lion's seat is covered with fine cloth, and is mounted by a jewelled footstool. The ordinary officials, according to their fancy, carve the frames of their seats in different ways, and adorn them with precious substances".
26. I.41-53; of Chakaldar, *op. cit.*, pp. 384 ff.
27. It is mentioned in the *Harṣacarita* and the Purāṇa.
28. Watters, *op. cit.*, p. 178. Idrisi says that the people of Antilwāṛā in Gujarat lived upon rice, peas, beans, haricots, lentils, mash, fish and animals, that die a natural death for they do not kill winged or other animals. Abu Zayd says that some Indians do not eat out of the same dish or upon guests they must have eat a separate dish. See Nainar, *op. cit.*, p. 100.
29. Watters, *loc. cit.*
30. Nainar, *op. cit.*, p. 102. For girls singing and dancing at the temples, see the *Rājataraṅgiṇī* account of Jayapedas stay at Puṇḍravardhana.
31. *Kāmasūtra*, VI.10.25; *Bhāgavata Purāṇa*, X.29.
32. For gambling, see Kane, *Hist. Dharm.*, vol. III, pp. 538 ff.
33. IX.221-22, 224-26.
34. II.203; cf. II.199 ff.
35. See his introduction to Yājñavalkya's *dyūta-samaḥ-vayaprakaraṇa* (II.199 ff).
36. See *SBE*, vol. XXXIII, pp. 385-86 (cf. verses 1.4,6, etc.).
37. XIX.2.
38. Nainar, *op. cit.*, pp. 100-10.
39. Elliot and Dowson, *op. cit.*, vol. I, p.1000.
40. Watters, *op. cit.*, p. 150: "Most of the people go barefoot and shoes are rare".
41. *Ibid.*, p. 148. The professional tailor called *tunnavaya* is mentioned in early works like the *Manusmṛti*, IV.412.
42. Sachau, *op. cit.*, vol. I, p. 180. The word *kurtaka* is not found in Sanskrit; but Pāli *kuttaka* means "a woollen carpet", and *kurtaka* seems to be used in this sense in a south Indian epigraph of the fourth century AD (*Ep. Ind.*, vol. XXXII, p. 88). The word *kurtā*,

now used in Hindi and other languages in the sense of "a shirt, etc.", is supposed to be of Turkish origin, borrowed from the Muslims.

43. For interesting details, see Moti Chandra, *Costumes and Coiffure*, 1973.
44. Watters, *op. cit.*, p. 148.
45. Nainar, *op. cit.*, p. 97.
46. Watters, *op. cit.*, p. 151. The various kinds of ornaments are illustrated by the images of gods, goddesses and others.
47. Indeed, most of the celebrated authors are known to have enjoyed and patronage of royal courts.
48. The astronomer Āryabhaṭa who was born in 476 AD and wrote his *Āryabhaṭīya* in 449 AD, belonged to Kusumapura (Pāṭaliputra) and was probably attached to the imperial court of the Guptas. The immortal Kālidāsa (fourth-fifth century author of such master pieces of classical Sanskrit literature such as the *Kumārasambhava*, *Raghuvaṁśa*, and *Abhijñānaśākuntalam* is traditionally associated with the Gupta Vikramāditya. The Prākṛt grammarian Vararuci and a number of other worthies are also similarly associated. The age of the Guptas was characterised by great activity in all the spheres of literature and the sciences. The Buddhist philosophers Asaṅga, Vāsubandhu and Diṅnāga, the lexiographer Amara and the grammarian Candragomin flourished in the same age. The great Varāhamihira, who belonged to a family of Māga brāhmaṇas (i.e., Persian Magi priests settled and naturalised in India) and probably to the Ujjain school of astronomy, wrote a number of works on astronomy and astrology in the sixth century. Another great astronomer and mathematician of the post-Gupta period was Brahmagupta (born 628 AD) of Bhillamala (Bīnmāl in the old Jodhpur State).
49. The celebrated Bāṇa, author of the *Harṣacarita* and *Kādambarī*, as well as Mayūra and others enjoyed the patronage of the Kanauj court under Harṣavardhana (606-47 AD). The great dramatist Bhavabhūti, author of the *Uttaracarita*, *Vīracarita* and *Mālatīmādhava*, flourished at the court of King Yaśovarman (*c.*725-53 AD) of Kanauj. His dramas were staged on the occasion of the annual festival of the God Kālapriyanātha at modern Kalpi in the Jalaun district of U.P. Vākpatirāja, author of the Prākṛt poem *Gauḍavaha* was another protege of Yaśovarman. Rājaśekhara wrote numerous works about the end of the ninth and the first part of the tenth century AD at the courts of the Kanauj king Mahendrapāla I and his son Mahipāla I of the

Gurjara-Pratihāra dynasty, as well as at that of King Yuvarāja I of Dahala ruling from Tripurī near Jabalpur. The poet-grammarian Bhartṛhari (sixth-seventh century) flourished at the court of the Maitrakas of Valabhī. The kings of Kashmir are known to have patronised scholars. In the eighth century, Udbhaṭa, the chief *paṇḍit* at the court of King Jayāpīḍa of Kashmir, is said to have enjoyed a daily pay of one lakh *dīnāra*s (i.e. cowries, or the value of that sum in Kharis of grain, corresponding to 28.1/2 rupees in steins' calculation). The famous Kashmirian critic Ānandavardhana, author of the *Dhvanyāloka*, appears to have enjoyed the patronage of Avantivarman (*c.*856-83 AD).

50. See Ray, *DHNI*, vol. I, pp. 23-24.
51. The Nālandā monastery was founded in the age of the imperial Guptas while the Vikramaśilā *vihāra* was established in the eighth or ninth century by either of the Pāla kings Dharmapāla and Devapāla. The Chinese pilgrim Hiuen-tsang received part of his religious education at Nālandā under the guidance of the great Buddhist teacher Śilābhadra. According to I-tsing, who learnt for some time at the Varāhamihira at Tāmralipti in the last quarter of the seventh century AD, Chinese students learnt Sanskrit with the help of the grammatical work, *Kāśikāvṛtti*, by Jayāditya and Vāmana (sixth-seventh century). Buddhist scholars attached to the monasteries of Bihar are known to have laid the foundation of Buddhism in Tibet. In the eighth century, Padmasambhava and Śāntarakṣita established the first regular Buddhist monastery of Bsam-ye in Tibet on the model of the Odantapurīvihāra in Magadha (probably at Bihar Sharif in the Patna district, Bihar). *Maṭha*s or colleges were attached to the important Brāhmanical temples in different parts of India.
52. Watters, *op. cit.*, p. 160.
53. For details of education, see A.S. Altekar, *Education in Ancient India*.
54. V.16-21.
55. I.122; cf. *Viṣṇu*, II.7-8.
56. See, e.g., Sircar, *Sel. Ind.*, vol. I, 1965, p. 293, text line 6.
57. See *Manu*, III.69.
58. Watters, *op. cit.*, p. 171. This is a general estimate. Sometimes he criticizes the character of the people of the particular areas. The people of the north-west from Laghman to Rajauri, as compared to Indians proper, are described as "coarse and plain in personal appearance, or rude violent dispositions, with vulgar dialects and of scant courtesy and little fairness; they do not belong to India

proper, but are inferior peoples of the frontier stocks." (*Ibid.*, p. 284. See also Sircar, *Problems of Kuṣāṇa and Rājpūt History*, pp. 27-28.

59. See Nainar, *op. cit.*, p. 97. For the prevalence of the customs in the Malabar coast. See *Ind. An.*, vol. VIII, p. 267.
60. Sircar, *Stud.Geog. Anc. Med. Ind.* 1971, pp. 219 ff., 275, 282 ff.
61. Sircar, *Stud. Rel. L. Anc. Med. Ind.,* pp. 206 ff.
62. *Ep. Ind.*, vol. XXXIII, p. 103.
63. Cf. Sircar, *Ind. Ep.,* p. 145.
64. Cf. *Kāmasūtra*, I.7 and 9.
65. *Bṛhatsaṁhitā*, chapters LXXX-XCVI.
66. I.271 ff., 295 ff.
67. For the numerous *vrata*s, see Kane, *Hist. Dharm.*, vol. V, pp. 1 ff.
68. See Sircar, *The Sakta Pithas*, 1973, p. 132, *Stud. Rel. L. Anc. Med. Ind.*, p. 230; cf. *Sachau, op. cit.*, vol. II, pp. 179-80 (pp. 182-83 possibly speak of Gauri worship on the 3rd of Mārgaśīrṣa and Māgha).
69. See Sircar *Ind. Ep.*, p.103.
70. See, e.g., *Ibid.,* p. 180, verse 23; p. 196, verse 131.
71. See e.g., *Ibid.*, p. 192, verse 113.
72. Cf. *Ibid.*, p. 142.

11

Vaiṣṇavism

A Fresh Look

R.N. Dandekar

Friends!

My first word this evening is one of gratitude to the authorities of the Atombapu Research Centre for having given me this opportunity to pay my tribute of piety and reverence to the adoringly cherished memory of Panditaraja Atombapu Sharma. It was nearly twenty years ago, while I was working as the Member-Secretary of the Sanskrit Commission appointed by Government of India, that I first came to know of the signal services rendered by the Panditaraja to the cause of Sanskrit and ancient Indian culture. In our report to government, we have made a special reference to those services. It is, indeed, highly gratifying to know that this Research Centre founded to commemorate the name of Panditaraja Atombapu has pledged itself to carry further his magnificent work. I wish it all success in its endeavours.

The subject which I have chosen for my Panditaraja Atombapu Memorial Lectures is "Vaiṣṇavism and Śaivism: A Fresh Look". However, in view of the limited time at my disposal, I shall restrict myself only to the consideration of the beginnings and the early stages of the development of these two religious sects.

It will be easily conceded that whosoever wishes to speak on this subject has necessarily to take as his starting point Ramakrishna Gopal Bhandarkar's (RGB's) Vaiṣṇavism, Śaivism *and Minor Religious Systems* (*VSMRS*), which was included in the "Grundriss der indoarischen Philologie" and which was first published in 1913. This monumental work represents a significant landmark in the study of the religious history of India. No doubt, since early times, single chapters on Indian religions, particularly Vedic religion, have been included in the histories of religions in general, such as those by E. Veron (*Histoire naturelle des religions*, 1885), C. Von Orelli (*Allgemeine Religionsgeschichte*, 1899), S. Reinach (*Orpheus. Histoiregenerale des religions*, 1907), and A.S. Bishop (*The World's Altar Stairs: Introductory Studies in the Religions of the World*, 1910). But these chapters are inevitably more or less superficial in character. It was Friedrich Max Müller, who, in his pioneering works like *Lectures on the Origin and Growth of Religion as Illustrated by the Religions of India* (1878), *Natural Religion* (1888), *Physical Religion* (1891), *Anthropological Religion* (1892), and *Theosophy or Psychological Religion* (1892), for the first time, occupied himself with the subject of Indian religions in a big way. His avowed aim, however, was to develop a science of comparative religion and comparative mythology. Naturally, therefore, his treatment was restricted to the "Aryan' or the Vedic religion. Moreover, his approach cannot be said to have been that of a historian of religion; he was primarily interested in the content of religion. The same was the case with works like L. Von Schroeder's *Arische Religion* (1914-16).

The scope of H.H. Wilson's *Essays and Lectures on the Religion of the Hindus* (1861-62) was certainly wider, but still, they did not constitute a regular history of the religion of the Hindus. Besides, these *Essays* were patently vitiated by the perversity of the author's approach to the subject. He is said to have publicly expressed the view (at the University of Oxford in 1840) that one needed to study the Hindu religion in order to be able to prove its erroneousness and to persuade the Hindu intelligentsia to adopt the Christian faith. Nevertheless, Wilson's English translation of the *Viṣṇu Purāṇa* was a laudable attempt to make the authentic sacred writings of the Hindus easily accessible to the Western public. The first proper history of the religions of India—a work which deals with both history and doctrines—must be said to be *Les religions del'Inde* (1879) by A. Barth. An authorised English translation of this book by J. Wood was published in 1882. The French scholar no doubt felt that Hinduism showed visible signs of decadence, but he was not inclined to believe that it would ever surrender to Christianity. Monier-Williams too, in his *Religious Thought and Life in India* (1883), took strong exception to Hindu religious leaders being characterised as "benighted heathens'. Barth's work was followed by *The Religions of India* (1895) by E.W. Hopkins (who sought to study these religions with a view to understanding the manner in which religions and theistic ideas arose and developed among a people and the light which they shed on the origin and development of similar ideas elsewhere), *Indische Religions geschichte* (1898) by E. Hardy, and *Ancient India: Its Language and Religions* (1898) by H. Oldenberg.

It was but to be expected that in such works as those mentioned above, the treatment of the two major sects of Hinduism, namely, Vaiṣṇavism and Śaivism, would be sketchy and inadequate. RGB, for the first time, undertook to trace the history of these sects in a comprehensive manner on the basis of all available literary, epigraphical, sculptural, and numismatic evidence. In keeping with the views regarding research methodology which he consistently advocated,[1] his approach to and treatment of the subject were eminently objective, critical, and comparative.

Many scholars have, in recent years, followed in the trail so finely blazed by RGB. Most of them have made RGB's *VSMRS* the very starting point of their theses. Verily they could not have done otherwise. However, they have had the additional advantage of much fresh material—literary and archaeological—which has become available since the publication of RGB's pace-setting work as also of new points of view derived from a new study of the related social sciences. It would, therefore, be interesting and instructive to review, in the light of this new knowledge, some of the questions pertaining to Vaiṣṇavism and Śaivism, which have been tackled by the great savant.

RGB's survey of Vaiṣṇavism from about the fifth century before Christ to the middle of the seventeenth century after Christ may be broadly divided into three main parts. In the first part he explains how that religious sect originated and how it passed through various stages of development before it finally came to be consolidated in the form of what may be called classical Vaiṣṇavism.

> While this first part is historical in character, the emphasis in the second part is more on the doctrine.

In the eighth century AD, Śaṅkarācārya vigorously promulgated "the doctrine of spiritual monism and world-illusion'—a doctrine which was considered to be highly detrimental to the basic tenets of Vaiṣṇavism. It had to be confronted and refuted on a logical-metaphysical level and the religion of *bhakti* had to be rehabilitated on sound rational basis. This is exactly what Rāmānuja (eleventh century) strenuously endeavoured to do. The same mission was carried forward, in their own distinctive ways, by Nimbārka (twelfth century), Madhva (thirteenth century), and Vallabha (fifteenth century). The second part of RGB's survey deals with the thought and work of these *ācārya*s. An active sympathy for the lower classes and the use of vernaculars for the propagation of *bhakti* with special stress on its emotional side had become evident in the history of Vaiṣṇavism ever since the days of Rāmānuja. The compositions of the Āḷvārs of the south would confirm this. But these traits became more marked with Rāmānanda (born 1300 AD). They continued to be the hallmark of the teachings and activities of the later Vaiṣṇava saints like Kabīr (1398-1518) and Tulasīdāsa (1532-1623) in the north, Caitanya (1485-1533) in the east, and Nāmadeva (born 1270?) and Tukārāma (1607-49) in the Deccan. The discussion of these teachings and activities may be said to constitute the third part of RGB's survey of Vaiṣṇavism. Out of these three parts it is the first which is particularly important from the historical point of view, the other two parts being more or less of the nature of factual statement. The first part is also more controversial and calls for a critical reappraisal, in the light of the fresh evidence that has become available, of some of the points made in it.

About the origin and growth of Vaiṣṇavism, RGB has to say this.

> It (Vaiṣṇavism) first appeared as a religious reform, like Buddhism and Jainism, but based on theistic principles. Its early name was Ekāntika Dharma, or the religion of a single-minded love and devotion to One. In its background stood the *Bhagavadgītā*, a discourse professing to be preached by Vāsudeva-Kṛṣṇa. It soon assumed a sectarian form and was called the Pañcarātra or Bhāgavata religion. It was professed by a tribe of *kṣatriyas* of the name of Sātvata and was noticed by Megasthenes, about the end of the fourth century before Christ, as the religion of such a specific people. This faith mingled itself with the existing one in Nārāyaṇa... and with that in Viṣṇu. In the *Bhagavadgītā* itself were embodied some of the teachings of the Upaniṣads. ... Soon after the beginning of the Christian era another element was contributed to this system of religion by the Abhīras, or cowherds, who belonged to a foreign tribe, in the shape of the marvellous deeds of the boy-Kṛṣṇa, who came to be regarded as a god, and of his amorous dalliances with cowherdesses. So constituted, Vaiṣṇavism went on till about the end of the eighth century....[2]

When RGB says that Vaiṣṇavism first appeared as a religious reform, he seems to suggest that it was orthodox in origin and that it represented an extension of Vedic thought in a particular direction. According to him, the tide of free speculations initiated by the Upaniṣads culminated in the east into such systems as Buddhism and Jainism and in the west into a theistic system with a god who had come to dwell among them. The tendency to trace all religious ideologies—indeed, the entire Indian culture—back to the Veda, in some way or the other, which characterised early Indology, is evident here. It must, however, be remembered that when the Vedic Aryans arrived in India, they did not by any means step into a religious vacuum. There is sufficient evidence to show that different religious sects prevailed in different regions of the pre-Vedic non-Aryan India. It is possible to identify at least two such pre-Vedic non-Aryan cults. One may designate them as the *muni-yati*-cult and the *bhakti*-cult with a view to distinguishing them from the exotic Vedic Aryan cult which may be called the *Ṛsi-cult*. The *muni-yati*-cult, with its emphasis on *yoga*, *tapas*, *Saṁnyāsa*, etc., was a characteristic feature of the pre-Vedic non-Aryan Śiva-religion of the Indus Valley as also of the ancient Magadhan religious complex which served as the fountainhead of Jainism and Buddhism,[3] while the autochthonous character of *bhakti*, as evidenced, among other things, by its connections with the indigenous worship of the Mother-Goddess and the *nāga*- and the *yakṣa*-cults, its vegetal and fertility symbolism, and the bacchalian element in it, is now generally accepted.[4] It can also be seen that the *muni-yati*-cult and the *bhakti*-cult did not fail to influence the *Ṛṣi*-cult, both positively and negatively. The Vedic religion adopted the pre-Vedic non-Aryan Śiva in the form of Rudra,[5] while it is not improbable that Vasiṣṭha's attitude towards Varuṇa reflects the influence of the *bhakti*-cult.[6] Negatively, the hieratic Vedic religion exhibited obvious loathness for the *yati*s, the Śiśnadevas, and the Mitra-devas.[7]

On account of its freshness, energy, and flush of victory, the Vedic religion succeeded in keeping the indigenous popular religious sects suppressed for a fairly long time. But when, about the end of the period of the major Upaniṣads (seventh-sixth centuries BC), the hold of Vedism, for obvious reasons, began to weaken, those popular religious cults again gathered strength—indeed, to such an extent that they soon posed a serious challenge to the Vedic religion itself.[8] There was, however, some difference in the attitudes of the religious sects mentioned above. While Jainism and Buddhism openly revolted against the hegemony of Vedism, the *bhakti*-religion, for some practical reasons, sought to establish a kind of liaison with it.

Bhakti for a personal God constitutes the very kernel of Vaiṣṇavism. It would seem that the theistic religion, with *bhakti* for the deified Vṛṣṇi hero Vāsudeva (who, it may be emphasised, is not mentioned in any early Vedic text) as its central tenet, was one of the several sects which re-emerged as powerful religious forces in the days of the decline of Vedism. Incidentally, it may be noted that, like Vāsudeva who belonged to the Kṣatriya tribe of the Vṛṣṇis, Mahāvīra and Gautama Buddha who consolidated their religious doctrines (the origin of which, as pointed out earlier, can be traced back to the pre-Vedic Magadhan thought-complex), at about this very time, also belonged to the Kṣatriya tribes of the Jñātṛkas and the Śākyas respectively. RGB has rightly indicated that the starting point of what we today understand by Vaiṣṇavism was not the worship of Viṣṇu—it was the worship of Vāsudeva. This Vāsudevism, which represented the primary phase of Vaiṣṇavism, must have become fairly well established in the days of Pāṇini (fifth century BC), for, Pāṇini was required to enunciate a special *sūtra* (IV.3.98) governing the formation of the word Vāsudevaka in the sense of a "*Bhakta* or devotee of the pre-eminently worshipful god Vāsudeva'.[9] The tradition of the supreme godhead of Vāsudeva and of Vāsudevism has been continuous since that time. Megasthenes (fourth century BC) speaks of the people of Sūrasena who held Heracles (by whom Megasthenes obviously meant Vāsudeva-Kṛṣṇa) in special veneration.[10] As pointed out by RGB, a *niddesa* passage also suggests that Vāsudeva-worship prevailed in the fourth century[11] BC. The *Bhagavadgītā* (third century BC) eulogises the man of knowledge, who at the end of several births, betakes himself unto the Lord in the conviction that "Vāsudeva is All" (VII.19). We then have the Besnāgar inscription, belonging to the last quarter of the second century BC, on the Garuḍadhvaja of Vāsudeva, the God of Gods, erected by Heliodoros, the Bhāgavata, the son of Dion and an inhabitant of Takṣaśilā.

The historical tradition that the god Vāsudeva originally belonged to the Kṣatriya family of the Vṛṣṇis is well attested. For instance, in the *Bhagavadgītā*, the Lord unequivocally declares that of the Vṛṣṇis he is Vāsudeva (X.37). The *Mahābhāṣya* of Patañjali (150 BC) also clearly speaks of Vāsudeva as belonging to the Vṛṣṇi family.[12] Again, Vāsudeva is closely related to the other deified Vṛṣṇi hero Saṁkarṣaṇa in the Ghosuṇḍī stone inscription of Śarvatata, belonging to the second half of the first century BC, and the Nānāghāṭ cave inscription of the Sātavāhana queen Nāgaṇikā of the first century BC.[13] The Kāśikā emphasises this close relationship between Saṁkarṣaṇa and Vāsudeva by giving the example, *dvandvamsaṁkarṣaṇavāsudevau*, to illustrate *P.* VIII.1.15, *atyantasahacarite lokavijñate dvandvamity upasaṁkhyānam*.

A striking point about the Vāsudeva-religion is that the word *vāsudevaka*, in the sense of a *bhakta* of Vāsudeva, is not attested in any available work.[14] On the other hand, since a descriptive grammarian like Pāṇini has devoted a separate *sūtra* to the morphology of that word, it must have been fairly common in his time. We are, therefore, constrained to assume that considerable literature of non-Vedic character[15] existed in Pāṇini's time but that it is now lost to us.[16]

RGB has not discussed the implication of the latter member of the compound *vāsudevārjunabhyām* in *P.* IV.3.98. It shows that, besides the Vāsudeva-religion, there also existed, in Pāṇini's time, a religious sect centering round Arjuna. But, unlike the Vāsudeva-religion, the religious history of India knows hardly anything of the Arjuna-religion. It is suggested that *P.* IV.3.98 does not presuppose two independent religious sects—one of the Vāsudevakas and the other of the Arjunakas—but that the *sūtra* refers to one single religious sect with Vāsudeva as the supreme god and Arjuna as the special devotee. Obviously, this suggestion is not supported by the wording of the *sūtra*. We have to accept that, in Pāṇini's time, there did prevail two independent religious cults, namely, the Vāsudeva-cult and the Arjuna-cult. Further, from the manner in which they have been referred to by Pāṇini, it may be assumed that these two cults were closely allied to each other—the Vāsudeva-cult having been regarded, even at that time, as being superior to the Arjuna-cult. In the *Ṛgvedic* mythology, Viṣṇu is closely associated with Indra.[17] According to *Śatapatha brāhmaṇa* II.1.2.11 and V.4.3.7, Arjuna is a secret or mystical (*guhya*) name of Indra, while, in later Vaiṣṇavism, the personality and character of Vedic Viṣṇu have been merged into those of Vāsudeva.[18] Therefore, the alliance between the Vāsudeva-sect and the Arjuna-sect, with which Pāṇini seems to have been familiar, may be said to correspond, in a way, with the alliance between Viṣṇu and Indra.[19] Another prototype of such an alliance is to be seen in the religious ideology pertaining to Nara and Nārāyaṇa,[20] wherein Nara may be regarded as the alter ego of Indra (of the *Ṛgveda*) and Arjuna (of *P.* IV.3.98) and Nārāyaṇa as that of Viṣṇu (of the *Ṛgveda*) and Vāsudeva (of *P.* IV.3.98). It would seem that, even in the initial stages of their history, the Vāsudeva-sect subdued and subsumed within itself the Arjuna-sect.[21] That would account for the fact that no traces of this latter sect have been preserved either in history or literature.

RGB has not said much about the Saṁkarṣaṇa-religion, though he has suggested that Saṁkarṣaṇa might have originally been a god outside the Vaiṣṇava pantheon.[22] Like the Arjuna-religion, the Saṁkarṣaṇa-religion also seems to have arisen as an independent religion; but unlike the former, its historical development can be reconstructed from literary and archaeological sources. In the *Mahābhārata*, Saṁkarṣaṇa or Balarāma is represented as a Vṛṣṇi hero, the elder son of Vāsudeva and Rohiṇī; but he does not play any significant role in the great epic.[23] The earliest literary reference to the Saṁkarṣaṇa-cult is to be found in *Kauṭilīya-Arthaśāstra* (fourth century BC) XIII.3.67, which speaks of the spies disguised as the ascetic worshippers of Saṁkarṣaṇa. Indulgence in intoxicating drinks seems to have been a special feature of that cult. Megasthenes says that Dionysus (-Bachhus, God of wine) is represented in India by three gods, and from the further description it becomes clear that, according to the Greek writer, one of them is Saṁkarṣaṇa. In the initial stages of its evolution, the Saṁkarṣaṇa-cult was closely related to the Nāga-cult—a fact which later led to the belief that Saṁkarṣaṇa was an *avatāra* of Śeṣa or Ananta-Nāga. Saṁkarṣaṇa's connections with inebriety and the snake-cult further led to his being often identified with Rudra-Śiva in the *Pāñcarātra-Saṁhitā*.[24] A further piece of evidence in support of the assumption that the Saṁkarṣaṇa-religion must have originated independently of the Vāsudeva-religion is the Mathura sculpture, of the second century BC, depicting Saṁkarṣaṇa by himself.[25] It is, however, not correct to say that Saṁkarṣaṇa was originally a non-Brāhmanical agricultural deity which later came to be identified with Balarāma,[26] for, Saṁkarṣaṇa and Balarāma nowhere appear as two separate individuals.

The worship of Saṁkarṣaṇa constituting an independent religious sect may be thus presumed to have arisen more or less contemporaneously with Vāsudevism; but its sphere of influence seems to have been rather restricted. Soon, the two independent religions, namely, the Saṁkarṣaṇa-religion and the Vāsudeva-religion, came to be closely allied to each other. It is this stage in the religious history which is reflected in the *Mahābhāṣya* of Patañjali, the *niddesa* text, and the Ghosuṇḍī and Nānāghāṭ inscriptions. Attention has recently been drawn also to a joint representation of Vāsudeva and Saṁkarṣaṇa belonging to the second century BC.[27] Two points need to be noted in this connection. The alliance between the Saṁkarṣaṇa-cult and the Vāsudeva-cult was not the result, as suggested by some scholars,[28] of a deliberate attempt to assimilate the Nāga-cult into the Vāsudeva-religion; rather it seems to have been prompted by the historical necessity of preserving and consolidating the religious cohesion of the

Vṛṣṇis-Sātvatas which would have been adversely affected if these two religious sects, which had arisen within the tribe, had been allowed to develop independently of each other. Second, the mention in the inscriptions of Saṁkarṣaṇa before Vāsudeva does not imply the precedence of the Saṁkarṣaṇa-religion over the Vāsudeva-religion.[29] Such a mention is only formal and is presumably occasioned by the historical fact that Saṁkarṣaṇa was the elder of the two Vṛṣṇi brothers who had been deified. It may be noted that the Ghosuṇḍī inscription characterises both the gods equally as *anihata*, *bhāgavat*, and *sarveśvara*.

The other development in the religious history of that same period a development which must have been independent of the first, namely, the alliance on equal terms between the Saṁkarṣaṇa-religion and the Vāsudeva-religion—was in the direction of the evolution of the doctrine of the *vyūhas*. Though the doctrine of the *vyūhas*, in its developed form, first occurs in the Nārāyaṇīya section (early centuries of the Christian era),[30] it is adumbrated even in the *Mahābhāṣya*. In his commentary on *vārttika* 2 of *P*. VI.3.5, Patañjali quotes the verse-quarter in the Upendravajra metre, *janārdanas tv ātmacaturtha eva*, which can be taken to allude to the four *vyūha*s. After Saṁkarṣaṇa had been included among the *vyūha*s,[31] the Saṁkarṣaṇa-cult must have ceased to exist as an independent religious cult.

RGB says that Vāsudeva was also called Kṛṣṇa because his *gotra* was Kārṣṇāyana.[32] In this connection, he emphasises the Vedic affiliations of Kṛṣṇa by pointing out that one Kṛṣṇa Aṅgīrasa is the Ṛṣi of Ṛgveda VIII. 74, that the same Kṛṣṇa Aṅgīrasa is mentioned in KB 30.9, and that Kṛṣṇa occurs in the *Chāndogya Upaniṣad* as the pupil of Ghora Aṅgīrasa. The Vedic seer Kṛṣṇa could thus have been a founder of a *gotra*. RGB further adds that, though Vāsudeva belonged to the kṣatriya family of the Vṛṣṇis, he must have adopted the *gotra* of his brāhmaṇa priest for sacrificial purposes.[33] In support of his assumption, RGB refers to the commentary of the *Ghaṭa-Jātaka* which seems to suggest that Vāsudeva belonged to the Kārṣṇāyana *gotra*. All this argument, however, is rather farfetched. Even assuming that Vāsudeva did adopt the Kārṣṇāyana *gotra*, one would not be able to explain why Vāsudeva was called Kṛṣṇa. He might have called himself Kārṣṇāyana, but not Kṛṣṇa. One hardly finds a person adopting the name of the founder of his *gotra* as his additional personal name. The commentary of the *Ghaṭa-Jātaka*, which too is a little confused about the *gotra* name and the personal name, obviously represents a later tradition. Incidentally, Kṛṣṇa of the *Chāndogya Upaniṣad* need not have been a brāhmaṇa seer.

Another assumption, which is often made in this context, is that, from the very beginning, Kṛṣṇa was an additional personal name of Vāsudeva of the Vṛṣṇis.[34] It is, however, rather unusual that an individual should have been originally given two equally important personal names. Pāṇini, who knows Vāsudeva as a god, nowhere alludes to Kṛṣṇa being the other name of that god. Similarly, in connection with the *vyūha*-doctrine, which is associated in a distinctive manner with the Vṛṣṇi heroes, the name Kṛṣṇa is hardly ever mentioned. It is also difficult to accept the suggestion that Vāsudeva was called Kṛṣṇa on account of his dark complexion[35] and that, in course of time, the epithet became a persona name.

As regards the names Vāsudeva and Kṛṣṇa, the view is sometimes put forth that Kṛṣṇa was the original name of the Vṛṣṇi hero and that Vāsudeva was just his patronym derived from his father's name Vāsudeva. This view cannot be accepted for various reasons. First, Patañjali's commentary on *Vārttika* 7 of *P*. IV.1.114[36] indicates that Vāsudeva (and not Vāsudeva) is the basic form of the name of the Vṛṣṇi hero and that the termination an affixed to this original name Vāsudeva also gives the form Vāsudeva. Second, if Vāsudeva was really a patronym, Balarāma or Saṁkarṣaṇa, who is represented as the elder brother of Kṛṣṇa, should have been more aptly called Vāsudeva. But that is not the case. On the other hand, we find Kṛṣṇa and Balarāma being specifically referred to by their matronyms, namely, Devakīputra and Rauhiṇeya respective The rivalry among some Kṣatriya princes for the real divine "Vāsudevahood" also clearly goes against Vāsudeva being regarded as a patronym.[37] Again, the etymologies of the word *Vāsudeva* given by the *Mahābhārata*[38] and Ujjvaladatta's gloss on *Uṇādisūtra* 1.1[39] would leave no doubt that Vāsudeva was regarded as the original name and not a patronym.[40] Jacobi mentions the fact,[41] which is particularly significant in the present context, namely, that the name Vāsubhadra sometimes occurs as an auxiliary of Vāsudeva.[42] We have, therefore, to conclude that, just as Kṛṣṇa was not an additional personal name of Vāsudeva, Vāsudeva was not the patronym of Kṛṣṇa.

The truth of this whole matter seems to be that Vāsudeva and Kṛṣṇa were originally two distinct personalities. As pointed out earlier, Vāsudevism must have originated at a fairly early date[43] so that it could become thoroughly well established in Pāṇini's time. Perhaps a little later than the Vāsudeva-religion, there grew another religious sect round the figure of Kṛṣṇa who had originally been the tribal hero and religious leader of the Yādavas[44] but who was subsequently made into a god. This Yādava Kṛṣṇa[45] may as well have been the same as Devakīputra Kṛṣṇa who is represented in *Chāndogya Upaniṣad* III.17.1 as a pupil of Ghora Aṅgīrasa and who is said to have learnt from his teacher the doctrine that man's life is a kind of sacrifice.[46] Chronology does not go against such an assumption; indeed, it supports it. Kṛṣṇa must be said to have developed his own philosophy (later embodied in the *Bhagavadgītā*), the main tenets of which were *lokasaṁgraha* and renunciation in action rather than of action. When, in course of time, the Vṛṣṇis and the Yādavas, who were already related to each other, came closer together presumably for political reasons, the divine personalities of Vṛṣṇi Vāsudeva and Yādava Kṛṣṇa were merged together so as to give rise to the new supreme god, Bhagavan Vāsudeva-Kṛṣṇa.[47] This must have happened not long after Pāṇini's time. *Kauṭilīya-Arthaśāstra* XIV.3 associates Kṛṣṇa with Kaṁsa, who is usually associated with Vāsudeva, thereby suggesting the identity between Kṛṣṇa and Vāsudeva. Megasthenes also seems to confirm this identity. He speaks of the "city of

Kṛṣṇa" (Kleisobora=Kṛṣṇapura) in the country of Śūrasena where the worship of Vāsudeva was prevalent. In the time of the *Bhagavadgītā*, and naturally also of the *Mahābhāṣya* of Patañjali,[48] the names Vāsudeva and Kṛṣṇa had come to be used indiscriminately to denote the same divine personality. In the new legends which grew round this composite supreme god Vāsudeva-Kṛṣṇa, the name Vāsudeva came to be interpreted as the patronym of Kṛṣṇa. Some Vāsudeva was imagined to have been Kṛṣṇa's father,[49] and Vṛṣṇi Saṁkarṣaṇa came to be regarded as his elder brother.[50]

Another hypothesis may also be hazarded in this connection. Since Vṛṣṇi Vāsudeva and Yādava Kṛṣṇa had originally been two distinct personalities, Vāsudeva could as well have been the name of Yādava Kṛṣṇa's father.[51] Kṛṣṇa would then be Yādava (tribal name) as well as Vāsudeva (patronym). The merger of Vṛṣṇi Vāsudeva and Yādava Vāsudeva Kṛṣṇa might have been facilitated by the common element Vāsudeva.

Though RGB does not consider Yādava Kṛṣṇa to have been distinct from Vṛṣṇi Vāsudeva, he does believe that the Gopāla Kṛṣṇa element was introduced into Vāsudevism at a fairly late stage in the development of the latter.[52] He points out that no reference to Gopāla Kṛṣṇa occurs in the epigraphical records like the Ghosuṇḍī and the Nānāghāṭ inscriptions; nor does it occur in the *Mahābhāṣya* of Patañjali or even in the Nārāyaṇīya section of the *Mahābhārata*. No doubt, in the Sabhā-Parva, Śiśupāla is represented as referring tauntingly to Kṛṣṇa's "exploits' in the Gokula, like the killing of Pūtanā,[53] but RGB regards that passage as an interpolation. Similarly, he accepts the interpretation of Kṛṣṇa's name Govinda, given in the Ādi-parva and the Śānti-Parva, as "finder of the earth", thereby rejecting any suggestion regarding Kṛṣṇa having been connected with the cows. However, he hastens to add that, more probably, the name means "finder of the cows". Finally, he concludes that the story of Kṛṣṇa's boyhood in the Gokula was unknown till about the beginning of the Christian era, that it occurs in its full-fledged form only in the *Harivaṁśa*, the *Vāyu Purāṇa*, and the *Bhāgavata Purāṇa*, that some of the elements in the Gopāla Kṛṣṇa mythology, which clearly betray Christian influence, such as, the worship of the boy-god and the story of his humble birth, his reputed father's knowledge that he was not his son, and the massacre of the innocents, were brought into India by the Abhīras when they migrated into this country in the first century AD, and that the Abhīras possibly brought with them also the name Christ, which probably led to the identification of the boy-God with Vāsudeva Kṛṣṇa.

There can be little doubt that the religion centering round the cowherd child-God Kṛṣṇa originated among the nomadic cowherd community of the Abhīras.[54] In the *Padma Purāṇa*, the supreme God is represented as announcing that he would be born among the Abhīras in his eighth incarnation.[55] Similarly, in the *Harivaṁśa*[56] and the *Balacarita*[57] of Bhāsa, Kṛṣṇa is said to have been brought up in a *ghoṣa*; and, according to the *Amarakośa*,[58] *abhīrapallī* is a synonym of *ghoṣa*. The religious cult of Gopāla Kṛṣṇa abjured the Indra-dominated Vedic religion (as is evidenced by the Govardhana-episode) and promoted religious sublimation of sensuous love (cf. the relationship between Kṛṣṇa and the Gopīs).

We need not here go into the question of the origin of the Abhīras. Whether they were a foreign tribe[59] or an aboriginal one living in Panjab,[60] there is sufficient evidence to show that they were in India already in the third century BC.[61] So RGB's suggestion regarding the Christian influences brought in by the Abhīras cannot be sustained.[62] Again, the so-called similarities between the legends pertaining to Gopāla Kṛṣṇa and Christ, to which RGB refers, are patently superficial. Attention may also be drawn to a Mathura sculpture, depicting Vāsudeva as crossing the Yamunā with the baby Kṛṣṇa in a basket, which has been assigned to the Kuṣāṇa period.[63] This may be taken to prove that the legend regarding Kṛṣṇa's transference to Gokula (which, in its turn, is the result of the merger of the Vāsudeva-Kṛṣṇa-religion and the Gopāla-Kṛṣṇa-religion, I had already been in common vogue even in the first century AD Similarly, a figure of Govardhanadhara Kṛṣṇa in red sandstone, from

Mathura, is assigned to the same period.[64] Bhāsa, who has to be assigned to a still earlier period, portrays, in his *Bālacarita*, various episodes in Kṛṣṇa's life in the cow-settlement. As for RGB's contention that the passage in the Sabhā-Parva, mentioned above, may be an interpolation, the evidence of the Critical Edition of the *Mahābhārata* goes counter to it. Indeed, there are a few other passages in the *Mahābhārata* which betray knowledge of Kṛṣṇa's life in the Gokula.[65] All the same, one does not fail to get the impression that the redactors of the *Mahābhārata* must have made deliberate attempts to suppress many of the episodes of Gopāla Kṛṣṇa's boyhood in the Gokula, particularly his amours with the Gopīs, presumably because those redactors wanted specially to highlight Kṛṣṇa's character as a divine teacher of new ethics.[66]

Just as the religion of Gopāla Kṛṣṇa, in its original form does not show any traces of Christian influence (as suggested by RGB), so too it cannot be shown to have originated from Vedic sources.[67] The word *gopa* is hardly ever used in the Ṛgveda in the specific sense of "cowherd'[68]; and the word *gavāḥ*, when associated with Viṣṇu, does not necessarily mean "cows'.[69] Reference to Gobāla Vārṣṇya in the *Taittirīya Saṁhitā* and the *Jaiminīya Upaniṣad brāhmaṇa*[70] also does not indicate the Vedic affiliations of Abhīra Gopāla Kṛṣṇa. As against this, Indra is often described in the *Ṛgveda* as *govid* (= finder of cows), but Gopāla Kṛṣṇa, as we have seen, asks his followers to desist from Indra—worship and to regard cows as their deities. The original non-Vedic character of the Gopāla-Kṛṣṇa-cult is thus beyond doubt.

It would seem that the Gopāla-Kṛṣṇa-religion of the Abhīras was, in course of time, engrafted on the organically united Vāsudeva-Kṛṣṇa-religion of the Vṛṣṇis-Yādavas.[71] This must have happened some time before the third century BC; for, the *Bhagavadgītā* contains the words Govinda[72] and Keśinīsūdana[73] which are reminiscent of Kṛṣṇa's boyhood days in the Gokula. Similarly, Kātyāyana (third century BC) found it necessary to add a *Vārttika* to *P*. III.1.138 to explain the morphology of the name Govinda[74] which must have become fairly common in his days. The words Dāmodara and Govinda, which definitely belong to the Gopāla Kṛṣṇa religious complex, also occur in the *Baudhāyana Dharmasūtra* (II.5.24) of about the same period.

The amalgamation of the Vāsudeva-reiligion of the Vṛṣṇis, the Kṛṣṇa-religion of the Yādavas, and the Gopāla-religion of the Abhīras gave rise to what may be called a new Kṛṣṇaism. If, as pointed out earlier, Vāsudevism represented the first phase of classical Vaiṣṇavism, this new Kṛṣṇaism represented its second (and perhaps most outstanding) phase. New legendary links were forged whereby Vāsudeva, Kṛṣṇa, and Gopāla were integrated into a single homogeneous mythological pattern. Vāsudeva, who, as the result of the merger of the Vāsudeva-religion and the Kṛṣṇa-religion, had already come to be regarded as Kṛṣṇa's father, was now represented as having transferred his infant son Kṛṣṇa to the care of his friend Nanda, the Abhīra leader of a ghoṣa with a view to guarding him against the misfortune of merciless slaughter which his earlier children had suffered at the hands of his brother-in-law Kaṁsa. There, in the Gokula, the boy Kṛṣṇa grew in the company of *gopa*s and *gopī*s as Gopāla Kṛṣṇa (Abhīra element). From there, he (with his elder brother Saṁkarṣaṇa-Balarāma) went over to Mathura, killed Kaṁsa, and thereby put an end to the latter's despotic rule (Vṛṣṇi element). Thereafter, Kṛṣṇa migrated to Dvāraka to found and foster the kingdom of the Yādavas (Yādava element). He also played the role of the friend and mentor of the Pāṇḍavas. Such was the composite mythology of Kṛṣṇaism. The religio-philosophico-ethical doctrine of this Kṛṣṇaism is embodied in the *Bhagavadgītā*.

The third century BC was the most eventful period in the history of Vaiṣṇavism. As we have seen, Vāsudevism-Kṛṣṇaism originated and developed as an essentially non-Vedic religious sect. Other heterodox religions, particularly Buddhism had also been flourishing, so much so that, in the third century BC, Buddhism reached almost the peak of its power. It must have, indeed, inspired the fear that it would soon overwhelm not only the declining Vedic religion but also other non-Vedic religious sects. Vāsudevism-Kṛṣṇaism, therefore, prepared itself to meet this serious challenge. It did so in two ways. First, it rallied together all the religious forces akin to it. The amalgamation of the Vāsudeva-Kṛṣṇa-religion and the Gopāla-Kṛṣṇa-religion and the consequent bringing into being of the new Kṛṣṇaism, to which a reference has been made above, was an important step in that direction. The other line of action, which it followed, may be said to have been rather unexpected. Non-Vedic in origin and development, Kṛṣṇaism now sought affiliation with Vedism—howsoever tenuous and formal that affiliation might be—so that it could thereby make itself acceptable to the still not inconsiderable orthodox elements among the people. The rearguards of the languishing Vedism, on their part, had also been wanting to reclaim its former position. For one thing, they tried to revive, reorganise, and revitalise the traditional Vedic way of life and thought. Among the literary monuments of this movement were the Vedāṅgas, particularly the Śrauta, the Dharma, and the Gṛhya-sūtras, as also the two Mīmāṁsā sūtras. As an additional measure, they must have welcomed the prospect of at least some Vedic elements being preserved through Kṛṣṇaism. The rapport which Kṛṣṇaism was striving to establish with Vedism was thus expected to prove beneficial both to Vedism and Kṛṣṇaism. This is the background on which the Viṣṇu-element and the Nārāyaṇa-element came to be merged into Kṛṣṇaism.

We need not here analyse in detail the Viṣṇu-mythology in the *Ṛgveda*.[75] Suffice it to say that it symbolises an important motif in the evolution of Vedic mythology, namely, hierarchisation of popular religion. Viṣṇu was originally a popular divinity of fertility and growth, conceived (as in several primitive mythologies) in the form of a bird.[76] However, popular pressure seems to have rendered it necessary to admit Viṣṇu in the hieratic Vedic pantheon. The artificiality of this mythological elevation of Viṣṇu is indicated by the forced manner in which he has been brought into association with Indra, who was, as it were, the philosophers' stone in the matter of hierarchisation. And, when Viṣṇu was thus being related to Indra, the Vedic poet-priests took care to suppress the original fertility traits in Viṣṇu's character and to superimpose on him the conventional solar character. The superimposition of solar character on Viṣṇu was presumably facilitated by the common symbol of "bird' which represented both the fertility-divinity and the sun. In the course of the further evolution of the Viṣṇu-mythology, Viṣṇu came to be regarded as the supreme (*parama*) God from the ritualistic point of view.[77] It was, however, his character as a god of fertility and growth which appealed most to the popular imagination and which consequently served as the most convenient point of contact between Kṛṣṇaism (particularly its Gopāla Kṛṣṇa aspect) and Vedism. It is also not unlikely that the popular understanding—or rather misunderstanding of the Ṛgvedic Viṣṇu's epithet *gopa* and of the *gavāḥ* in his highest abode[78] also helped the identification of the popular god Kṛṣṇa with the Vedic Viṣṇu.

The assimilation of the Viṣṇu-element[79] by Kṛṣṇaism, resulting in Kṛṣṇa being identified with Viṣṇu, must have occurred before the final redaction of the *Bhagavadgītā*. In the *Bhagavadgītā*, Lord Kṛṣṇa is addressed as Viṣṇu.[80] Attention may also be drawn to Arjuna's prayer to Kṛṣṇa that he should again appear before him in "that same four-armed form".[81] Further, as RGB has pointed out,[82] the Viśvarūpa manifested to Arjuna by Lord Kṛṣṇa[83] is almost similar to the Vaiṣṇavarūpa mentioned in the *Anugītā*.[84] This fact would confirm Kṛṣṇa's identification with Viṣṇu. Again, in the *Baudhāyana Dharmasūtra*,[85] which belongs to about the same period as the *Bhagavadgītā*, Viṣṇu is called Govinda and Dāmodara,[86] and in the *Taittirīya Āraṇyaka*,[87] which is a little posterior to the *Bhagavadgītā*, he is identified with Vāsudeva and Nārāyaṇa. The identity of Vāsudeva with Viṣṇu is also suggested by the fact that, in the Besnagar inscription,[88] Vāsudeva's column is called Garuḍa-column. Incidentally it may be mentioned that, in the *Mahābhārata*, the name Viṣṇu occurs less frequently than the names, Vāsudeva, Kṛṣṇa, and Nārāyaṇa.

Two points need to be specially noted in connection with the assimilation of the Viṣṇu element by Kṛṣṇaism. First, when Viṣṇu came to be assimilated into Kṛṣṇaism, there occurred a vital change in his character. In the Ṛgvedic mythology, Viṣṇu is represented as a subordinate ally of Indra. In Kṛṣṇaism, Viṣṇu not only supersedes Indra but, in his role as Kṛṣṇa, he actively antagonises him. The legends concerning the Govardhana mountain and the *pārijāta* tree would confirm this.[89] Second, it is not quite correct to characterise the assimilation of the Viṣṇu-element into Kṛṣṇaism as the "Brāhmanisation" of Kṛṣṇaism,[90] for, it actually resulted in the Kṛṣṇaisation of Viṣṇu rather than in the Viṣṇuisation of Kṛṣṇa. No significant Brāhmanic traits are seen to have been introduced into Kṛṣṇaism together with the Viṣṇu-element. Indeed, the position of Viṣṇu in this entire newly evolved religious complex is such as would hardly justify that religious complex being designated as Vaiṣṇavism. The only indication of Viṣṇu's predominance is to be found in the newly propagated belief that Kṛṣṇa was an avatara or incarnation of Viṣṇu.

The *Bhagavadgītā* reflects the stage of Kṛṣṇaism after it had assimilated the Viṣṇu-element. It would seem that, in the matter of essential attitude and doctrine, the *Bhagavadgītā* represented a kind of reaction against the prevailing Vedic ideology. It must be said to have adequately responded to the needs of the hour. Broadly speaking, the major Upaniṣads, which mark the acme of the religio-philosophical culture of the Vedas, teach that the ultimate goal of human life is the realisation of the essential identity of the individual soul and the universal soul which results from the complete withdrawal from the fundamentally unreal phenomenal world. The Upaniṣadic attitude is thus individualistic and, to a large extent, negative. As against this, the *Bhagavadgītā* emphasises the ideal of *lokasaṁgraha*—of the stability, solidarity, and progress of the society. The society can function properly only on the principle of the ethical interdependence of its various constituents. Man must, therefore, see to it that, as an essential constituent of society, he furthers this process of *lokasaṁgraha* through an active awareness of his social obligations (*svadharma*). The *Bhagavadgītā* countenances neither the complete abnegation of action (*saṁnyāsa*) as implied in the Upaniṣads nor the mechanical observance of the ritual practices (*karma kaṇḍa*) enjoined by the brāhmaṇas. The *karma yoga*, which is verily the central theme of the *Bhagavadgītā*, tries to combine the ideals of *lokasaṁgraha* and *mokṣa* by stressing the *anāsakti yoga*, that is, renunciation in action and not of action. The elaborate ritualism of the brāhmaṇas and the contemplative spiritualism of the Upaniṣads were both beyond the common man. The *Bhagavadgītā*, therefore, emphasises the way of *bhakti* for a personal god, which, as we have seen, was the very starting point of Vāsudevism-Kṛṣṇaism. But it seeks to harmonise *bhakti* with *karma-yoga*. The true *Karma-yogī* is also a true *bhakta*, for, by following his *svadharma*, the former devotedly participates in the divine project. The *Bhagavadgītā* cannot boast of any distinct philosophical system of its own; it has eschewed the metaphysical dogmatism of the prevailing schools of philosophy and has sought to evolve a loose philosophical synthesis.[91] Synthesis in all fields was, verily, the watchword of the new Kṛṣṇaism. Another significant trait of Kṛṣṇaism, which is not reflected in the *Bhagavadgītā* but which is clearly brought out by Kṛṣṇa's character as represented in the *Mahābhārata*, is its new political ethics which insists on the urgency of attaining the end, which one considers to be right, by any means even if they sometimes do not appear to be so right.[92]

Presumably, the religio-philosophical teachings of Kṛṣṇaism were originally embodied in an independent popular text. This text was later interpolated, obviously after suitable modifications, into the bardic-historical poem *Jaya*, in the form of the *Bhagavadgītā*, whereby it served as the cornerstone of the Kṛṣṇaite super structure which transformed the *Jaya* into the *Bhārata*.[93]

The assimilation of the Nārāyaṇa-element into Kṛṣṇaism,[94] which is generally regarded as the second major factor in the process of the so-called Brāhmanisation of Kṛṣṇaism, does not seem to have been known to the *Bhagavadgītā*. The name Nārāyaṇa does not occur in the *Bhagavadgītā*, nor does the doctrine of the *vyūhas* which is believed to have been taught to Nārada by the Great Being in the Śvetadvīpa (that is, Nārāyaṇa).[95] It would seem that, very soon after the final redaction of the *Bhagavadgītā*, Nārāyaṇa became an essential constituent of Vāsudevism-Kṛṣṇaism. The *Taittirīya Āraṇyaka* X.11 clearly identifies Nārāyaṇa, Vāsudeva, and Viṣṇu.[96] The association of Nārāyaṇa with Vāsudevism-Kṛṣṇaism must have become well established since then. The Ghosuṇḍī inscription of Sarvatata speaks of the *nārāyaṇa-vaṭaka* for the place of worship[97] of Saṁkarasaṇa and Vāsudeva. In the *Mahābhārata* XII.321.16-17, the supreme God is said to have manifested himself in the four forms—Nara, Nārāyaṇa, Hari, and Kṛṣṇa. Nārāyaṇa is also glorified there as *sātvatadharmagopta* (XII.322.5). He declares that he can be seen only by those who devoutly follow the *ekāntika-dharma* (XII.326.12). In the *Devabodhisattva Śāstra*, Āryadeva (second century AD) quotes certain sayings of Nārāyaṇa which are quite similar to what Lord Kṛṣṇa has said in the *Bhagavadgītā*.[98] Similarly, the episode described in the *Mahābhārata* III.186.39ff. of Mārkaṇḍeya's having entered into the mouth of Nārāyaṇa and having seen the entire universe subsisting within that God's body would remind one of Arjuna's *viśvarūpadarśana* as described in the *Bhagavadgītā* XI. It may also be pointed out that the Ājīvikas, who flourished in the sixth-fifth centuries BC as a non-Vedic religious sect but who came to be later closely associated with the Vāsudevakas, were characterised as *nārāyaṇāśrita*.[99]

The name Nārāyaṇa is variously explained. On the face of it, it looks like a *gotra*-name (like Kātyāyana or Vātsyāyana), derived from the name Nara. Nārāyaṇa was accordingly regarded as a sage born in the family of another sage called Nara. It was further suggested that both these sages, who were later deified, were originally great sun-worshippers, which fact facilitated the later identification of Nārāyaṇa with Viṣṇu. However, in the *Mahābhārata*, it is Nara who is represented as having been born as the result of the austerities of Nārāyaṇa. There is also no evidence to suggest their connection with sun-worship. Further, doubt is expressed as to the propriety of the highest God being the descendant of anyone else.[100] According to *Manusmṛti* I.10, Nārāyaṇa was so called because his primary abode (*pūrvāyana*) was waters (*nārah*).[101] But there Nārāyaṇa is obviously represented as being identical with Brahma-Prajāpati rather than with Viṣṇu. Bhandarkar accepts the formation of the word *nārāyaṇa* according to *P.* IV.1.99, but explains its meaning in quite an ingenious way. He understands *nara* in the sense of a collection of *nara*s or men, and *ayana* in the sense of a resting place or goal.[102] The god Nārāyaṇa is thus the resting place or goal of men. Bhandarkar refers, in this context, to the statement made by *Keśava* or Hari to Arjuna that he is known as the resting place or goal of men (*narānām*).[103] The form *nara* is no doubt possible, but it is by no means common. Bhandarkar's explanation is accordingly, far-fetched and, therefore, not very convincing.[104] It would rather seem that Nara and Nārāyaṇa originally constituted one single personality conceived as having been made up of two closely related aspects and that the essential idea underlying it was that of the "cosmic male" or *Puruṣa*.[105]

RGB's analysis of the Nārāyaṇa[106] is excellent; but it does not throw much light on how and why the Nārāyaṇa-element might have been merged into Vāsudevism-Kṛṣṇaism. The several references to the ascetics-*yogī*s associated with Nārāyaṇa in Badari or Śvetadvīpa[107] would indicate that the Nara-Nārāyaṇa cult had originated independently of the Veda; but the connection of Nārāyaṇa with the Indus valley civilisation cannot be validly established.[108] Tradition invests the Nārāyaṇa-cult with great antiquity, for Nārāyaṇa is described as *yo' sau nārāyaṇo nāma pūrveṣām api pūrvajaḥ*.[109] It is not unlikely that this very same Nārāyaṇa was adapted into the Vedic ideology in the form of Puruṣa Nārāyaṇa of the *Śatapatha brāhmaṇa*.[110] According to the *Śatapatha Brāhmaṇa* XII.3.4, Prajāpati urged Puruṣa Nārāyaṇa to perform a sacrifice. He did so and, as the result of it, he "placed himself in all the worlds, in all the gods, in all the Vedas, and in all the vital airs, and they were placed in him".[111] In the *Śatapatha Brāhmaṇa* XIII.6.1, Puruṣa Nārāyaṇa is said to have performed a Puruṣamedha extending over five nights whereby he superseded all beings and himself became identical with the All. Presumably, it was this latter reference which gave rise to the tradition of Nārāyaṇa being associated with the famous cosmological hymn, the Puruṣa Sūkta (*ṚV* IX-90),[112] as its *Ṛṣī*. But what seems to have facilitated the merger of Nārāyaṇa into Vāsudevism-Kṛṣṇaism (which was intended to serve the same purpose as the merger of Viṣṇu) was not so much his cosmic character and function as his dual personality as Puruṣa Nārāyaṇa. Correspondence could be easily established among the four pairs, namely, Nāra-Nārāyaṇa of Badarikāśrama, Puruṣa-Nārāyaṇa of the *Śatapatha Brāhmaṇa*, Indra-Viṣṇu of the Ṛgvedic mythology, and Arjuna-Vāsudeva of Vāsudevism-Kṛṣṇaism.

Once Nārāyaṇa was assimilated into Vāsudevism-Kṛṣṇaism, he came to be represented as the propounder of a specific aspect of Vaiṣṇavism, namely, the Pāñcarātra.[113] This was presumably due to the reference in the *Śatapatha Brāhmaṇa* to the Pāñcarātra Sattra which Puruṣa Nārāyaṇa is said to have performed (see supra). However, neither the Nārāyaṇa[114] nor any other part of the *Mahābhārata* gives a consistent and detailed account of the Pāñcarātra doctrine. Whatever might have been the original significance of the term *pāñcarātra*,[115] there should be no doubt that the doctrine was closely related to the historically authentic Vṛṣṇi heroes. An inscription from the Mora well (about 7 miles from Mathura), belonging to the time of the Śaka chief Ṣoḍaśa (first century AD), speaks of *bhāgavatam vṛṣṇinām pañcaviranām pratimāḥ* installed in a stone temple by a lady named Tosa. These five *vīra*s must be the same as the five *vaṁśavīra*s of the Vṛṣṇis mentioned in the *Vāyu Purāṇa* 97.1-2, namely, Saṁkaraṣaṇa, Vāsudeva, Pradyumna, Śāmba, and Aniruddha.[116] It seems most likely that each of these Vṛṣṇi heroes originally had his own independent religious sect. When attempts were being made to consolidate classical Vaiṣṇavism, these various sects were presumably integrated into one single religio-philosophical pattern.[117]

Notes

1. Cf. RGB's *Collected Works*, vol. I, pp. 362-93.
2. RGB's *Collected Works*, vol. IV, pp. 142-43.
3. Dandekar, *Some Aspects of the History of Hinduism*, Ch. I and p. 87.
4. Cf. Ted. J. Solomon, "Early Vaishnav Bhakti and Its Autochthonous Heritage", *Hist. Rel.*, X.32-48.
5. Dandekar, "Rudra in the Veda", *FUPHS* 1:94-148.
6. Dandekar, "Varuṇa, Vasiṣṭha, and Bhakti", *Wijesekera Fel. vol.*, Peradeniya (Ceylon), 1970, 77-82.
7. See ref. in footnote 5.
8. Dandekar, "Cultural background of the Veda", *UCR* 11: 135-51.
9. For details See Dandekar, "The beginnings of Vaiṣṇavism", *Indologica Taurinesia III*, 1975.
10. It is suggeted that Megathenes must have rendered Hari-Kṛṣṇa as Heracles.
11. RGB's *Collected Works*, vol. IV, pp. 3-4.
12. *Vārttika* 7 of *P.* IV.1.114: *vṛṣnyaṇo'vakāśaḥ/vāsudevaḥ, baladevaḥ.*
13. RGB's *Collected Works*, vol. IV, pp. 4-5.
14. In the few passages where the word does occur, it invariably occurs in grammatical contexts.
15. Most of the pre-Pāṇinian literature, which has come down to us, is Vedic.
16. Much other evidence is available to support this assumption.
17. See Dandekar, "Viṣṇu in the Veda", *Kane Comm.* vol., pp. 95-111.
18. See infra.
19. The precedence between the two Vedic gods was reversed in Vaiṣṇavism.
20. See the Nārāyaṇīya section in the *Mahābhārata*. Also see infra.
21. This may also reflect Viṣṇu's having superseded Indra in Vaiṣṇavism. For details, see Dandekar, "The beginnings of Vaiṣṇavism".
22. Cf. S. Chattopadyaya, *Evolution of Hindu Sects*, p. 44. It is suggested that Baladeva and Vāsudeva were originally conceived as the associate male gods of the older female divinity Ekānaṁśā (S. Jaiswal, *The Origin and Development of Vaiṣṇavism*, p. 67).

23. In the *Mahābhārata*, Saṁkaraṣaṇa is shown to have particularly favoured Duryodhana.
24. Schrader, *Introduction to the Paṣcartāra and the Ahirbudhnya Saṁhita*, p. 36.
25. The Jaina *Aupapātikasūtra* mentions Balarāma as one of the eight renowned kṣatriya teachers (Leumann's edn., pp. 69-70).
26. S. Jaiswal, *op. cit.*, p. 60.
27. J. Filliozat, "Representation de Vāsudeva et Saṁkarṣaṇa au sircle IIe avant J.C.", *Arts Asia,* 26, pp. 113-24.
28. S. Chattopadhyaya, *op. cit.*, p. 47.
29. R.P. Chanda has suggested (*Archaeology and Vaiṣṇava Tradition,* p. 403), that in the second century BC, there were two forms of Vāsudeva worship—one in which Vāsudeva was worshipped as the supreme God and the other in which he was worshipped as a god second to Saṁkaraṣaṇa.
30. In the Bhiṣma Parva and the *Ahirbudhnya Saṁhitā*, Saṁkaraṣaṇa is represented as an exponent of the Sātvata or Pāṣcarātra system (D.C. Sircar, *Studies in the Religious Life of Ancient and Medivial India*, p. 36).
31. For a discussion of the *Mahābhāṣya*-passage, see Dandekar, "The beginnings of Vaiṣṇavism".
32. *Op. cit.*, pp. 14-17.
33. This is prescribed by *Āśvalāyana Śrautasūtra,* XII.15.
34. B.B. Majumdar, *Kṛṣṇa in History and Legend*, p. 5.
35. Cf. D.G. Sircar, *op. cit.*, p. 25.
36. See footnote 12.
37. Among the princes involved in such rivalry may be mentioned Pauṇḍraka Vāsudeva (*MBh.* II.13.17-19) and Śṛgāla Vāsudeva (*Harivaṁśa*, Appendix 18).
38. *MBh.* V. 683: *vasanāt sarvabhūtānāṁ vastuvād devayonitaḥ/ vāsudevas tato vedyaḥ.*
39. *vāsuś ca deva ceti vāsudevaḥ.*
40. For further discussion, see: Dandekar, "The beginnings of Vaiṣṇavism".
41. Hermann Jacobi, "Ūber Viṣṇu-Nārāyana-Vāsudeva", Streitberg Festgabe, p. 163.
42. E.g. in *Bhāsa's Dūtavākya,* V.6.
43. According to the *Uttarādhyayanasūtra* XXII, Vāsudeva was a contemporary of the twenty-second *tīrthaṅkara* Ariṣṭanemi whose date would be about seventh century BC. In Pataṣjali's time, Vāsudeva (or rather Vāsudeva-Kṛṣṇa) had already come to be regarded as a religio-legendary figure belonging to a remote past. (For details, see: Dandekar, "The beginnings of Vaiṣṇavism").

44. The historicity of Yādava Kṛṣṇa cannot be doubted; the genealogy of the Yādavas is traditionally well preserved (B.B. Majumdar, *op. cit.*, p. 279). Barth, Hopkins, and Keith think that Kṛṣṇa was not a human being but a popular divinity. According to Barth, he was a solar god who was regarded as *kuladevatā* by some Rājpūt tribes. Hopkins accepts Kṛṣṇa's solar character and considers him to be a tribal god of the Pāṇḍavas. Keith believes that Kṛṣṇa was a vegetation-divinity.
45. Cf. *Bhagavadgītā*, XI.41: he Kṛṣṇa he Yādava....
46. The identity of Yādava Kṛṣṇa with Devakīputra Kṛṣṇa is questioned by some scholars. The only point of contact between the two, it is argued, is that the role of Yādava Kṛṣṇa as a religious teacher is derived from his namesake mentioned in the *Chāndogya Upaniṣad* (S. Jaiswal, *op. cit.*, pp. 70-71). There should, however, be no doubt about some doctrinal similarity between the *Bhagavadgītā* and *Chāndogya Upaniṣad,* III.17.1.
47. It may be noted that the teacher of the *Bhagavadgitā* is referred to by the name Kṛṣṇa far more frequently than by any other name. It is also significant that in the *Bhagavadgitā*, which embodies his philosophy, Kṛṣṇa identifies himself with Vāsudeva of the Vṛṣṇis (X.37).
48. See Dandekar, "The beginnings of Vāsudeva".
49. Vāsudeva is obviously an artificial back-formation from Vāsudeva. Though Jacobi does not subscribe to the view that Vāsudeva was the patronym of Kṛṣṇa, he says that the etymologically correct name would be Vāsudeva (*op. cit.,* p. 165). Sukumar Sen points out (SP: 14th *AIOC*, p. 103) that *vasu* and *vāsu* are respectively the normal and the lengthened grades of IE *wesu*. Therefore, according to him, Vāsudeva = Vāsudeva. Jacobi mentions the case of Narasiṁha = Nārasiṁha (*op. cit.*, p. 164).
50. According to the *Ghaṭa-Fāṭaka,* Vāsudeva and Baladeva were the sons of Upasāgara and Devagabbhā. The *Mahomagga Fātaka* mentions Jāmbavatī as beloved Vāsudeva-Kāṇhā. *Viṣṇu. P.* V.17.26 speaks of Kṛṣṇa and Balarāma as the manefestations of Vāsudeva.
51. Jacobi suggests (*op. cit.*, p. 163) that the name of Kṛṣṇa's father was Ānakadundubhi (*MBh.* II.30.12; III.21.7; XVI.7.1; *Harivaṁśa* 24.15-16.)
52. RGB's *Collected Works*, vol. IV, pp. 49-54.
53. *MBh.* II.38.4, 8, 9.
54. In the *Harivaṁśa* (59.20) Kṛṣṇa says: "We are cowherds wandering in forests, maintaining ourselves on cows, which are our wealth",

RGB points out that the Āhīrs, who are the descendants of the old Ābhīras, still follow the occupation of cowherds.

55. *Padma Purāṇa,* Sṛṣṭikhaṇḍa, V.17.1-19.
56. *Harivaṁśa,* 51.28 ff.
57. Act I.
58. II.2.21.h
59. As suggested by D.R. Bhandarkar (*Some Aspects of Ancient Indian Culture*, p. 62).
60. As suggested by V.V. Mirashi (*CII*, V, p. xxxi ff).
61. The *Divyāvadāna* mentions two Ābhīra contemporaries of Aśoka. The word *ābhīra* occurs also in the *Mahābhāsya* of Pataṣjali.
62. According to Elliot, *Hinduism and Buddhism*, vol. III, p. 427, Christianity did not appear in India in an influential form before the sixth century AD.
63. *ASI*, *Annual Report*, 1925-26, pp. 283-84.
64. S. Chattopadhyaya, *op. cit.*, p. 68.
65. Cf. *MBh.* V.128.45-46. In the Epic, Kṛṣṇa is often called Keśiniṣūdana (II.30.11; 36.2; III.15.10); this epithet is reminiscent of an exploit of boy Kṛṣṇa.
66. See *supra.*
67. H.C. Raychaudhuri says (*Early History of the Vaiṣṇavia Sect*, p. 3) that it is possible that the legend of the pastoral Kṛṣṇa arose from the Vedic legend of Viṣṇu Gopā. Also see S. Chattopadhyaya, *op. cit.*, p. 73.
68. As suggested by H.G. Raychaudhuri, *op. cit.*, p. 28. In *Ṛgveda* I.22.18, to which the author refers, *gopā* clearly means "guardian", "wächter".
69. According to Geldner, the word *gāvah*, occurring in the Viṣṇu hymn (*Ṛgveda* I.154.6), rather denotes the stars.
70. H.G. Raychaudhuri, *op. cit.*, p. 28.
71. It may be emphasised that such engrafting was facilitated on account of the cultural and political affinity among the Vṛṣṇis, the Yādavas, and the Ābhīras. The commonness of the name Kṛṣṇa may also have served as a supporting factor.
72. I.32; II.9.
73. XVIII.1.
74. *gavi ca vindeḥ saṁjñāyam.* The word *govinda* has also been derived from *gopendra.* Recently, S.K. Chatterji (*Ruben Fel. vol.*, 1970, 347-52) has connected the word govinda with the Old Irish boand, so that *govinda* would mean "fair or beautiful on account of cows".
75. See Dandekar, "Viṣṇu in the Veda", *Kane Fel. vol.,* 95-111.
76. The word *viṣṇu* is to be derived from the root *vi* (= to fly).

77. Cf. *Aitareya Brāhmaṇa* I.1 (The idea expressed in this passage that Viṣṇu was *parama* may have been derived from that of the *parama pada* of Viṣṇu mentioned in the *Ṛgveda*); *Śatapatha Brāhmaṇa* I.9.3.9; *Taittiriya Āraṇyaka* V.1. In the *Maitri Upaniṣad* (VI.13), food is called Bhagavān Viṣṇu.
78. See *supra*.
79. It must be emphasised that there did not exist any religious cult as such centering round Viṣṇu. To understand the word *sūrayah* in *Ṛgveda* I.22. 20 more or less in the sense of *bhakta*s (D.C. Sircar, *op. cit.*, p. 7) is unwarranted.
80. XI.24; 30. In these passages, the word *viṣṇu* certainly does not mean merely "the luminous one". It is also not clear why the Lord should have said that, among the Ādityas, he was Viṣṇu (*BG* X.21). In the *Ṛgveda*, Viṣṇu is not included among the Ādityas. According to a later tradition, there are twelve Ādityas representing the sun in the twelve months of the year, and Viṣṇu is included among them. But these Ādityas do not seem to be intended here, for, Varuṇa, Aryaman, Rudra, who are according to that tradition, included among the Ādityas, are mentioned separately in this context. Incidentally, the *Bhagavadgītā* does not seem to accept Viṣṇu's identity with the sun, for, Ravi (= the sun) is mentioned separately in the very verse-half in which Viṣṇu is mentioned.
81. *BG* XI.46.
82. RGB's *Collected Works*, vol. IV, p. 48.
83. *BG* XI.
84. *MBh.* XIV.53-55 (*Anugītā*).
85. II.5.24.
86. In his original character, Viṣṇu was closer to Gopāla Kṛṣṇa; the names Govinda and Dāmodara are derived from the Gopāla Kṛṣṇa complex.
87. X.1.6.
88. See *supra*.
89. This being so, it is, indeed strange that in the *Bhagavadgītā* Lord Kṛṣṇa declares that he is Indra among the gods (X.22). But, after all, the whole catalogue of the *vibhūti*s appears to be rather conventional.
90. As one is often tempted to do. Cf S. Jaiswal, *op. cit.*, p. 51.
91. For a more detailed discussion, see Dandekar, "Hinduism and the Bhagavadgitā: A Fresh Approach", *FOIB* 12, pp. 232-37.
92. This was also the teaching of Kauṭilya, who lived not very long after the teacher of the *Bhagavadgītā*.

93. See Dandekar, "The Mahābhārata: Origin and Growth", *UGR* 12. pp. 65-85.
94. Nārāyaṇa cannot be regarded to have been the centre of Vaiṣṇavism as suggested by some scholars. Cf. S. Jajswal, *op. cit.*, p. 32. It is also suggested that Nārāyaṇa was original and that Viṣṇu came later.
95. It is very difficult to accept the view that Nārāyaṇa, though not mentioned in the *Bhagavadgītā*, is its Bhagavān—Its Real Lord. Cf. S. Jaiswal, *op. cit.*, p. 37.
96. *nārāyaṇa vidmahe vāsudevāya dhīmahi/tan no viṣṇuḥ pracodayāt.* The Gāyatrī-*mantra* in the *Maitrāyaṇī-Sāṁhitā* II.9.1 implies that Keśava Nārāyaṇa, and Viṣṇu are identical; but this cannot be taken to suggest the merger of the element into Nārāyaṇa Vāsudevism-Kṛṣṇaism. The same is true of the mention of Viṣṇu and Nārāyaṇa side by side in the *Maitrī Upaniṣad* VII.7. The *Baudhāyāna-Dharmasūtra* II.5.24 does not connect Nārāyaṇa with Vaiṣṇavism, as suggested by some scholars. Gf. D.C. Sircar, *op. cit.*, p. 23.
97. *pūjāśilāprākāra.*
98. S. Jaiswal, *op. cit.*, Appendix B.
99. A reference may be made here also to an incscription from the Guntur district, belonging to the fourth century AD, which mentions a *devakula* of Bhāgavat Nārāyaṇa.
100. Jacobi, *op. cit.*, p. 161.
101. *āpo nārā iti proktā āpo vai narasūnavaḥ,*
    tā yadasyā 'yanaṁ pūrvaṁ tenanārāyaṇa smṛtaḥ.
102. It is suggested (L.B. Keny, "The origin of Nārāyna", *ABORI* 23: 250 ff.) that Nārāyṇa is a deity of Dravidian origin and that word in Dravidian means "one lying among waters". Keny further identifies Nārāyaṇa with an of the Moheñjo-Daṛo triad.
103. *MBh* XII.328.35.
104. There is hardly any evidence to support the views that Nārāyaṇa signified the collectivity of man, that Nara represented an individual, and that Puruṣamedha was intended for providing food to the entire community of men. Cf. S. Jaiswal, *op. cit.*, p. 35.
105. Bhandarkar also says (*op. cit.*, p. 43) that originally Nārāyaṇa has a cosmic character and is not a historical or mythological individual.
106. *Collected Works*, vol. IV, pp. 6-11.
107. The Gandhamādana, where the Badarikāśrama was situated, may be identified with the northern ridge of the great Hindukush

arch with its northern extension, the Khwaja Mohammad range. It extended south-north to the south of the Pāmīrs (Meru?) and farther to the west in the southwesterly direction. To the north of the Gandhamādana mountain was the Nīla mountain (Zarafshan-Trans-Alai-Tien Shan range) and to the south the Niṣādha mountain (Hindukush-Kunlun chain). cf. S.M. Ali, *The Geography of the Purāṇas*, pp. 58-59.

108. See Keny's view mentioned in fn. 101. According to Kosambi (*ISIH*, p. III; *FESHO* 4, p. 210), Nārāyaṇa has some features in common with the Sumerian god Ea or Enki.
109. *MBh.* VII.172.51.
110. The popular God Viṣṇu was similarly elevated to the hieratic Vedic pantheon. See *supra*.
111. *Collected Works*, vol. IV, p. 44.
112. The central theme of the Puruṣa Sūkta is the self-immolation of a hermaphrodite god-man for the creation of the universe and the procreation of mankind.
113. *MBh.* XII.326.100-101. It may be pointed out that this sect is also known as Pāñcarātra; but the form Pāñcarātra, used by RGB, is adopted in this paper. Incidentally, it is strange that Nārāyaṇa does not occur as a *vyūha* in this doctrine. It is Vāsudeva who represents the highest soul. Nārāyaṇa is, however, called Pāñcarātrika in *MBh.* XII.325.4 (59). The Pāñcarātra also knows hardly anything of Gopāla-Kṛṣṇa. However, as pointed out by RGB (*op. cit.*, p. 57), the glories of boy Kṛṣṇa are sung in the *Jñānāmṛtasāra* contained in the *Nāradapāñcarātra* published by the Asiatic Society of Bengal.
114. The view of some scholar that the Nārāyaṇa implies an actual journey of some Indian Vaiṣṇavas to Christain countries and the subsequent inclusion of some inclusion of Christ among the incarnations of Nārāyaṇa is now proved to be quite unwarranted. It is suggested (S. Chattopadhyaya, *op. cit.*, p. 56) that, since Pāmīr (Meru) was the provenance of the Pāñcarātra doctrine, it may have received some inspiration from the Central Asiatic region in the Kuṣāṇa age.
115. Some of these meanings are *Nārada-Pāñcarātra* (I.1.44): *P.* = knowledge (*rātri*) of five (*paṣca*) kinds, namely, *tattva, muktiprada, bhaktiprada, yaugika*, and *vaiśeṣika*. *Iśvara-Saṁhitā* (XXI): *P.* = doctrine taught by the Great God to the five sages in the course of five successive days and nights. *Śri-Kṛṣṇa-Saṁhitā* (II.40): *P.* = doctrine which destroys (*pac*) ignorance (*rātri*). *Padma-Tantra*: P. = destroyer of the five erroneous systems,

namely, Sāṁkhya, Yoga, Buddhism, Jainism, and Pāśupata. The term *pāñcarātra* is also connected with the five elements forming the body of Brāhma, or the five forms of the Great God, namely, *para*, *vyūha*, *vibhāva*, *antaryāmī*, and *arcā*, or the five methods of worship, namely, *abhigamana*, *upādāna*, *ijyā*, *svādhyāya*, and *yoga*.

116. Luders identifies them with Baladeva, Akrūra, Anādhṛṣṭi, Śarana, and Vidūratha.

117. It is, however, difficult to say why and how, out of the five *mahāvīras*, only four were made to represent the four *vyūhas*.

12
Śaivism
A Fresh Look

R.N. Dandekar

Compared to Vaiṣṇavism, the origin of Śaivism is more obvious and its historical evolution less complex. According to RGB, the beginnings of Śaivism have to be traced back to the Vedic god Rudra who personified the dreadful and destructive phenomena of

> the storms that uproot trees and even demolish houses, accompanied by the thunderbolt which strikes down men and beasts dead in a moment and the epidemics that rage and carry off numbers of men.[1]

Rudra (from the root *rud* "to howl") went about howling with the stormy winds (Maruts) who were his sons (Rudrīyas). RGB further adds that these dreadful phenomena were the result of the wrath of Rudra, which, however, could be appeased with prayer, praise, and offering. Rudra then became Śiva or the benignant one. In the *Ṛgveda,* Rudra stood for the destructive agency of lightning. But when he was duly propitiated with prayers, he became *paśupa* "protector of the cattle" (I.114.9). Rudra caused diseases, but he also possessed the healing remedies (I.43.4). This ambivalent character of

Rudra was often emphasised in the *Ṛgveda.* The conception of the Vedic Rudra gradually developed further until, as seen in the *Śatarudrīya* (TS IV. 5.1; F5 16), he became the God

> of wild and awful scenes, such as cemeteries, mountains and forests. Of the beasts and savages that dwelt in these last and of the thieves and outcasts that resorted to them, he became the lord.[2]

Subsequently he developed into the God who pervaded the universe, dwelt in fire and water, in all beings, and in herbs and trees, and thus became the supreme ruler of all. Indeed, as pointed out by RGB, even in the *Ṛgveda,* Rudras was represented as having risen to supreme power (VII.46.2). It was in this form that the god became "the subject of Upaniṣad speculation, by meditating on whom and seeing whom everywhere in the universe a man attained blissful serenity".[3]

This hypothesis put forth by RGB is characterised by the two common assumptions of early Indology, namely, (1) that the origin of everything Indian has ultimately to be traced back to the Veda, and (2) that the Vedic gods are basically personifications of natural phenomena. It, however, needs to be emphasised that the real popular religion, which was essentially distinct from the Vedic religion, remained outside the purview of the Veda. The Veda, it must be realised, does not teach us everything on ancient social and religious conditions of even Aryan India. It may be said to have emanated from a narrow circle of poet-priests, and reflects a somewhat singular view of things.[4] Long before the advent of the Vedic Aryans, there had prevailed in various parts of India widely spread and deeply rooted popular religious cults. Though they might have apparently suffered a kind of setback on account of the onslaught of the freshly vigorous Vedic way of life and thought, some of them proved influential enough to compel the sponsors of Vedism to accommodate them, in one form or another, in the framework of their religious ideology And when, in the course of the religious history of India Vedism began gradually to decline, these popular religious cults again came into their own and confirmed themselves as the religion of the people. Such, in broad outline, is the genesis of Vaiṣṇavism, Śaivism, and other minor religious sects which together constitute the major part of classical Hinduism. It has been rightly observed that these religious sects are of a fairly ancient date though their positive history is comparatively modern.

How a pre-Vedic non-Aryan religion was adopted into the Vedic religious ideology is perhaps best illustrated by the personality and character of Vedic Rudra.[5] From a cursory study of the various references to Rudra in Vedic literature, one generally gets the impression that two distinct Rudras are presented in that literature—the Ṛgvedic Rudra,[6] who is a heavenly god with Maruts as his hosts, and the post-Ṛgvedic Rudra, who is earthly in character and is associated with evil spirits and dreadful beings. However, the basic identity of these two Rudras is quite unmistakable. A critical consideration of the name, the outward appearance, and certain special features of these two Rudras would leave no doubt about this. The distinction between the two Rudras is only apparent and is occasioned by varying emphasis.

Rudra is essentially ambivalent in character. He is described as a fierce God (II.33.9,11; X.126.5), destructive like a terrible beast (II.33.11), unassailable and unsurpassed in might (I.114.4; II.33.3). According to the *Aitareya Brāhmaṇa* (III.3.9), Rudra is the compound of the terrible forms of the gods, while the *Śatapatha Brāhmaṇa* (IX.1.1.1,6) says that even gods are afraid of him. But Rudra is not exclusively malevolent and maleficent. For, he is said to bestow blessings on his worshippers (I.114.1-2; II.33.6) and generally look after the welfare of man and beast (I.43.6). He sees to it that the inhabitants of a village are well-fed and free from disease (I.114.1). But by far the most significant reference in this connection is the one to Rudra's great healing powers. He is the physician of physicians (II.3.4), whose remarkable remedies are often praised by the Ṛgvedic poets (I.114.5; II. 33.7, 12; V.42.11; VII.46.3). Rudra's healing powers are referred to also in the post-Ṛgvedic literature (*AV* II.27.6; *VS* 3.59; 16.5, 49), but less frequently than his frightful and destructive nature. This "double personality" of Rudra seems to have been regarded by the Ṛgvedic poets as the special distinguishing feature of that God. A *brahmodya* stanza (VIII.29.5) indirectly speaks of Rudra as a God, who is at once ferocious (*ugra*) and bright and holy (*śuci*), and who wields in his hand a sharp weapon (*tigmāyudha*) and at the same time possesses marvellous healing powers (*jalasabheṣaja*).

Similarly, on the one hand, Rudra is called the ruddy boar of the heaven (I.114.5) or the great *asura* of the heaven (II.1.6), while, on the other, the *Śatarudrīya* associates him with various kinds of people and places on the earth. He is glorified as the lord of thieves, pilferers, and plunderers (*VS* 16.20-22). Not only this; he is himself characterised as robber and prowler (even in *ṚV* I.114.4, Rudra is referred to as *vaṅkukavi*), cheater and deceiver (*ibid.*).[7] In the *Śatarudrīya*, Rudra is presented with all the characteristics of purely popular origin—as a figure so real in popular consciousness. As so appositely observed by Barth, "we can conceive nothing more life-like than the figure which stands out from this piece of rude realism, but nothing, at the same time, less Brāhmanic".[8] In this unusual litany, we hardly come across any expression bearing on ritual or any allusion to a sacred custom. Rudra certainly does not appear here as a sovereign God, but there are clear indications that he must have originally been one.

Rudra does not enjoy any position of prominence and honour in the *śrauta* ritual. He is either "driven back to his home" as in the Agnihotra,[9] or only the remnants of oblations are assigned to him.[10] As against this, Rudra plays a particularly important role in certain *gṛhya* or popular rites such as the Śūlagava,[11] the Aśvayuji, and the Pṛṣṭaka. Thus, while Rudra is generally excluded from the *homa*s offered in hierarchical ritual, he is very positively represented as being entitled to the *bali*s offered in folk-cult rites.

But it is Rudra's unmistakable connection with certain religious cults of ancient times which throws a very suggestive light on the essential personality and character of that god. The Keśin-hymn (X.136), for instance, relates to the orgiastic cult of the *munis* who are said to have worn long hair, indulged in a sort of ecstasy-producing medicament, and attained certain miraculous powers which were comparable to those attained through *yoga*; and, in that hymn, Rudra is represented almost as the leader of that cult (X.136.7). The cult of the *brahmacārins* is glorified in AV XI.5.[12] These *Brahmacārnis* practised severe penance and thereby became endowed with peculiar virile powers which enabled them to undertake even cosmic activities. The description of the *brahmacārī* tends to remind one of Vedic Rudra. Similar is the case of the Vrātyas (*AV* XV) who had developed their own distinctive religious ideology, social order, and general way of life. Vedic Rudra betrays many points of contact with their supreme god whom they called Ekavrātya.[13]

Among the features of the Vedic Rudra which differentiate him from the major Vedic gods must also be mentioned his association with what may be broadly called the demon-world, with the serpents, and, as indicated above, generally with non-social, non-divine, fear-inspiring elements. It is, however, not correct to conclude on the strength of such references, as RGB does, that "the sentiment of fear is at the bottom" of the worship of Rudra-Śiva.[14]

The most common theory regarding the character of Rudra is that he is the roaring storm-God who is both frightful and beneficent. RGB has endorsed this theory without any discussion, but specifying that Rudra represented the destructive agency of lightning. According to him, the simple folk working in the field saw in the black cloud tinged red by the soft glow of the lightning God Rudra with his blue neck and red complexion.[15] In the present context, it is neither possible nor necessary to subject this theory to any critical examination. Suffice it so say with Oldenberg that, in the Vedic descriptions of Rudra, lightnings do not flash, rains do not pour down, winds do not rush forth.[16] Therefore, at least in the consciousness of the Vedic poets, Rudra was not a god of tempest.[17] Moreover that theory miserably fails to explain, rationally and satisfactorily, the complex personality of Rudra with its distinctive and exclusive features as set forth above. As for Rudra's identification with Agni, it can easily be shown to be just incidental and not essential.[18] According to Oldenberg,[19] who considers Rudra's connection with mountains and forests to be far more vital and essential than that with storm and lightning, characterises that God as the old man of the mountains, a demon of disease coming from forest and mountain, like Mars Silvanus. But, while emphasising one significant aspect of Rudra's character,[20] Oldenberg has completely ignored other equally or even more important aspects. Arbman,[21] like Oldenberg, rejects the theory that Rudra is the God of thunderstorm or that he personifies any other phenomenon of nature. According to him, Rudra is an unheavenly product of lower mythology, an earthly, demonic, fearful God who has originated from the primitive concepts of death and its fears. He further asserts that Ṛgvedic Rudra represents an artificial side-growth of the continuous line of development from the original primitive non-Vedic Rudra to the later Vedic Rudra, and then to the epic Śiva.

There is no doubt that in the Vedic literature, particularly in the *Ṛgvedic*, greater emphasis is put on Rudra's association with death and its horror than on any other aspects of his complex personality and character. Rudra's *sāyakas* (II.33.10) are the death-bringing arrows shot by Rudra, the sender of disease and death. In I.114.10, Rudra's missiles are unequivocally characterised as "cow-slaying" and "man-slaying". In IV.3.6, that God is directly called *nṛhan*, the slayer of men. A reference has already been made to the significance of the relationship which was tendentiously established between Rudra and Maruts (who originally represented the spirits of the dead), after that God had been admitted to the Vedic pantheon.[22] Rudra's character as the God of death is further concretised, so to say, in later Veda. In the *Atharvaveda*, for instance, he is very significantly deseribed as assailing his victims with diseases (XI.2.22, 26; VI.90; 93). Rudra's doubles, Bhava and Śarva, also are addressed in that Veda as gods of death (*AV* XI.2.2). Various details of the Vedic ritual in which Rudra figures confirm his character as God of death. In the Sākamedha, for instance, there is a funeral ceremony which includes an offering to Rudra. Incidentally it may be pointed out here that, according to the primitive belief, the God of death and his hosts also bestowed fertility on land, animals, and human beings. It also needs to be added that, since the entire concept relating to Rudra was foreign to the Vedic ideology, the character of that God was not clearly defined in the Veda, and the emphasis often shifted from one aspect of his character to another. That is why Rudra cannot be said to have been represented in the Veda as God of death either exclusively or consistently.

The following points will now have been clear from the foregoing discussion:

(1) that Rudra was essentially different from the normal hieratic Vedic gods;
(2) that he belonged to a milieu which was foreign to the Vedic poet-priests;
(3) that the Vedic poet-priests must have accommodated him in their religious complex under the pressure of circumstances, and, therefore, reluctantly and almost under protest;
(4) that, while doing so, they either suppressed or transformed many of that god's essential traits; and
(5) that, as a result of this, only one aspect of Rudra's original complex character, namely, that of the God of death came to be generally emphasised in the Vedic literature.

One does, however, get a few glimpses of Rudra's original complex character from various stray references to that God in the Veda. Indeed, some indications are available in the Vedic literature itself of the rise of Rudra, in the form of Rudra-Śiva, to the position of supreme godhead. For instance, various references in *AV* XV suggest Rudra's correspondence with Ekavrātya (XV.1) and with Bhava, Śarva, Paśupati, Ugradeva, Mahādeva, and Īśāna (XV.5). And, already in the *Maitrāyaṇī Saṁhitā* II.9.1, Rudra is identified with Puruṣa and Mahādeva.

There is sufficient evidence to justify the assumption that Rudra is but the Vedic version of a well-established pre-Vedic non-Aryan popular god. The religious cult centering round this proto-Indian God had spread far and wide—different aspects of that God and different forms of his worship having been emphasised in different regions of the country. The essential common basis of that religion is, however, quite unmistakable. This popular proto-Indian religion differed from the Vedic religion in many significant respects. For instance, that religion was iconic, that is to say, the followers of that religion worshipped their God in the form of some concrete symbol which was installed either in the open or within some temple-like structures which were usually erected away from the main settlements. The Vedic religion, on the other hand, generally did not know of any temple or image-worship. Perhaps the earliest suggestive literary reference to idols is to be found in Pāṇini V.2.101 (*area* : also *pratikṛti* in V.3.96: also cf. V.3.99). Idol-worship, accordingly, seems to have come into vogue among the followers of Brāhmanism not very long before Pāṇini's time. It may be suggested that, with the beginning of the movement for revitalising and popularising Brāhmanism which crystalised in the Sūtra-Vedāṅga period, several elements of the popular proto-Indian religion came to be assimilated into the Brāhmanic religion, idol-worship being perhaps one of such elements. The proto-Indian worship consisted mainly of *pūjā*, that is, besmearing the icon of the god with some sacred substance, and *bali*, that is, the offering, made directly to the God, of raw flesh and blood. This mode of worship thoroughly contrasted with the Vedic ritual or *homa* in which usually cooked oblations (or *soma*) were offered to the gods, not directly but through the sacrificial fire, in the accompaniment of *mantras*. Like idol-worship, the word *pūjā* and also the religious practice denoted by that word were adopted by Brāhmanism during the Sūtra-Vedāṅga period—and that too presumably for the very reason for which idol-worship was adopted. Some of the other features of the proto-Indian religion which clearly differentiated it from the

Vedic religion were yoga, penance and austerities, phallic cult, the God's lordship over animals and association with serpents, fertility rites, importance given to Mother Goddess and to female divinities, and the propitiation of the spirits of the dead and their leader. To anticipate, most of these features are present, in one form or another, in the religious ideology relating to Vedic Rudra.

The proto-Indian god was celebrated as "red god" in some circles, particularly among the proto-Dravidians. They called him by the name Śiva (which proto-Dravidian word means "red one"), because they worshipped him, among other things, by pouring over (Tamil *pucu* from which the word *pūjā* is derived) his icon the blood of the animal, more particularly the buffalo (or, in some cases, even the human being), which was offered to him, and, as a consequence of this, the god actually looked red. Vedic Rudra has borrowed not only the name but also some characteristics of the red god. The word, *rudra*, has to be derived from a hypothetical lost root, *rud*, which must have meant "to be ruddy or red".[23] Thus, Rudra, like proto-Dravidian Śiva, also means the red God. Rudra is actually associated with the red colour in a variety of ways. He is described as being Āruṣa (I.114.5), Babhru (II.33.5), Tāmra, Arum, Vilohita, Nīla-lohita (*TS* IV5.1; *VS* 16.6-7). Like the proto-Indian Śiva, Rudra also is offered *bali* (and not *homa*) as in the Śūlagava rite. Rudra's fondness for blood is frequently referred to. The *TS* (II.1.7.1ff.), for instance, narrates the legend of *Vaṣaṭkāra* breaking open the head of *Gāyatrī*. On that occasion, we are told, the gods took the various juices issuing out of that head. But Rudra chose only the blood. The *Āpastamba Śratasūtra* (X.13.11) seems to refer to blood as Rudra's water. In the Aśvamedha, the blood of the horse is assigned to Rudra (*TS* I.4.36), and according to the *Śatapatha Brāhmaṇa* (V.3.1.10), Rudra longs for the cows slaughtered in the royal palace in the Rajastiya. Red colour is also suggestive of death, magic, evil omen, swearing, cursing, misfortune, etc. And it can be shown that both proto-Dravidian Śiva and Vedic

Rudra were intimately connected with these concepts implied by the red colour.

When the Vedic poet-priests felt constrained by the force of circumstances to admit the popular proto-Indian red God to their pantheon, they naturally sought either to suppress or to transform many of his characteristic features. For instance, they retained the name of the God, but in a different form. They called him Rudra instead of Śiva. As has been pointed out earlier, it was the frightful, demonic aspect of Rudra's character that was specifically stressed in the Vedic literature. This fact made his name almost a taboo. The Vedic poet-priests tried to get over this contingency by referring to that god euphemistically.[24] They gave him the epithet *śiva*, which in Sanskrit meant "gracious benevolent". Several other Vedic gods also were characterised as *śiva*, but it was only in the case of Rudra that the epithet became, in course of time, the proper name of the God. It is not unlikely that this happened under the influence of what may be called folk-philology. For, the word *śiva* was phonetically similar to the name of the proto-Dravidian God (who was the direct ancestor of Vedic Rudra), but which (in Sanskrit) denoted just the opposite of what Rudra generally represented in the Veda. The name Śiva as such seems to be unknown to the Saṁhitās (except perhaps in *Ṛgveda* VII.18. 7 where Śiva seems to be the name of a tribe), the brāhmaṇas, and the old Buddhist literature. It is only in the *Śvetāśvatara Upaniṣad* that the word is first used as a proper noun. Thereafter, both Rudra and Śiva began to be used as the names of one and the same God.

There are indications that the Indus Valley religion was related to the proto-Dravidian Śiva-religion; both were iconic; both sponsored phallus-worship; the buffalo played a special role in both; both served as the fountain head of the religion of epic Śiva. In the pre-Vedic Indus Valley civilisation, the proto-Indian God was represented as ithyphallic Yogīśvara *Paśupati*. The famous Moheṅjo-Ḍaṛo seal,[25] for instance, shows

> the God, who is three-faced, is seated on a low Indian throne in a typical attitude of *yoga* with legs bent double beneath him, heel to heel, and toes turned downwards. His arms are outstretched, his hands, with thumbs to front resting on his knees.... The lower limbs are bare and the phallus seemingly exposed.... Crowning his head is a pair of horns meeting in a tall headdress. To either side of the God are four animals, an elephant and tiger on his proper right, a rhinoceros and buffalo on his left. Beneath the throne are two deer standing with heads regardant and horns turned to the centre....[26]

It is needless to add that all the typical features of this God are evidenced in the conception of Vedic Rudra and epic Śiva. As has been already pointed out, Rudra is connected with *yoga* through his association with the *muni*-cult, while epic Śiva[27] is often glorified as Yogīśvara. The hieratic Vedic attitude towards *yoga* and related practices, like renunciation, austerities, and wandering mendicancy, is reflected in Indra's antagonism to the *yati*s (*TS* 6.2.7.5; *Ait. Br.* VII.4.2). The Indus Valley religion, like the classical Śiva-religion, promoted the worship of the anthropomorphic ithyphallic god as well as of the separate phallic symbol. The description of some of the Vrātyas as *Śamanīcamedhra* and of the *brahmacārīn* as *bṛhacchepa* tends to establish Vedic Rudra (who was associated with those cults) as representing a significant stage in the almost unbroken continuity from the Indus Valley Paśupati to epic Śiva.[28] As in the case of *yoga*, so too in the case of phallic worship, the attitude of Vedism was contentious. The *śiśnadeva*s (phallus-worshippers) were regarded as the enemies of the Vedic Aryans.[29]

The Indus Valley God's lordship over animals is clearly suggested by the Mohenjo-ḍaṛo seal. Vedic Rudra (as also epic Śiva) is actually called Paśupati (*VS* 16.17, 40), while most of the animals shown on the Mohenjo-Ḍaṛo seal are brought into relation with epic Śiva in a special manner.[30] The Indus

Valley Paśupati's tall headdress perhaps reappears in the form of Rudra's *uṣṇīṣá* (*VS* 16.22) and *kaparda* (*VS* 16.43). And though, neither Vedic Rudra nor epic Śiva is represented with horns, there is hardly any doubt that the horns do reappear in the form of the crescent moon which Śiva bears on his forehead.[31] Another Indus Valley seal[32] provides evidence for the assumption that the serpent cult was an integral part of the Indus Valley Śiva-religion. Vedic Rudra also is associated with serpents in various ways. For instance, *Atharvaveda* III.27 and VI.56.2-3, which are said to pertain to Rudra, are regarded as serpent charms.[33]

Apart from the proto-Dravidian Śiva and the Indus Valley Paśupati (whose identity will have now become quite manifest), two other forms of the same proto-Indian god are referred to in the *Śatapatha Brāhmaṇa* (I.7.3.8)—Śarva[34] who was glorified by the Eastern people and Bhava who was glorified by the Vāhikas.[35] It is significant that both these regions lay outside the brahmanised country.

Thus, Rudra is not a storm-God, but represents just the Vedic version of the proto-Indian Śiva-Paśupati. It is to this latter God, and not to Vedic Rudra (as RGB says), that the origin of Śaivism is to be traced back. Indeed, most of the essential features of Śaivism are anticipated by the proto-Indian religion of Śiva-Paśupati and consequently by the religious complex pertaining to Vedic Rudra.[36]

I have suggested[37] that the word *śivasaḥ* occurring in *Ṛgveda* VII.18.7 may denote the people who worshipped Śiva as their chief God.[38] The passage mentions various tribes who tried to win over Indra to their side—of course, hypocritically—against the Vedic Aryan leader Sudās in the Daśarājña. The Visānins, that is, the people wearing a headdress adorned with horns (presumably, like their God depicted on the Mohenjo-Ḍaṛo seal) are mentioned side by side with the Śivas. This may be understood as confirming the character of the Śivas as the worshippers of Śiva. It would appear that the Śivas, the Visānins, and the *iṣṭa-deva*s, who are represented in the

Ṛgveda as the enemies of the Vedic Aryans, professed the same proto-Indian Śiva-religion. Apart from this solitary and not improbable reference, the word *śiva* does not occur in the Saṁhitās or the Brāhmaṇas in the sense of either God Śiva or the worshipper of Śiva. As pointed out by RGB,[39] in the *Śatapatha Brāhmaṇa* VI.1.3.7 and the *Kauṣītaki Brāhmaṇa* VI.1.9, Rudra is referred to as the son of Uṣas. Prajāpati is said to have given him eight names, seven of which are the same as those mentioned in the *Atharvaveda* XV.5.1-7 while the eighth is Asani. More significant is the reference to Rudra roving from place to place, hankering after the sacrificer's cattle and then being propitiated by an offering on the cross-road (*Śatapatha Brāhmaṇa* II.6.2.6). It may also be noted that the cult of the Vrātyas receives special attention in the *Pañcaviṁśa Brāhmaṇa*, while the references to Muni Aitaśa in the state of ecstasy (*Ait. Br.* VI.5.7) and to Keśin Darbhya (*Kaus. Br.* VII.4) remind one of the *muni*-cult. All this does not, however, imply any particular development in the Rudra-Śiva religion as reflected in the Brāhmaṇas.

Pāṇini refers in IV.1.49 to the gods Bhava, Śarva, and Rudra, without, however, hinting, in any way, at their essential identity; but he does not seem to know of Śiva as the name of a God.[40] Pāṇini IV.1.49 explains the formation, among others, of such names as Bhavānī, Śarvāṇī, and Rudraṇī, from Bhava, Śarva, and Rudra respectively, denoting the wives of those gods.[41] The name Śivānī, derived similarly from Śiva, occurs in classical Sanskrit literature, but Pāṇini does not mention Śiva in that *sūtra*. According to some scholars,[42] the *ayaḥtūlikā* implied by *P.* V. 2.76 is a kind of Śaiva ascetic, but the wording of the *sūtra*[43] does not seem to support such an assumption.[44] Megasthenes mentions two gods who had become known to him in India—Hercules of the plains and Dionysos of the mountains. Hercules is usually identified with Kṛṣṇa, and it is suggested that Dionysos may stand for Rudra-Śiva who is described as Girīśa or Giritra. But the essential character of Dionysos is that of a God of wine, and, as pointed out elsewhere, he is to be identified with Saṁkaraṣaṇa-Baladeva rather than with Śiva.[45] Nevertheless, soon after Pāṇini's time, Śiva seems to have begun being recognised, by that name, as a prominent god of the people. For, Kauṭilya recommends the construction of a temple of Śiva in the centre of a city.[46]

The *Śvetāśvatara Upaniṣad* (*SU*) represents a very significant landmark in the history of Śaivism. That Upaniṣad is in respect of Śaivism what the *Bhagavadgītā* is in respect of Vāsudevism-Kṛṣṇaism. There is, however, no doubt that the *Bhagavadgītā* is chronologically later than the *Śvetāśvatara Upaniṣad*. It can, indeed, be shown that many concepts occurring in the *Śvetāśvatara Upaniṣad* have been further developed in the *Bhagavadgītā*.[47] The *Śvetāśvatara Upaniṣad* V.2 mentions Kapila, the founder of the Sāṁkhya system,[48] who may be taken to have belonged to the sixth century BC. That would fix the *terminus ante quem non* for the origin of that *Upaniṣad*. Further, from the grammatical point of view, that *Upaniṣad* is clearly post-Pāṇinian.[49] The *Śvetāśvatara Upaniṣad* may accordingly be assigned to about the end of the fifth century BC. Conceptually, the *Śvetāśvatara Upaniṣad* may be placed between the *Kaṭha-Upaniṣad* and the *Bhagavadgītā*.[50]

The *Śvetāśvatara Upaniṣad* is essentially monotheistic in character. *Eko devaḥ*[51]—these words may, indeed, be said to be the keywords of this philosophical tract. This One God is beyond all contingency and variation, and yet he is the creator as well as the Destroyer—the *Urgrund*—of the world. He also sustains everything: *bhārateviśvamisaḥ* (I.8). It is verily through his greatness that this *brahmacakra* is set in motion (VI.1). He is described as being immanent (I.16; II.16) as well as transcendent (III.10, 14)—a kind of polarity which is poignantly expressed and which deeply touches the heart.[52] And, manifestly, this *eka deva* is Rudra: *eka evarudro' vaṭasthe na dvitīyo ya imām! lokān īṣata iṣinibhiḥ* (III.2).[53] He is now definitely identified with Śiva (IV.14, 15, 18), and is also referred to as Hara (I.10), Maheśvara (VI.7), Bhāgavat (V.4), Giriśānta-Giritra (III.5, 6) and Mahān Puruṣa (III.8). His description as *vṛkṣaivastabdhaḥ* (III.9) seems to suggest his name Sthānu. In its glorification of Rudra-Śiva as the One

God, the *Śvetāśvatara Upaniṣad* is evidently influenced by the concept of *eka-vrātya* (*AV* XV) and the descriptions in the *Śatarudrīya*[54], Verily, the *Śvetāśvatara Upaniṣad* represents a kind of philosophical continuation of the ancient *Śatarudrīya*.

Rudra being thus represented in the *Śvetāśvatara Upaniṣad* as the Supreme Being, it is difficult to agree with RGB's observation that this *Upaniṣad* "does not appear to be composed in a sectarian spirit".[55] Again, Rudra in the *Śvetāśvatara Upaniṣad* is not, as RGB seems to suggest,[56] the result of the personalisation of the impersonal *Brahman*. There are clear indications in the *Upaniṣad* that the God is actually superior to *Brahman*—he is *brahmayoni* (V.6) and *brahmapara* (III.7). It is true that Sāṁkhya (VI.13), Yoga (VI.13), and Vedānta (VI.22)—all these three are mentioned by name in the *Śvetāśvatara Upaniṣad*, but the teachings of that *Upaniṣad* are basically Sāṁkya-Yoga-oriented,[57] the Vedāntic elements in them, if any, being only superficial.[58] The word *māyā* occurring in this *Upaniṣad* is, for instance, to be understood not in the strict Sāṁkya-Vedāntic sense of illusion, but rather in the Ṛgvedic sense of the *māyā* of ***Asura*** Rudra—the *devātma-śakti* and its creation.

Mokṣa is naturally the goal according to the *Śvetāśvatara Upaniṣad*, and it is to be attained by means of the knowledge of the One God: *jhatvadevammucyatesarvapasaiḥ* (II.15). The *Upaniṣad* does not seem to tire of repeating this dictum (IV.14-15). But far more important in this connection is *bhakti* for god Rudra-Śiva. Indeed, as has been rightly observed, the most characteristic feature of the religious sects of India, in general, is that they subordinate knowledge to a psychical fact of a totally different nature, namely, *bhakti*, that is, faith, humble submission, absolute devotion, love for God, without which knowledge is either vain or impossible.[59] It has been already pointed out that the cult of *bhakti*, which was presumably pre-Vedic and non-Aryan in origin, must have come to be revived some time before Pāṇini's time.[60] It is but natural that the *bhakti*-cult should have been specifically related, first of all, to the god who had been known to the people from very early times, namely, Rudra-Śiva. As required by the doctrine of *bhakti*, the worship of Rudra-Śiva was open to all people irrespective of race, *varṇa*, or *āśrama*. The *Śvetāśvatara Upaniṣad* emphasises that it is through meditation on,[61] application to, and identification with Hara that the unreality that the world is finally comes to an end: *tasyabhidhyanadyojanattattvabhavadbhityas ca 'nteviśvamayanivṛttiḥ* (I.10). And even the fact that *Svetāśvatara* is enabled to impart his esoteric teaching to a person who has the deepest *bhakti* for the God and for the *guru*[62] is itself the result of his *tapas* but more particularly of the grace of God (VI.21, 23).[63]

It is particularly noteworthy that, though the *Mahābhārata* (*MBh*) is generally conceived in the interest of Vaiṣṇavism (Vāsudevism-Kṛṣṇaism), Kṛṣṇa being represented almost as the *primo motore* of the Great Epic, the cultus which is often quite emphatically glorified in the epic is that of Śiva. One would, therefore, be justified in assuming that, long before the *Mahābhārata* assumed its final form, the Śiva-cult had re-established itself as a dominant force in the religious history of India. The two major characters of the epic, namely, Kṛṣṇa and Arjuna, are represented to have been the special proteges of Śiva. They are shown to have survived unscathed the horrendous onslaught which Aśvatthāmā had mounted against the Pāṇḍava army after the death of his father. When asked by Aśvatthāmā how that could have happened, Vyāsa narrated to him how formerly Nārāyaṇa had practised penance on the Maināka mountain for 60,000 years, how, as the result of it, he had seen Rudra-Śiva appear before him, how he had then praised Śiva as the highest God, and how, finally, Śiva had granted to him the boon of invincibility in battle. The privilege of this favour of Śiva was shared also by Nara who was born of Nārāyaṇa's *tapas*. Nārāyaṇa and Nara, who, in the epoch of the *Mahābhārata*, incarnated themselves as Kṛṣṇa and Arjuna respectively, continued to enjoy that favour of Śiva (Droṇa-Parva. 172). A similar explanation was given by Vyāsa in another context. While Arjuna was routing the Kaurava forces, he saw that a resplendent person bearing a *śūla* was actually doing so for him. When he reported this to Vyāsa, the latter told him that it was Śiva who had been constantly guarding him throughout the war. Vyāsa then praised Śiva with what is referred to as a *caturvidhastotra* (Droṇa-Parva. 173).[64] Verily, as described in the Āraṇyaka-Parva (38-41), Arjuna had obtained his strongest weapon, namely, the *pāśupata-astra*, from Śiva himself whom Arjuna had propitiated through *tapas* and who, in the guise of a Kirāta, had subsequenty to test Arjuna's fortitude and valour.[65]

In the first episode mentioned above, a hint was incidentally given by Vyāsa that Aśvatthāmā also was in a way cherished by Śiva (Droṇa-Parva 172.82). This very point seems to have been further developed in the Sauptika-Parva (6-7). When, after having been temporarily dissuaded from his proposed nocturnal raid, Aśvatthāmā returned to his camp, he saw a gigantic apparition blocking his way. He attacked that phantom with all his might, but to no avail. He suspected that the phantom was born from his own evil inclinations; he, therefore, surrendered to Śiva, sang him a hymn of praise, and then actually prepared to offer himself as an oblation to the God. Śiva was thereby propitiated. He then told Aśvatthāmā of the rigorous austerities which Kṛṣṇa had practised for the sake of his favour and declared that no one was more beloved to him than Kṛṣṇa (Sauptika-Parva 7.61: *tasmādistatamaḥkṛmadanyo mama navidyate*). Further, in the same Parva, it is narrated that Yudhiṣṭhira asked Kṛṣṇa how Aśvatthāmā, single-handed, had dared perpetrate the atrocity during the night and that Kṛṣṇa replied that it was all due to the credulous favour of Śiva. Kṛṣṇa further took that opportunity to expatiate on Śiva's greatness. Brāhma, he continued to tell Yudhiṣṭhira, implored Śiva to create the world and procreate the human race. Śiva agreed and undertook severe penance for that purpose. Having waited for the God for a long time, Brāhma decided to bring about creation through another agency. Śiva returned from his penance and saw that the world had already been created. Greatly enraged, he cut off his generative organ and violently planted it upon the earth, for, he thought, it was no longer needed. Kṛṣṇa also told Yudhiṣṭhira of the sacrifice of the gods in which no portion was offered to Śiva and which, therefore, Śiva had ruthlessly exterminated (Sauptika-Parva 17-18).

But Śiva's unquestioned supremacy is perhaps best illustrated by the Kṛṣṇa-Upamanyu episode described in the Anuśāsana-parva (14-18). Jambuvatī desired a son from Kṛṣṇa. Having known that Rukmiṇī had given birth to valiant sons as the result of Kṛṣṇa's worship of Śiva, she importuned Kṛṣṇa again to worship that God for her sake. Kṛṣṇa went to the Himalaya mountain for penance and casually came to the hermitage of Upamanyu. Upamanyu asked Kṛṣṇa to practise penance there only, for, Śiva himself was residing there. Upamanyu then told Kṛṣṇa how he had practised penance in order to propitiate Śiva, how he had refused to accept boons from any God other than Śiva, and how, in the end, Śiva had manifested himself before him and had fulfilled all his desires (14). Kṛṣṇa, too, is then said to have propitiated Śiva through penance and to have thereby obtained the desired boons (15-16). This narrative is followed by the *Śiva-aṣṭottara-sahasranāma-stotra* (17) and the eulogy of that *stotra* by different sages (18). In another context, on having been asked by Yudhiṣṭhira what specific knowledge he had obtained from Durvāsā,[66] Kṛṣṇa responded by glorifying the supreme greatness of Rudra-Śiva (Anuśāsana-Parva 145) and by explaining the significance of the great God's various names, such as Maheśvara, Rudra, Mahādeva, Śiva, Sthānu, Puśupati, etc. (Anuśāsana-Parva 149). It is noteworthy that, in both these cases, a special mention is made of the *Śatarudrīya* (Anuśāsana-Parva 145.4; 146.23).

Various occasions have been manoeuvred by the redactor of the *Mahābhārata* to introduce—appositely or otherwise–hymns of praise of Śiva. Some of the more important of these *Śivastuti*s are: by Kṛṣṇa in Droṇa-Parva 172, by Vyāsa in Droṇa-Parva 173, by the gods and the *brahmarṣi*s on the eve of the destruction of Tripura (Kama. 24), by *Aśvatthāmā* in Sauptika-Parva 7, by Upamanyu in Anuśāsana-Parva 14, by Kṛṣṇa in Anuśāsana-Parva 15, and the *Śiva-aṣṭottara-sahasra-nāma-stotra* (Anuśāsana-Parva 17).[67] It may also be mentioned that many *tīrthas* spread over different regions of the country are described in the epic as having been sanctified by association with Śiva, in one form or another—a fact that would indicate the wide sphere of the influence of the Śiva-religion.

Attention may now be drawn to some characteristic features of the Śiva-religion which become evident from the many allusions to Śiva occurring in the epic. In the epic Śiva-religion, greater importance is attached to *tapas* than to *bhakti* or any other form of worship. And this is in full conformity with the proto-Indian character of that religion. Whoever seeks to propitiate Śiva practises penance—for instance, Nārāyaṇa, Upamanyu, and Kṛṣṇa did so. Even Śiva, who is naturally enough represented as the supreme God, himself takes to *tapas* whenever he wants to accomplish something. That phallus worship is an integral part of the Śiva-religion is also frequently emphasised in the epic. Indeed, Upamanyu argues that Śiva is the greatest of the gods because it is only his *liṅga*—and of no one else—that is worshipped by gods (Anuśāsana-Parva 14.100-102: *nasuiruma yad anyasya litigant abhyarcyatesuraiḥ*). The suggestion that *liṅga* here means merely a concrete symbol or an indicatory mark would not carry conviction. For, the symbols of even other gods are seen to be actually worshipped. But it is only in the case of Śiva that his generative organ is worshipped. That *liṅga*, in the context of Śiva, invariably signifies the generative organ is confirmed by the legend narrated by Kṛṣṇa to Yudhiṣṭhira regarding Śiva having cut-off his *liṅga* when he discovered that it was no longer needed since the process of creation had already been accomplished (Sauptika-Parva 17.24). Again, the *Mahābhārata* is definitely familiar with the circumstance that Śiva is worshipped in two different forms—in the human form and in the form of *liṅga* (Droṇa-Parva 173. 94: *pūjayedvigrahamyastu liṅgam vā 'pi samarcayet*; also Anuśāsana-Parva 146.15-17).

One is often reminded of Śiva's ancient character as the God of fertility in respect of man, animal, and land, when one reads in the epic, not infrequently, of persons propitiating Rudra-Śiva for the sake of progeny (cf. Anuśāsana-Parva 14-16). The almost unbroken continuity of the Śiva-religion from the proto-Indian period to the epic—Paurāṇic period is further evidenced, among other things, by Śiva appearing as a Kirāta (Āraṇyaka-Parva 38-41) or as a *Puruṣa* bearing a *śūla* (Droṇa-Parva 173) and by his being denied a share in the sacrifice (Sauptika-Parva 18; Śānti-Parva 274).[68] Similarly, some of the ideological features of Śaivism which were first introduced in the *Śvetāśvatara Upaniṣad* are seen to have been delineated also in the epic such as, for instance, its Sāṁkhya-Yoga orientation.[69] Supreme godhead of Śiva, which is frequently emphasised in the epic, may also be mentioned in this very context. As for this last, however, it needs to be pointed out that, though Nārāyaṇa-Kṛṣṇa is usually represented as a protege of Śiva, the redactor of the epic, presumably with a view to stressing the Vaiṣṇava genesis of the epic, has introduced some episodes wherein Rudra-Śiva is said to be just a product of the wrath of Nārāyaṇa (Brahmā being the product of his grace)[70] or Nārāyaṇa is shown to have seized Rudra by the throat[71]or Rudra is made to surrender to Nārāyaṇa.[72] But, even in such cases, the redactor either betrays his bias in favour of Śiva (Śānti-Parva 328.21: *tasmādātmanameva 'grerudramsampūjyamyaham*) or seeks to establish a kind of equipoise between the two gods (Śānti-Parva 330.64: *na 'vayorantaramkiñcin ma tebhudbuddhiranyathā*).[73]

The tradition of phallus-worship in India is, indeed, very ancient. It has been suggested that the Neolithic people in south India were primarily worshippers of *liṅga*. Evidence, is produced in this connection of the Kapagallu Hill in Bellary district, where one sees a *liṅga* together with a bull in a crouching position.[74] Be that as it may, there is certainly far more definite and far more profuse evidence regarding phallus-worship which has been unearthed in the Indus Valley. The conical terracotta objects with rounded tops and the ringstones discovered in the Indus Valley are, without doubt, the symbols of *liṅga* and *yoni* respectively. We have already seen that the chief god of the Indus Valley people was the ithyphallic Yogīśvara Paśupati (who has been depicted on the Moheṅjo-Ḍaṛo seal and who is identical with the proto-Dravidian god Śiva).[75] The ithyphallicism of the Moheṅjo-Ḍaṛo figure and the large number of *liṅga-yoni*-like objects discovered in Indus Valley may be presumed to have been closely related to each other verily, they have to be regarded as denoting the two aspects of the phallic worship which was an integral part of the proto-Indian Śiva-religion. It is not unlikely that the worship of the phallus, which, as evidenced by its almost universal dissemination, must have been a natural development in the history of human culture, had grown in India independently in the hoary past,[76] and that it came to be associated with the religion of the ithyphallic God only at some later date. Whatever that may have been, one thing seems to be quite certain, namely, that, in the proto-Indian religion of the Indus Valley period, the two had already become organically connected with each other. It is believed that an oblong terracotta sealing discovered in the Indus Valley actually shows the figure of Śiva with his three symbols, namely, the bull, the trident, and the phallus.[77] We may, therefore, assume that in the proto-Indian Śiva-religion the God was worshipped both in the anthropomorphic ithyphallic form and in the form of a separate *liṅga*. This practice of the worship of Śiva has continued even in historical times,[78] though the *liṅga-pūjā* seems to have become more common in course of time.

As phallus-worship was supposed to have been unknown to the Veda, it was suggested that it had originated among the Dravidian races[79] or among the Western nations and even among the Greeks.[80] For one thing, it is not correct to say that phallus-worship was unknown to the Vedic poet-priests; indeed, they knew it and abhorred it as is indicated by their attitude towards the Śiśnadevas. And, second, in view of its universal diffusion in very ancient times, the question regarding its origin is rendered almost irrelevant.[81]

There has been a tendency among Indian scholars—a tendency which is perhaps quite natural—to reject the assumption that the *liṅga* is a phallic emblem. It is suggested, for instance, that the idea of the *liṅga* originated out of an attempt to express the inexpressible, to make Śiva perceptible to the mental eye.[82] The *liṅga* is Maheśvara himself, and not merely the emblem of his *membrum virile* (*liṅgamsaksanmaheśvaraḥ*).[83] It was also claimed that the *liṅga* signified a protest against. It was also claimed that the *liṅga* signified a protest against idolatry. According to another interpretation, the Śiva-*liṅga* is the closest possible approximation to the cosmic *Puruṣa*—the hemispherical top of the *liṅga* consists of thousands of heads (*sahasraśīrṣa*), each of the size of a point. The *liṅga* represents the double idea of the "formless" and the "all-formed" Śiva.[84] But the more common idea which is presumed to underlie the *liṅga* is that of the *axis mundi* (which is also implied by the Atharvavedic Skambha and the Buddhist *stūpa*). Recourse is also taken in this connection to the Purāṇic account of the quarrel for precedence between Brahmā and Viṣṇu and the appearance before them of Śiva in the form of a blazing column the ends of which the two gods were asked to find but which, to their chagrin, they could not. This blazing column, it is pointed out, came to be later represented through the *liṅga*.[85]

The close relationship between the ithyphallic god and the *liṅga-yoni*-like objects, which is clearly implied in the Indus Valley religion, should, indeed, put an end to all such speculations. There is also the strong corroborative evidence provided by the Gudimallam *liṅga* of the second century BC[86] whose similarity to the human male's generative organ is quite unmistakable. And the still more pertinent point is that, at Guḍimallam, an anthropomorphic figure of Śiva, in standing position and with two arms, and the *liṅga* appear to be inseparably connected with each other.[87] This would put beyond all doubt three facts, namely (1) that the Śiva-cult and the *liṅga*-cult organically constituted a single religious complex, (2) that the *liṅga* signified the phallus and (3) that, as in the proto-Indian period so too in historical times, Śiva was worshipped in two forms—in the human form and/or in the *liṅga*-form. The Bhītā *liṅga* (first century BC) which, like Śiva, has five faces,[88] and the many *liṅga*s with figures of Śiva belonging to the Kuṣāṇa period, which have been discovered at Mathura,[89] would further confirm these facts if any such confirmation was at all needed. It is also noteworthy that Lakulīśa, the founder of the Pāśupata sect, who was often identified with Śiva himself, was sculpturally represented as seated in a Yogic posture, adjoining a *liṅga* and, at the same time, with a prominent generative organ. Similarly, the Pāśupatas are known to have worshipped the *liṅga* as well as the *mūrti* of Śiva (*Pāśupatasūtra* I.6, 9).

As for the literary evidence in this connection, reference may be made to the description of Rudra-śiva in the *Śvetāśvatara Upaniṣad* as the God, who, being one, rules over every single *yoni* (V.2: *yoyonimyonimadhitiṣṭhatyekaḥ*), or as a person who is of the measure of a thumb[90] (III.13: *aṅguṣṭhamātraḥpuruṣaḥ*; also V.8); to Upamanyu's unequivocal assertion (mentioned above) that Śiva was the greatest of all gods because it was only his *liṅga* which was worshipped[91]; and to the Purāṇic account that the sages of the Pine Forest, accusing Śiva of seducing their wives in disguise, cursed him, that, as the result of the curse, the generative organ of Śiva dropped down, and that Śiva, revealing himself to them, taught them, to worship his fallen *liṅga*.[92] It may, however, be added that, in the Purāṇas as also elsewhere, we do come across passages wherein attempts are made to foist some mystic or philosophical meaning on the concept of *liṅga*. All such attempts have proved to be manifestly artificial and unconvincing. We may also incidentally note that, notwithstanding the wide diffusion of phallus-worship in India since very ancient times, the word *liṅga* in the sense of phallus is, strangely enough, not seen to have been used in early literature. The word occurs in that sense for the first time in the concluding portion of the *Mānava-Śrautasūtra* which presumably belongs to the third century BC.[93] *Mānava-Śrautasūtra* 11.7.1.13 reads: *suguptadeśegocarma-mātre 'sthānsvanuliptevaliṅgapadmakṛtimprakalpyaprokṣya "ma no mahāntam" itisthāpayed "namaḥśambhave" ce 'tyarcayet.* The fact that this whole section is called *rudrajapasya vidhānakalpa*[94] and the specific context in which the *sūtra* occurs confirm that the word *liṅga* here means "phallus".[95] From the *Mahābhārata* onwards, the word *liṅga* in the sense of "phallus" seems to have obtained wide currency.

The few references to the Śiva-cult which we come across in the *Mahābhāṣya* of Patañjali clearly indicate that that cult had become firmly established long before his time. Commenting on *P.* V.3.99,[96] Patañjali seems to suggest that, even in the fourth century BC the Śiva-worship had become so common that the Mauryas got the images of gods like Śiva, Skanda, and Viśākha[97] prepared and sold to the people. In another context, Patañjali apparently hints that Śiva did not formally belong to the hierarchical Vedic pantheon. In his commentary on Vārttika 2 of *P.* VI.3.26,[98] he specifically mentions the *dvandva* compounds formed with the names of the gods Brahmā and Prajāpati, Śiva and Vaiśravaṇa,[99] and Skanda and Viśākha as not being covered by the category of what he calls *lokavedayoṅ devatādvandva*. But perhaps the most significant reference in the *Mahābhāṣya*, from the point of view of the history of the Śiva-religion, is that to the Śivabhāgavatas.[100] The Śivabhāgavatas must have constituted a specific sect of the followers of the Śiva-religion—the distinctive characteristics of that sect being *bhakti* for Śiva[101] and bearing of an iron lance (trident) in the hand. According to Patañjali's commentary on *P.* V.2.76, a Śivabhāgavata cannot be called *ayaḥśūlika* though he carries an *ayaḥśūla* in his hand. The word *ayaḥśūlika* is not to be understood in the literal sense, but only in the metaphorical sense. It denotes a person who takes recourse to harsh measures in order to accomplish some work which can be accomplished by milder methods. The context seems to suggest that the *ayaḥśūlika* was a kind of extortionist false ascetic, like the *daṇḍajinika*, but his connection with the Śiva-religion, if any, is not clear.

The numismatic evidence for the prevalence of the Śiva-religion, particularly in the first couple of centuries before and after Christ, is also not inconsiderable. It is noteworthy that most of this evidence is derived from north-western India. For instance, a bronze seal, discovered by Marshall at Taxila and belonging to the first century BC shows the figure of Śiva and the legend *śivarakṣitasa* in Brāhmī and Kharoṣṭhī characters.[102] The coins of the *arjunāyānas* (*cir.* 50 BC) and the Yaudheyas (*cir.* 150 AD) show the bull which is obviously a Śaiva emblem. The Auḍumbaras (end of the first century BC) issued their coins in the name of the God Bhāgavat Mahādeva. A reference may also be made to the coins of Wema Kaḍphises who called himself Maheśvara. One of the prominent Śaiva sects was called Maheśvara; but it is doubtful whether the term was used on Wema's coins in the strict sectarian sense as suggested by RGB.[103] A coin of the Kuṣāṇa king Huviṣka (106-138 AD) is said to have a motif similar to that of the Moheṅjo-Ḍaṛo seal of Paśupati.[104] The end of the Kuṣāṇa power synchronised with the rise of the Bhāraśivas in northern India (*cir.* 150 AD). As their name clearly indicates, the Bhāraśivas were staunch followers of the Śiva-religion. So were the Vākāṭakas who were matrimonially related to the Bhāraśivas, Gautamīputra, the son of the Vākāṭaka sovereign Pravarasena I, having been married to a daughter of the Bhāraśiva king Bhavanāga.[105] The period of about two hundred years from 150 AD, which was dominated by these two dynasties, saw a kind of upsurge of the Śiva-religion. The Guptas, who came to real power in the first decades of the fourth century AD, exhibited a remarkable catholic spirit in the matter of religion. Epigraphic and numismatic evidence indicates that most of the Gupta sovereigns were devout Vaiṣṇavas or Bhāgavatas,[106] but there is also evidence to show that they and their ministers respected and patronised Śaivism without any inhibition.[107] The prevalence of Śaivism in northern India in the post-Gupta period may very well be inferred from the statement of Hieun-Tsang (second decade of the seventh century). The Chinese pilgrim, who mentions the Pāśupatas as many as twelve times, says that there were temples of Maheśvara at which the Pāśupatas worshipped; in one or two of them they even resided. And at Varanasi Hieun-Tsang found about ten thousand sectaries who honoured Maheśvara, besmeared their bodies with ashes, went naked, and tied their hair in knots. It may be added that when Hieun-Tsang travelled in India, Buddhism was rapidly disappearing from the south, while Śaivism, and especially Jainism, were the popular faiths in that region.

It has already been seen that south India was the provenance and the stronghold of a prominent aspect of the proto-Indian Śiva-religion. The various other original popular religious cults of south India also showed many traits similar to those of the early Śiva-religion. Indeed, they all seem to have formed a more or less integrated religious complex under the supreme godhead of Śiva. It was, therefore, no wonder that Śaivism, in its new sophisticated form, found in south India a most suitable soil for a rapid and exuberant growth. What the religious situation in south India had been when Śaivism made its reentry in its ancient home is not clear. Buddhism is known to have become firmly established in the Deccan by the third century BC. It continued to flourish during the Sātavāhana period (*cir.* 200 BC - 250 AD), as is evidencced by the various monuments, big and small, which are scattered in the valley of the Kṛṣna and its environs. There are also indications that Buddhism, Jainism, and Brāhmanic Hinduism co-existed in the south during the early centuries of the Christian era. Soon, however, Buddhism gradually disappeared from the religious scene in that region, and as elsewhere so too here, it was Śaivism which profitted most by the expulsion of Buddhism. Śaivism had thus to contend mainly with Jainism.

And now to conclude with a reference to some distinctive features of Śaivism, it may be recalled that Vāsudevism-Kṛṣṇaism originated from and centred round a human hero who came to be deified in course of time. One of the purposes of the *avatāra*-theory seems to have been to provide a kind of rationalisation—and also substantiation—for such godship of a human being. Śiva, on the other hand, has been conceived as a god from the very beginning. And moreover he is conceived essestially as an earthly god—as a God who, being ever present, is intrinsically interested and involved in the affairs of man. Naturally, therefore, Śaivism does not countenance any *avatāra*s of Śiva. The tradition that, in each Kalpa, Śiva appears along with his four disciples is obviously sectarian and conventional. Actually, Śiva is believed to operate either directly or through the medium of the *guru*. The peculiar concept of the *guru*, which, incidentally, is not of Vedic origin,[108] constitutes one of the important characteristics of the Śaiva religious ideology. In a sense, the *guru*-tradition is to Śaivism what the *avatāra*-theory is to Vaiṣṇavism.[109]

Paradox, it is rightly observed, is the very heart of the Śaiva mythology. For instance, Śiva is often represented both as creator and destroyer. He is even said to be that power in the universe which causelessly destroys and causelessly creates.[110] But there is nothing inherently paradoxical in this. The creator is also the destroyer, neither in anger nor by caprice but by the very nature of his activity.[111] This ambivalence of Śiva's nature is best reflected in his dance which typifies the eternal rhythm and polarity which are at the root of the infinite creative process.[112] Through the various movements in the course of his dance, Śiva brings into being the corresponding cosmic forces—his dance is, indeed, "a piece of animated symbolism".[113] Śiva, the Naṭarāja, through the sheer rapture of exuberant power, dances the creation into existence[114] but, through his frenzied *tāṇḍava*, he also destroys what he has created, in order that he may re-create it and thereby perpetuate the rhythm of the creative process.

But the apparent paradox in Śiva's personality and character is far more emphatically expressed in his portrayal as an ithyphallic *yogī*. Śiva's sexuality, it needs to be noted, has mystical rather than libidinous implications. It is the manifestation of an upsurge of a kind of cosmic energy and life-force. Through his asceticism, Śiva is enabled to keep that creative energy or life-force under control. Śiva personifies the ideal which rejects both the licentious indulgence and the stifling continence and which promotes the controlled release of power. *Tapas* and *kāma* may be diametrically opposed, but they are by no means mutually exclusive.[115] Indeed both are regarded as being of the nature of fire or heat. These two polar opposites, namely, asceticism and sexuality, are believed to lead to the same condition, namely freedom from contingency. It is wrong to bifurcate the personality of Śiva and argue that eroticism belongs to the Śiva of the Tantras and asceticism to the Brāhmanic Śiva. This apparent *coincidentia oppositorum*—this concept of the erotic ascetic—is to be understood as the expression of the essential polarity of one single integrated whole. Śiva comprehends within himself, superbly balanced, the supreme aloofness and contemplativeness of *tapas* as well as the hectic fervour and involvement of *kāma*. Indeed, all opposites are beautifully reconciled in his personality and character.[116]

The inadequate understanding and appreciation of the essentially integrated character of Śiva and the consequent emphasis on one or another aspect of his superficially multiple nature have given rise to an intriguing variety of Śaiva sects—the Kāpālikas with their bloody and revolting *aghora* practices; the Vāmācāra-Tāntrikas with their orgiastic rites; the ecstatic Pāśupatas; the mystic Śaiva-Siddhāntins of Kashmir; the aggressive Vīraśaivas; and the saintly Śaiva *bhakta*s of south India about whose fine devotional poems it is said that in them is to be found the frankest and the profoundest delineation of the individual religious life with its struggles and dejections, its hopes and fears, its confidence and its triumph.[117] Such evocation of heterogeneous responses by a single godhead constitutes yet another noteworthy feature of Śaivism.

It is perhaps on account of its erotic mysticism that we see in Śaivism a comparatively heavy preponderance of the female divinity. As indicated above, tendencies are evident even in the proto-Indian Śiva-religion towards the worship of the male and the female aspects of divinity in a joint divine sovereignty. In classical Śaivism, Śakti, the metaphysically derived cosmic potence of Śiva, was granted an independent status and a separate personality. Indeed, in the cosmogony of the Tantras, the role of the creator actually belongs to her—Śiva being represented as a mere immobile spectator.[118] But, here too, in conformity with the usual tendency of Śaivism, the two poles, namely, the male and the female aspects of divinity, are re-united, through a balanced integration, to form the magnificent godhead of Ardhanārīśvara.[119] Kālidāsa has very poetically brought out the paradox of Śiva, who is ever united with his consort, being the foremost among the all-adjuring ascetics.[120] It is further paradoxical, in a sense, that the lord of the *yogī*s and the ascetics should have been regarded as the originator and the presiding deity of drama and dance.[121] But, obviously, this idea has its origin in the cosmic dance of Naṭarāja Śiva. Mention may be incidentally made in this very context of the tradition that the first fourteen *sūtra*s of his grammar, which form the basis of a part of his terminology, were revealed to Pāṇini by Śiva himself.[122]

Having originated as a religion of the people (rather than of hieratic circles) Śaivism has been more or less non-conformist in character in the sense that it generally did not make much of the traditional varṅāśrama dharma. It also promoted equality of sex. Some of the Śaiva sects, like the Liṅgāyatas, even went to the extent of denouncing *vedaprāmāṇya*, Brāhmanic orthodoxy, image-worship, and the doctrine of transmigration. They removed the bar to widow-remarriage and strongly protested against child-marriage.

There is no doubt that Śaivism is more ancient than Vaiṣṇavism, but the lattar is said to be more expansive, more attractive, and more favourable to community of worship and religious sentiment.[123] Both Śaivism and Vaiṣṇavism sponsor a personal monotheism (as against the earlier pantheism), but ritual practices are perhaps more in evidence in Śaivism than in Vaiṣṇavism. While Śaivism regards the universe as the source of pain and misery—as the *pāśa* of the *pasu*—and, therefore, as worthy of being repudiated, Vaiṣṇavism looks upon it as an evidence of the Lord's omnipotence and, therefore, as worthy of being cherished. But it may not be valid to assert that, on account of this attitude of Vaiṣṇavism towards the universe, its contributions to arts and literature have been richer and more profuse than those of Śaivism.[124] Śaivism is known to have dominated the religious scene till eleventh century AD; but thereafter Vaiṣṇavism, which had been infused with new life in respect of both philosophy and devotionalism by the *ācārya*s beginning with Rāmānuja, started to look up. And, though, today, Śaivism may reckon more sanctuaries, it is Vaiṣṇavism which is generally in ascendancy. Whatever that may be, perhaps the greatest glory of the Śiva-religion is that it can justifiably boast of the longest continuous and living tradition among the religions of the civilised world.

Notes

1. RGB's *Collected Works,* vol. IV, p. 145.
2. *Ibid.,* p. 222.
3. *Ibid.*
4. Cf. Barth, *The Religions of India,* 1882, Preface, xiv.
5. For a comprehensive study of Rudra, see Dandekar, "Rudra in the Veda", *JUPHS,* I: 94-148.
6. So far as the number of hymns in which he is celebrated in the *Ṛgveda* is concerned, Rudra will have to be regarded as occupying a very subordinate position in that Veda.
7. Such descriptions can by no means be ignored as being merely fantastic.
8. Barth, *op. cit.,* p. 162. C.V. Nārāyaṇa Ayyar (Śaivism *in south India*) tries to reconstruct from such allusions in the *Śatarudrīya* as *upavīti* (*VS* 16.17: sacrificer-ruler-punisher) the social background of Rudra being conceived as "fierce".
9. *ĀpŚS* VI.11.3.
10. Rudra is accordingly characterised as *uccheṣaṇabhāga* (*TB* I.7.8.5; comm.on *TS* I.8.14).
11. The *ŚSS* and the *ĀśGS* regard the Śūlagava as a *śrauta* rite.
12. Bloomfield (*JAOS* 15: 167 ff.) thinks that *ṚV* X.136 and *AV* XI.5 refer to a common theme.
13. The reference to *vrāta* and *vrātapati* occurring in the *Śatarudrīya* (*VS* 16.25) may be regarded as significant in this connection.

14. RGB's *Collected Works*, vol. IV, p. 151. It is difficult to agree with Barth's suggestion (*op. cit.*, p. 160) that the god who inspires terror and strikes dread is religiously more acceptable
15. *Ibid.,* p. 146. cf. *nīlagrīvo vilohitaḥ* (*TS* 4.5.1). Incidentally it may be pointed out that RGB's views that in the rising sun the Āryas found Mitra, a friendly god, and that in the sun, who vivified the world at the end of the night, they found Savitṛ (p. 145) are quite unacceptable.
16. *JAOS* 16, p. cl.
17. Some of the other naturalistic theories about Rudra are that he is the celestial father (Bergaigne) or that he is Vedic Apollo (Kuhn) or that he is the moon-God (Siecke).
18. Hillebrandt (*VM* II: 179-208) thinks that Rudra is the god of tropical heat before the rainy season.
19. *RdV* 215-25.
20. Rudra is regarded as a mountain-deity (later known as Mallayyā) of the Dravidians who were wild mountain-dwellers (Sakhare, *History and Philosophy of the Lingayat Religion,* p. 133). RGB thinks that Rudra is called Girīśa or Giritra "probably because the thunderbolt that he hurls springs from a cloud which is often compared to a mountain and in which he was believed to dwell" (*op. cit.,* p. 146). According to Ravindra Kumar Sastri (Śaivism *through the Ages,* p. 36), Girīśa signifies the minute form of Rudra in one's body (*giri*) or the presiding deity of some incantations (*giri* from *gīḥ*)
21. E. Arhman, *Rudra: Untersuchungenzumaltindischen Glauben und Kultus,* Uppsala, 1922.
22. When later, in the evolutionary Vedic mythology, Yama came to be regarded as the regular god of death, the relationship between Rudra and Maruts was brought to an end and Maruts began to be represented as the hosts of Indra.
23. Cf. *ZDMG* 40, 120. The word rudra is derived from various roots: *rud* (to howl or to crackle); *ru* (to roar) and *dru* (to spread forth); *rud* (to shine); *ruj* (to shatter). Sāyaṇa, in his commentary on *ṚV* I.114.1, explains the word in six different ways. All these etymologies are linguistically unsound.
24. In this context, reference may be made to the fact that, for a similar reason, Erinyes or Greek Furies was renamed as Eumenides. Adoption of a euphemistic name represents an attempt to civilize a terrible deity.
25. Marshall, *Mohenjo-Ḍaṛo and the Indus Civilisation* (*MIC*), I, pl. xii, fig. 17.

26. *Op. cit.*, pp. 52 ff.
27. Some scholars do not accept the suggestion that the Mohenjo-Ḍaro God is the direct precursor of epic Śiva.
28. A. Ghosh (*IC* 2, 763-71) thinks that Vedic Rudra is a storm god; and yet he links him up with the Indus Valley god on the strength of the evidence of the ellipsoid stones, which, in the context of Rudra, are to be regarded as thunderbolt stones. This is obviously not convincing.
29. Cf. *ṚV* VII.21.5; X.99.3.
30. Śiva is described as wearing the skin of an elephant (*Kumāra.* 5.67; *Megha*-Purva, 38). Communal offerings of buffaloes were made to the proto-Dravidian Śiva. The buffalo, as the vehicle of the God of death, may also have been originally connected with Śiva. As the "Old Man of the Mountains" and as an archer, Vedic Rudra and epic Śiva are closely connected with wild animals like rhinoceros and tiger (cf. *AV* XI.2.24: *āraṇyāḥpaśavaḥ* mentioned in connection with Rudra). Śiva is referred to as *hariṇeśa* and *mṛgarūpa* in a *stotra* occurring in the Himavat-khaṇḍa of the *Skanda Purāṇa*. His characterisation as *ekaśṛṅga* in that very *stotra* may remind one of the unicorn bull which is frequently represented on the Indus Valley seals. See Dandekar, *Some Aspects of the History of Hinduism*, p. 6. Also R.P. Goswami, *Ekaśṛṅgāṇipaśupati* (Marathi), *Jñāneśvara*, November 1974, pp. 10-15.
31. Only in one passage in the *Mahābhārata* (Bom. Edn.: III.88 8), which, significantly, is not included in the critically constituted text, there is a reference to the *viṣāṇa* (horn) of *Śūlin* (Śiva). The bull must have been regarded as the vehicle of the Indus Valley god (as of the epic Śiva), and, as it often happens, some special feature of the vehicle is transferred to the God himself and sometimes also to his worshippers. In later literature, Śiva and his attendants are openly called *śṛṅgin*. Incidentally, it does not seem likely that the horns have taken the form of Śiva's *triśūla* in later times.
32. MIC III, pl. cxvii, fig. 11.
33. The existence of the serpent cult is also confirmed by Rudra-Śiva's connection with mountains and forests and with fertility rites.
34. According to Machek (*Arch. Or.* 22, 544-62), Śarva is the original name of Rudra, the latter being merely an epithet. It is also suggested that the ancient Iranian Saurva Daeva is identical with Vedic Śarva (Haug, *Essays on the Religion of the Parsis*, p. 272). According to Rabindrakumar Bhattacharya (*JOIB*, 24: 285),

Śarva represents the malignant form and Bhava the benignant form of Rudra.

35. The Vāhlīkas are presumably the Bāhlīkas. Their way of life and their religious cult (which is more or less similar to that of the later Vāmācāra-Śaivas) are described in *Mahābhārata* (Bom. Edn.) VIII.44. There the Vāhlīkas (Crit. Edn. elsewhere reads Bāhlīkas) are associated with the Vrātyas. It may also be pointed out, in this context, that *AV* XV.5 assigns Bhava to the eastern region and Śarva to the southern region. Both are there referred to as "archers" (though, etymologically, Śarva is the proper archer).
36. Also see: Dandekar, "Rudra in the Veda", *JUPHS*, 1: 94-148; *Some Aspects of the History of Hinduism*, ch. I.
37. Dandekar, *Some Aspects of the History of Hinduism*, p. 5.
38. Geldner, in his translation of the *Ṛgveda*, understands the word *śivāsaḥ* in the sense of "friends". He also suggests that the word may stand for the tribe of the Śibis. Sāyaṇa interprets the various names mentioned in this context ritualistically.
39. *Op. cit.*, p.149.
40. In *P.* IV.1.112, *śivādhibhyo'n*, a person named Śiva is obviously intended.
41. *indra varuṇa bhavaśarvarudramṛdahimāranyayavayavanamā tu-lācoryānāmānuk.* Mṛda as a name (of Rudra-Śiva) does not occur either in the *Ṛgveda* or in the *AVŚ.* The word *mṛda* does occur in *Kāṭhaka Saṁhitā* 37.13-14, but whether it denotes god Rudra-Śiva is not clear from the context. The same may be said about *AVP* XX.42.3-6.
42. V.S. Agrawala, *India as known to Pāṇini*, p. 388.
43. *ayaḥśūladaṇḍājinābhyāṁṭhakṭhaṣau.*
44. Also see *infra.*
45. Dionysos is said to possess the characteristics of several Indian gods and is accordingly identified with each of them. A reference may also be made here to the suggestion that the Siboi and the Oxydrakai were worshippers of God Śiva (S. Chattopadhyaya, *op. cit.*, p. 94).
46. *Kauṭilya Arthāśātra* II.4.
47. For instance the concept of *uttama puruṣa* in the *Bhagavadgītā* (XV. 17) is presumably developed out of the concept of *mahān puruṣa* in *Śvetāśvatara Upaniṣad* (III.8.19).
48. Max Müller (*SBE* XV, p. 255), among others, understands the word *kapila*, in this context, to mean "fiery" or "ruddy". Deussen identifies Kapila or "the savant" with Hiranyagarbha.
49. Cf. Kirfel, *Beitrage zur Geschichte der Nominakomposition in den Upaniṣads und im epos*, Bonn, 1908; Wecker, *Der Sprachgebrauch*

der alteren Upaniṣads, KZ 47, pp. 1 ff. It is also suggested that the form brahman occurring in *Śvetāśvatara Upaniṣad* I.12 betrays the influence of Prākṛtis.

50. The *Śvetāśvatara Upaniṣad* belongs to what Deussen has called the "middle group" of the Upaniṣads. From the lexical point of view, Jacobi supports this view (*Die Entwickelung der Gottesideebei den Indern*, pp. 20 ff.).
51. Cf. I.10; III.3; etc.
52. Cf. J.W. Hauer, *ZDMG*, 84: 99.
53. This is the reading accepted by R. Hauschild in his edition of the *Śvetāśvatara Upaniṣad* (Leipzig 1927: Reprint, 1966).
54. *AV* X.8 must also be mentioned in this connection.
55. *Op. cit.*, p. 151. The Śaiva character of this *Upaniṣad* may be said to be further evidenced by its reference to *atyāśramin* (VI.21), *tapas* (VI.21), *saṅgha* (VI.21), *yoni* (V.2), and *guru* (VI.23). Hauer (*op. cit.*) even suggests that Śvetāśvatara may have been a name of Rudra-Śiva. Incidentally, the *Śvetāśvatara Upaniṣad* is referred to in the commentary as the *Mantropaniṣad* of the Śvetāśvataras. Traditionally, the Śvetāśvatara is regarded as a branch of the Taittirīya school of *KYV*. The commentary, however, speaks of *ātharvaṇikāḥ śvetāśvatara.*
56. *Op. cit.*, pp. 151-52. Macnicol (*Indian Theism*) characterises Rudra in the *Śvetāśvatara Upaniṣad* as "a deity of agnosticism".
57. Cf. E.H. Johnston, "Some Sāṁkhya and Yoga conceptions of the *Śvetāśvatara Upaniṣad*", *JRAS* 1930, 855-78. Johnston, indeed, regards the *Śvetāśvatara Upaniṣad* as "the oldest document we have giving an adequate account of Sāṁkhya views. In the paper mentioned here, he discusses *Śvetāśvatara Upaniṣad* I.4-5, for the explanation of which, according to him, one has to look to the Sāṁkhya system. He concludes that "the author of the Upaniṣad was fully acquainted with the Sāṁkhya conceptions of *prakṛti* its evolutes and subordinate categories, but in a form more primitive than that of the *SK* (*Sāṁkhya-Kārikā*)". Johnston further discusses in that paper *Śvetāśvatara Upaniṣad* II.8-15 (particularly II.10) which refer to Yoga practices. The *Śvetāśvatara Upaniṣad* is also regarded (A.G. Kṛṣṇa Warrier, *ALB* 17, p. 96) as the earliest authentic source of our knowledge of Yoga. The *Upaniṣad* contains many technical terms from Sāṁkhya-Yoga (I.8,10; IV.5). Strangely enough, Deussen thinks (*Sechzig Upaniṣad's des Veda*, 1921, p. 301) that Sāṁkhya and Yoga in the *Śvetāśvatara Upaniṣad* are to be understood not as systems, but in the sense of *vaidikaṁ jṣānaṁ dhyānaṁ ca.*

58. According to Kunst, *BSOAS* 31, p. 307, the *Śvetāśvatara Upaniṣad* "certainly defies the monistic Brahmā = *āiman* interpretation of the advaitins". Hopkins, however, observes (*JAOS,* 22: 386): "The great value of the Śvetāśvatara Upaniṣad lies in its showing that with the first formal appearance of (*māyā-*) Vedānta the ancient Sāṁkhya had already passed into the Sāṁkhya-Yoga stage of deism."
59. Cf. Barth, *op. cit.,* p. 218. Also Renou, *Religions of Ancient India,* p. 93.
60. See Lecture I.
61. The knowledge of the God, mentioned above, is actually included in meditation.
62. The Guru-tradition is peculiar to the Śiva-religion as is evidenced by the *Brahmacārī-sūkta* in the *Atharvaveda* See *infra.*
63. *Prasāda* or grace of God is an essential element of the *bhakti* doctrine.
64. Cf. Droṇa-Parva 173.103.
65. It is suggested (Renou, *op. cit.,* p. 62) that this struggle of Śiva against Arjuna reflects the opposition which the Śiva-cult met with before it was finally established.
66. It is not unlikely that Durvāsā (mentioned in Anuśāsana-Parva 144) was just a form of Śiva himself.
67. Dakṣa is represented as having praised and propitiated Śiva after the latter had destroyed his sacrifice. This passage (Bom. Edn. Śānti-Parva 248) is, however relegated to the Appendix in the Critical Edition (XII. App. I. 28).
68. Accoding to Śānti-Parva 224.45, a *Puruṣa* was born from the sweat of Śiva after the latter had exterminated Dakṣa's sacrifice. This Puruṣa was Jvara or fever personified. One would be reminded here of Vedic Rudra's character as a sender of diseases.
69. Cf. Karṇa-Parva 24.39. Rudra-Śiva is referred to as the *ṣaḍviṁśaka tattva* (Anuśāsana-Parva 14.181).
70. Śānti-Parva 328.12: *yasya prasādajo brahmā rudraś ca krodhasaṁbhavaḥ.* In Śānti-Parva 338-339, Tryambaka-Śiva is shown to have approached his father, Brāhma, to seek enlightenment on the nature of Virāṭ Puruṣa. The *Viṣṇu* Purāṇa refers to Rudra-Śiva as being born from Viṣṇu's frown, while the *Mārkaṇḍeya* Purāṇa speaks of Rudra-Śiva as the child of Brāhma.
71. Śānti-Parva 330.47.
72. Śānti-Parva 330.61.
73. It is noteworthy in this connection that Śiva and Viṣṇu have several names in common (cf. the *Sahasranāmastotras* relating to

the two gods, which occur in the *Mahābhārata*). It should also be noted that there are hardly any indications in the epic of a rivalry between the followers of the two sects. The *Rāmāyaṇa* adds little to our knowledge of the history of Śaivism. Rāma is said to have broken the bow of Śiva on the eve of his marriage to Sītā and also to have performed *liṅga pūjā* before invading Laṅkā. Rāvaṇa is represented as a devotee of Śiva. As for the Śaiva Purāṇas (the description of some Purāṇas as Śaiva is doubted by scholars), Barth appropriately characterises them as "spiritless" (*op. cit.*, p. 197). In them, legendary narrative (mostly developed out of the pre-existing seeds) abounds; it has little historical or doctrinal value.

74. V.R.R. Dikshitar, *Prehistoric south India*, pp. 89 and 238. The association of the *liṅga* and the bull is noteworthy.
75. R.D. Banerji has suggested that the water-reservoir at Mohenjo-Ḍaṛo and Haṛappā, provided with a narrow covered channel, was presumably a receptacle for holy water for washing the sacred image of the God. This is a feature of Śiva-worship even today.
76. It is suggested that the primitive phallic cult was closely connected with ancestor worship and also with the serpent-cult. The Nāgas were phallus worshipper (K.R. Subramanian, *Madras Univ. Journal*, I, 2).
77. *MIC* I, pp. 129-30, pl. XCIII, 303.
78. It may be noted that not all the varieties of Śiva-image, in historical times, have the *ūrdhvaliṅga* feature. However, all the Śiva-images found in eastern India show this feature without exception.
79. Stevenson, "On the Ante-Brāhmanical religion of the Hindus", *FRAS* 8.
80. F. Kittel. *Uberden Ursprung des Lingakullus in Indien*, p. 46.
81. In the context of the origin of the *liṅga*, Barth observes that "the Hindus, once in search of symbols with figures, must have found it out of themselves, which could not have been difficult to a people with whom the names for "male" and "bull" had for long been synonyms of "God" (*op. cit.*, pp. 261-62).
82. Cf. V.S. Agarwala, *Pur.* 7, 291 ff. The author also says: The *liṅga* form implies the source of creativity that is invisible and unmanifested. The *liṅga* is the concrete manifestation.
83. *Linga Purāṇa*. 20.15-21; 16.1.
84. The *liṅga* is also believed to symbolise *nāda* supervening the *pīṭha* like a cylinder (cf. Sakhare, *op. cit.*, pp. 303 ff.).

85. According to V.M. Apte, "From the Ṛgvedic Rudra to Purāṇic Śiva", *Journal of the University of Saugar* 6), the pouring of melted butter upon the tapering flame of Agni enclosed within the Vedī is reminiscent of the *liṅga*-worship.
86. D.R. Bhandarkar takes the fourth century AD to be the date of the Guḍimallam *liṅga*. He suggests—not at all convincingly that the *liṅga*-worship was foisted on the Śiva-cult in the beginning of the Gupta period (*Lecture on Ancient Indian Numismatics,* pp. 19-20).
87. Cf. Gopinath Rao, *Elements of Hindu Iconography* II,1, pp. 65-69. The *liṅgas* at Kulattūr and Kudumiyāmalai may also be mentioned in this context.
88. *ASI, Annual Report, 1909-10*, p. 148.
89. V.S. Agrawala, *Handbook to the Sculptures of the Curzon Museum of Archaeology*, p. 42.
90. For *aṅguṣṭha* as a symbol of the generative organ, see Dandekar,"Viṣṇu in the Veda", *Kane Fel. vol.,* p. 109.
91. *MBh,* Anuśāsana-Parva 14.100-102. A passage, which the Bom. Edn. gives in this context (13.14.33-35) but which is relegated to the App. in the Crit. Edn., purports to say: The procreated beings (*prajā*) are not characterised either by the lotus (the emblem of Brāhma) or by the *cakra* (the emblem of Viṣṇu) or by the *vajra* (the emblem of *Indra*); but they are characterised by the *liṅga* (the emblem of Śiva) and by the *yoni*. Therefore, the *prajā* belongs to Maheśvara ... all males bear the visible mark of Hara's *liṅga* ... know Īśāna to be the male organ and Umā to be the female organ.
92. This account occurs in various Purāṇas Cf. *Śiva Purāṇa*: 4.12. 1-54; *Linga Purāṇa:* 1.29; 1.31; 1.33.34.
93. It must have preceded the *Manusmṛti* (which is believed to have been based on the lost *Mānava-Dharmasūtra*) at least by a century.
94. J.M. Van Gelder translates this (Śatapiṭaka Series, vol. 27) as "the ritual of the prescription for the murmured prayers to Rudra". The section ends with: *it imānavagṛhyapariśiṣṭe nityajapavidhānam*.
95. The translator renders the word *liṅga* with "member". Accoding to Przyluski, the words *lāṅgūla* (plough) and *liṅga* (phallus) are of Austro-Asiatic origin. They are connected wilh the concept of fertility, vegetation, procreation, etc.
96. *jīvikārthecā 'paṇye.*
97. Viśākha is usually understood to be just another name of either Skanda or Śiva. The present context would, however, show that Pataṣjali knew a God named Viśākha who was different from

both Skanda and Śiva. J.N. Banerjea, *op. cit.*, p. 117, identifies Viśākha with the mount of Śiva.

98. *devatādvandveca: brahmaprajāpatyādināṁ ca.*
99. As pointed out earlier, Kauṭilya mentions the temples of Śiva and Vaiśravana. Incidentally, the compound *śivavaiśravaṇau* mentioned by Patañjali does not denote any distinct Śaiva sect as seems to be suggested by B.N. Puri, *India in the time of Patañjali*, p. 188.
100. In the commentary on *P.* V.2.76 : *ayaḥśūladaṇḍājinābhyāṁ-ṭhakṭhaṣau.*
101. The word *śivabhāgavata* is explained as *śivo bhagavān bhaktir asya.* Incidentally, the use of the epithet *bhāgavat* more or less exclusively in Vaiṣṇava contexts seems to have been later than the third century AD.
102. *Comprehensive History of India,* vol. II, p. 401.
103. *Op. cit.,* p. 167. Incidentally, RGB assigns Wema Kadphises to the middle of the third century AD.
104. It may be mentioned in this context that Renou (*op. cit.*, p. 102) speaks of a secondary identification of with Mitra, as the result of which Śaivism took the lead even under the foreign rulers like the Hephtalites.
105. Dandekar, *A Hisory of the Guptas,* p. 18.
106. At least one Gupta sovereign, namely, Vainya Gupta, was a Śaiva. The Gunaighar copperplate of 507 AD would show that Vainya Gupta was professedly a Śaiva (Dandekar, *A History of the Guptas,* pp. 141-42).
107. For details, see Dandekar, "Religion and Philosophy in the age of the Guptas", *RO* (Poland) 21: 35-107.
108. The word *guru* (in the sense of "preceptor"), which is so common in later literature, does not occur in the early Veda. Perhaps the earliest suggestion of this concept is to be found in the reference to the *ācāryā-brahmacāri* in relationship in the *Brahmacārī-Sūkta* (*AV* XI.5).
109. One may mention, in this context, the Bhaṭṭāra Guru of the Indonesian Śaivism.
110. Cf. Macnicol, *op. cit.,* p. 161.
111. Cf. Eliot as quoted by Bouquet, *Hinduism,* p. 94.
112. Cf. V.S. Agrawala, "The meaning of Mahādeva", *Pur.* 7(2).
113. Renou, *op. cit.,* p. 65.
114. Cf. Zaehner, *Hinduism,* p. 85.
115. See W.D.O. Flaherty, "Asceticism and Sexuality in Śiva-mythology", *Hist. Rel.* 8(4), 330-37; (9), 1-41; "Symbolism of the

Third Eye of Śiva", *Pur.* 11(2). Pārvatī said to have loved Śiva not in spite of his ascetic accoutrements and third eye, but because of them. They made him unique; in Śiva's ascetic powers there is implicit great erotic power.

116. Kālidāsa has given a fine poetic expression to this feature of Śiva's character in the Nāndī verse of the *Mālavikāgnimitra.*
117. Cf. Eliot, *Hinduism and Buddhism,* vol. II, p. 217. It is certainly not correct to say, as Macnicol (*op. cit.,* p. 160) has done, that Śiva is the God least likely to attract a theistic devotion. Indeed, the south Indian Śaivism gave *bhakti* to the north and borrowed philosophy from it.
118. This is reminiscent of the Prakṛti-Puruṣa relationship of the Sāṁkhya. The deep-seated and primitive faith in the mother-principle as the ultimate secret of the universe must have substantially influenced this elevation of Śakti. Similar tendency is discernible also in respect of Lakṣmī, Sarasvatī, Rādhā—but only rarely and certainly not in such an emphatic manner.
119. Marshall, *Excavations at Taxila,* p. 158, mentions an early terracotta bust which is believed to be that of Ardhanārīśvara. It is suggested that this form was conceived by the Kūsāṇa and Greek sculptors and perfected by the Gupta sculptors. Incidentally, the concept of the hermaphrodite divinity is to be met with also in the Veda (see Dandekar, "Yama in the Veda").
120. *Mālavikāgnimitra,* Nāndī: *kāntāsaṁmiśradehopyaviṣayamanasāṁ yaḥ purastād yatīnām.*
121. Cf. *Mālavikāgnimitra* I.4: *rudreṇedam umākṛtavyatikare svāṅge vibha- ktaṁdvidhā.* The Nāndīs of most of the Sanskrit dramas are related to Śiva. Like the dramatic literature, the ancient Sanskrit works of romance also show the patronage of Śiva. The *Bṛhatkathā,* for instance, begins with a dialogue between Śiva and Pārvatī.
122. According to the *Kathāsaritsāgara* I.4, his entire grammar was revealed to Pāṇini by Śiva.
123. Cf. Barth, *op. cit.,* p. 216.
124. On this whole subject one may be referred to Gonda, *Viṣṇuism and* Śaivism*: A Comparison,* University of London, 1970.

Index